There are ONLY seven ways to get rich:

1. Inherit it

2. Marry it

3. Invest for it

4. Get lucky, the lottery or win it

5. Work for a company

6. Break the law: Steal, deal or con

7. Entrepreneur/Work for yourself

The best way to become wealthy –
honestly, ethically, legally and morally –
is number 7.

BE AN ENTREPRENEUR
AND
WORK FOR YOURSELF!

The Internet is the most powerful business tool in the history of mankind. It can help you make money, save money, network and communicate easily and quickly, often without the need for start-up capital. It levels the playing field so individuals, entrepreneurs and small companies can compete with large, multinational corporations and win!

You can work smart. You can work hard. I'll show you hundreds of ways to work smart using the Internet. But only you can decide whether you want to work hard. In my experience, the best way to make more money in this world, to help your company get ahead of the competition, to truly get ahead financially and be your own boss, is to work smart and hard!

– Marc Ostrofsky

"The future potential of Internet-based businesses is staggering. This easy-to-follow book will teach you the ropes of this business and give you great tips and suggestions on achieving financial success."

– **Dr. Stephen R. Covey**, author of
The 7 Habits of Highly Effective People and *The Leader In Me*

"I've asked thousands if they will be one of the millionaires made by the recession. If you read and apply what Marc has laid out in Get Rich Click, you will be well on your way. It's actionable information you can apply now!"

– **David Bach**, *New York Times* best-selling
author of *Start Over, Finish Rich*

"Marc Ostrofsky delivers in Get Rich Click. His approach will change how people think about the role of the Internet in business and delivers on teaching you how to make money online."

– **Jack Canfield**, *New York Times* best-selling
coauthor of *Chicken Soup for the Soul* series

"The 800-pound guerrilla when it comes to finding unique ways to make money on the Internet is Marc Ostrofsky. He has made $100 Million+ and his book Get Rich Click will teach you how to do it too."

– **Jay Conrad Levinson**, author of *New York Times* best-selling
Guerrilla Marketing series of books

"With so much noise in the Internet business sector, it's refreshing to see practical advice from someone who has been there, done that. Marc Ostrofsky's Get Rich Click lays out an easy-to-navigate blueprint to making money online for anyone with a dream and a willingness to work the plan. Packed with checklists, bullet points and no-nonsense advice from someone who has made millions online, this book is a no-brainer for anyone wanting to mine gold from the Internet."

– **Joel Comm**, *New York Times* best-selling author of *Twitter Power*

"There's a golden opportunity today . . . with an idea, a domain name and a bit of gumption–you can Get Rich Click. Marc Ostrofsky gives you the low-down on what he's done to make it happen in several different marketplaces and businesses. Everyone from the bootstrapping start-up to the next Internet tycoon can pick up something from the guy who's been there and done it."

– **Yanik Silver**, serial Internet entrepreneur and founder,
Maverick Business Adventures

"If you are looking for a way to build a successful online business without sacrificing lifestyle, you can learn the secret in Marc Ostrofsky's book, Get Rich Click."

– **Marci Shimoff**, *NY Times* best-selling author of *Happy for No Reason*
and *Chicken Soup for the Woman's Soul*

"Personal brand is a key to success in my world. I would say that Marc's personal brand is teaching others how to gain a competitive advantage by strategically leveraging the power of the Internet in business. Buy this book and learn how this serial technology entrepreneur has done it . . . over and over again."

– **Steve Harrison**, creator of National Publicity Summit

"If you want to change your life by focusing on the ability to obtain greatness from within and live up to their potential, Get Rich Click is the book for you!"
— **Bill Walsh**, author, speaker and world-renowned marketing expert

"Get your hands on Get Rich Click and you'll have gold in the palm of your hands. Marc's approach to the Internet and how to make money online will give you a headstart and turn your obstacles into opportunities."
— **Sharon Lechter**, coauthor of *Three Feet from Gold: Turn Your Obstacles Into Opportunities!* and *Rich Dad Poor Dad*

"Just when I thought I knew enough about online marketing and sales, I get your book. It's filled with ideas that, when implemented can make millions for the reader. I plan on having my whole team get a copy and read it now!"
— **John Assaraf**, *New York Times* best-selling author, *The Answer* and featured in *The Secret*

"The only problem I have with Get Rich Click is that it isn't a video . . . yet! Marc breaks the model of the traditional online marketer by showing you how to open your mind to thinking differently about how to use the Internet."
— **Mike Koenigs**, Cofounder of Traffic Geyser

"Get Rich Click is a blueprint for making money on the Internet and teaches all ages how to profit online. Author Marc Ostrofsky is a successful serial entrepreneur that supports young entrepreneurs and the NFTE. Buy this book and start your online business today."
— **Steve Mariotti**, founder, Network for Teaching Entreprenership

"Marc Ostrofsky's Get Rich Click will give you the tools, tactics, and most importantly, the confidence, to dramatically increase your income by building your business online. Go for it!"
— **Keith Ferrazzi**, *New York Times* best-selling author of *Never Eat Lunch Alone* and *Who's Got Your Back?*

"Internet marketing is a mix of art, science, knowledge and a never ending quest to learn where the gold is buried for that day, hour or even minute. Marc has proven to know how to do successfully . . . over and over again. If you want to make money from home, online, part time or full time, Get Rich Click is the book to read!"
— **Mike Filsaime**, marketing expert, President and CEO, MarketingDot-com.com

"The fastest fortunes today are made on the Internet. Marc's book, Get Rich Click shows you hundreds of ways to make serious money online. It's an absolute MUST for any online entrepreneur."
— **Robert Allen**, author of *Creating Wealth*, *The One Minute Millionaire* and many other best-selling books

"Great read . . . a winner."
— **John DiMartini**, author and speaker as seen in *The Secret*

"Marc is one of the smartest Internet business experts in this country. We have become good friends and talk all the time about ways I can use the Internet to help my business. His advice is worth millions to me and I highly recommend listening to what he has to say."
— **Peter Max**, world-renowned contemporary artist

"As a successful author and internet entrepreneur, I know the tips and tricks of making money online! Marc Ostrofsky has an astounding success story and Get Rich Click is an incredible book. It's easy to read, follow and will put you on the right track to making money online!"
— **Anthony Morrison**, successful online entrepreneur
and author of *Advertising Profits from Home*

"I teach people the secrets to master sex, money and power. Marc teaches people the secrets of how to master the online world and the ways to turn that mastery into dollars. Get Rich Click is hypnotic in its brilliance and practicality."
— **Marshal Sylver**, *The Millionaire Maker*

"Marc has that rare ability to identify and often create new and unique technology applications and opportunities and then turn them into income-producing companies. If you want to make money on the Internet, Get Rich Click is full of ideas, applications and real-world examples of exactly how to go about doing just that."
— **Paul Frison**, CEO, Houston Technology Center

"Creativity is a necessary key to success in today's competitive marketplace. Marc is one of those creative genius types that are always coming up with new and innovative ways of making money online. This book outlines a clear-cut path to teach anyone how to use the Internet to make money. I highly recommend it!"
— **Liz Kalodner**, Executive Vice President
and General Manager, CBS Consumer Products

"Marc Ostrofsky knows how to Get Rich Click! Each of his wildly successful ventures started from a simple, low-cost idea. What sets Marc apart is his revolutionary way of viewing the Internet. He has more ideas and ways to make money on the Internet than anyone I have ever met. If understanding an insider's mind is what you are looking for, Get Rich Click is for you."
— **Jan E. Smith**, Former President, Disney Interactive

"I've often said, 'In imagination, there is no limitation.' Marc Ostrofsky is proof of this! His book, Get Rich Click is BRILLIANT. If you want to make money 24/7/365, this book is your key to financial success!"
— **Mark Victor Hansen**, *New York Times* best-selling
coauthor of *Chicken Soup for the Soul* series

"Think differently! Think online! If you are going to survive, thrive and grow in this interconnected world we now live in, you need to read Get Rich Click!"
— **Brian Tracy**, *New York Times* best-selling author and management expert

"Taking action is my mantra for success. Get Rich Click will show you how to take action online. This is a book that will move you toward your dream of building an online business."
— **Les Brown,** best-selling author & motivational speaker

Get Rich CLICK!

THE ULTIMATE GUIDE TO MAKING MONEY ON THE INTERNET!

If you can click a mouse,
you can make money on the Internet!
This book is filled with HUNDREDS of ways
to make you money and save you money.
Learn more about "Reverse e-Commerce,"
Pay-Per-Action, Internet Real Estate,
Blog Marketing, 100+ SEO tactics
and much, much more.

Marc Ostrofsky

For general information on our other products and services, please contact us online at
GetRichClick.com

To purchase bulk copies of this book, please contact us online at
GetRichClick.com/bulk

ISBN(13): 978-0-9827696-0-7
ISBN(10): 0-9827696-0-1

Published by:
Razor Media Group, LLC.
Houston, Texas
E-mail: info@razormediagroup.com
Web: razormediagroup.com
Book Distribution: The BookMasters Group/Atlas Books
Available From Major Wholesalers: Ingram, Baker and Taylor, Bookazine,
Gazelle and others

12 11 10 9 8 7 6 5 4 3 2 1

I dedicate this book to the
memory of my mother,

Shirley Ostrofsky,

who died while I was doing the
final edits on this book,
just before it went to press.
She was truly a class act and always
seemed to turn the bad into the "not so bad."
She taught me the true meaning of
unconditional love!
I will miss her terribly.

Preface

I met Marc Ostrofsky at the National Speakers Association annual convention. It's kind of blurry there because every one of the 1,500 people in attendance is trying to out do, and out talk the other. So as Marc was telling me "his story" I admit my listening skills were less than stellar. I only remember the words CuffLinks.com and millions.

But he followed up after the event and snapped me into focus. His story is off the chart both entrepreneurially and financially. We kept up the conversation, he came to Charlotte for a visit, spoke at my annual boot camp and introduced me to several of his friends of distinction.

Marc Ostrofsky is a warm fuzzy guy, who has made a ton of money on the Internet, and from the Internet. This book is a cold slap in the face to wake up and smell the URLs. And this book is the *first* reality book of how-to-do-it-NOW!

Marc is not one of these "Here's how I did it and let me sell you the secret" guys. This book IS the secret.

The Internet is the future of marketing, sales, information and e-commerce and will grow for the next hundred years. And *Get Rich Click* is a road map for how to capture it, take advantage of it and monetize it while it's still the new frontier.

Everyone looks at the Internet with a sense of awe, wonder and bewilderment. They look at a website or URL and say, "Why the hell didn't I think of that?" You've said it. I've said it. Not Marc. He immediately saw the opportunity of the Internet and seized it.

Marc didn't invent the Internet. (Everyone knows Al Gore did that.) He capitalized on the Internet, cashed in and is still cashing in . . . 24 hours a day, 7 days a week, 365 days a year.

And so can you.

This book explains the game and gives a simple game plan that anyone (even you) can understand and execute for as little as the cost of registering a URL. And Marc even tells you the best places where and how to do that.

What's missing from this book is *you*. The keys to understanding and execution are contained herein, but *you* must pull the trigger to get the money-ball rolling in your direction.

This book gives you the understanding that it's not too late to score big on the Internet and motivates you to fire the pistol to hit yourself in the butt to take action. And if you fire the shot correctly, the bullet will hit you right in the wallet.

– **Jeffrey Gitomer**,
author of *The Little Red Book of Selling*

Foreword

As CEO of ClickBank, my primary focus day in and day out is to ensure that ClickBank provides individuals and businesses with better, more profitable ways to make money online. Since we are in the business of enabling success, when I see an Internet marketing resource as valuable as this book come along, I pay attention. This book will open your eyes to a world of opportunity you probably didn't know existed. In the pages that follow, you'll read about everyday people just like you who have made money online.

Also, you'll read about the many different ways people have become successful online, and it's never been clearer than it is today that the opportunities are endless. At ClickBank we understand this firsthand, because many of the success stories feature our clients! Over the past 12 years, since the early days of e-commerce, we've focused primarily on digital products like eBooks, software and membership sites and have helped hundreds of thousands of product creators and their affiliates become successful in an incredible variety of niches. Additionally, many of the tools set forth in this book have been employed by ClickBank clients to make money online.

One ClickBank success story that you'll read about highlights Jacob Hiller, an innovator who has become wildly successful by teaching people how to jump higher. You'd think that might be a niche product, but Jacob has already made over $1 million to date. Despite the many success stories I've seen, I continue to find it fascinating that someone can take an avocation and convert it into a lucrative vocation. Each of these amazing stories is unique, inspiring and true.

One notable characteristic of successful ClickBank clients is that they are incredibly good at keeping an eye on trends, and must do so to stay on top of their game in the continually changing world of Internet marketing. Many of those clients then take advantage of the trends by forming partnerships with subject matter experts in the markets or verticals they want to target.

In the spirit of great partnerships, when I first met Marc Ostrofsky it didn't take long for us to realize that we needed to find a way to combine our efforts to provide people with valuable resources to make money online. We have recently done just that through the creation of a bi-weekly video newsletter. ClickBank is pleased to partner with *Get Rich Click* to deliver this newsletter (www.getrichclick.com/withclickbank) not only to affiliate marketers, but to anyone who has ever aspired to make money online. It is full of success stories, trends and tips and tricks to help people achieve their goals online, and I invite you to see for yourself.

My hope is that you will use this book (and the newsletter) as a resource in your Internet marketing efforts. Everyone has a passion – something they're good at and can share with others. I encourage you to use the success stories in this book as inspiration and fuel for your business. Use the business models and techniques covered in this book to help you get started, or take your business a step further. And be sure to keep an eye on the trends and the new ways you'll learn about people making money online so that you can incorporate them into your own efforts. I assure you that the content you'll find within these pages is useful and relevant. Marc Ostrofsky has an incredible Internet marketing success story of his own and serves as a great guide through the world of making money online.

– Brad Wiskirchen
CEO, ClickBank

Table of Contents

Introduction

The Internet is quickly changing the world as we know it. For the first time in history, a single businessperson can compete on equal footing with large, multinational firms. Anyone can sell something, collect the money for the item, then go purchase it and send it to the buyer. Today, armed with nothing more than information and a little bit of know-how, people are becoming millionaires. Thanks to the Internet.

The Internet is today's gold rush, creating more millionaires and doing so faster than any other medium in history.

The Internet has created more opportunities for "the rest of us" to get wealthy than did the telephone, the telegraph, radio or television. As an interactive tool, the Internet is redefining the way people around the world work, play, socialize and communicate.

This book is filled with stories of people, just like you, who wanted to create wealth using the Internet. The only difference is that they acted on their ideas. Many had little or no start-up money. *Get Rich Click* contains hundreds of ideas and real-life stories from entrepreneurs from all ages that show exactly how easily and quickly you can make money on a full- or part-time basis.

In these pages, you will learn about:

- New money-making ideas and opportunities others are doing on the Internet
- Advertising commissions
- Getting paid for simply providing leads to others
- Making money with information and knowledge
- Creating a website that's made up entirely of others' content and ads
- Unique ways of making money with eBay
- Making money with affiliate programs
- Website marketing
- Creating simple e-commerce, retail sites that make money the same day they are created
- Making money on the Internet with no website
- Selling a product on the Internet, getting paid for it and then buying it to fulfill the order

And much more. This book will help you turn the gray matter in your brain to virtual gold!

Technology Wildcatting™

The profit potential from the Internet is staggering. It may take only one tip from this book, one story, one bit of information showing how someone else did it and you find a way to adapt that story to your situation. Now is the time to get your share of this enormous, amazing and growing pie.

Wildcatters are independent prospectors searching for new deposits of wealth. It used to take a lot of luck to dig a hole and strike oil. Today, drilling for oil is as much a science as it is an art. Drilling firms today use a host of scientific methods to minimize the number of dry holes they dig.

Making money on the Internet is really no different. Online, entrepreneurs – the technology wildcatters of the Internet – use knowledge, data, upside potential and an understanding of the market and the players within that market to know where to drill and how to play.

"Learn More . . . Earn More™"

– Marc Ostrofsky

Success comes from a combination of knowing what's going on in the market, knowing where the market is headed, planning to be in the right place, at the right time, arming yourself with the right products, having the right information and taking advantage of the opportunities.

The Internet Is the Ultimate Business Tool

I believe I may have been one of the first to view the Internet as a medium to conduct business. My beliefs and viewpoints were so strong that I decided to purchase the domain name business.com. In 1995, I paid $150,000 for the domain name to a British Internet service provider. At the time, industry insiders and the media were baffled to discover anyone would pay such an absurd amount of money for a simple dictionary word between a "www." and a ".com."

Future events justified my huge outlay of cash. In 1999, only four years later, I resold the domain name to eCompanies, an Internet incubator (investing company) looking for an easy-to-remember name that would save millions in advertising costs. The sticker price: $7.5 million. That sale landed in *The Guinness Book of World Records* for the largest amount anyone had ever paid for a web address to date. There was no website, no product, services or sales.

So often people say to me, "I wish I had done that!" or "It was so simple, why didn't I think of that?" Well, you still can. We are truly in the bottom of the first inning when it comes to the potential for growth and opportunity on the Internet. There are hundreds of ways to make money using the Internet. Domain names.

Pay-Per-Click advertising. Mobile content. Social network marketing. Search engine optimization. Blogs, affiliate marketing and more. You can even get paid to read e-mail and take surveys at home!

The Internet Approach Is Really Simple

You'll learn how to make money on two fronts:

1. Using the Internet to enhance your business, increase sales and decrease your cost structure regardless of whether you are a retailer, wholesaler, supplier, service provider, content provider, entrepreneur or multinational company.

2. Using the Internet as the primary business model in your chosen market, often without maintaining a physical office or location other than your home office or a laptop.

Using the Internet as your primary business tool comes in many forms: selling a product; selling services; providing or selling information. You'll learn all about affiliates – how to team up with others, sell their products and earn big commissions from them. You'll learn how to buy, sell, lease and even rent domain names, and how website traffic is the most powerful factor for any web-based business. For that, I have included over a hundred ways to optimize and increase traffic to your website.

Think of traditional business models in nontraditional ways.

Spotting Nuggets of Gold: Understanding Markets

Get Rich Click helps you understand the opportunities available to you on the Internet and identify new and ongoing, significant, recurring income streams.

The key word here is "ongoing." One time transactions typically don't produce significant long-term revenue. If all you want to do is make a one time $5,000 or $50,000 sale on the Internet, this isn't the book for you. Ongoing sales is the method I have used to make money. Think of the old adage, "Give a man a fish; he eats for a day. Teach a man to fish and he eats for a lifetime." I'll teach you how to fish – how to spot, understand and profit from these new and ever-changing opportunities on the Internet – so you, too, can eat for a lifetime.

"To create a new standard, it takes something that's not just a little bit different; it takes something that's really new and really captures people's imagination." – Bill Gates

Tom Peters, one of the world's most innovative management gurus and coauthor of international best sellers *In Search of Excellence* and *Re-imagine!* says, "Nothing is unimaginable!" When you consider the power, reach, size and nominal costs involved in using the Internet, then, without question, absolutely nothing is unimaginable!

Three years ago, no one would have imagined the power of a handheld device such as Apple's iPhone. It's an entrepreneur's dream. Hundreds, if not thousands, of entrepreneurs are creating amazing iPhone applications, letting Apple handle all of the heavy lifting by selling them on every iPhone at the push of a button and paying the entrepreneur 70 percent of every dollar generated from the sale of these applications.

This is how you learn to be successful and *Get Rich Click*. The Internet gives you access to the magic button that makes your dreams reality. Just imagine it, and the Internet can help you or your business make it happen – faster, more efficiently and at a lower cost than ever before.

No Technical Knowledge Required!

Some people won't buy this book because they have "technophobia," but making money on the Internet does not require you to be a "techie" at all!

Many of the people in the success stories you'll read have no programming or graphic design skills. I'm living proof you don't need technical skills, as mine are few and far between. I am a marketing guy, not a tech guy.

Above all else, making money on the Internet involves understanding opportunities. If you add in selling, marketing, market dynamics, knowing what you don't know, understanding people and how they behave, and having the ability to balance your weaknesses and strengths, you have a recipe for success.

All you need to mine this new gold field are the right tools. The Internet is one big jump in the right direction to finding these tools.

Every technological revolution creates bigger, better and more abundant tools. We are still in the "tool-creation" phase of the Internet. Compared to picks and shovels, this tool is much more efficient, a quantum leap forward in the world of tools. It offers us a new way of thinking and "clicking" to make money. It truly is a tool that will allow many to cash in on what is fast becoming known as the "gold rush of the 21st century," a tool that will allow individuals and businesses to start and continue a journey to *Get Rich Click*.

The market, technology, the defining qualities of relevance are all changing at light speed. In five years, we will be looking at a different Internet landscape, and that will be as filled with opportunity as is the one right now. Everyone transacting on the Internet is trying to achieve the same goal: increase sales and decrease expenses. Those who succeed find the answer to this balancing act.

Everyone thinks they need to create the next Facebook or become the next Microsoft or Google to get rich. It's simply not true. The real person on the street can make money and get rich by following the strategies I've written about here. I know they work because I have done them! Even if you simply help others implement some of the ideas in *Get Rich Click*, you can and will be successful.

Get Rich Click is one tool to help you learn from the experience of others!

– Marc Ostrofsky

FREE Digital premiums

Get Rich Click is the ultimate source for making and saving money online. As an added incentive for buying this book, the GRC team has assembled offers totaling more than $500 in digital premiums! The offers include terrific discounts from our own online companies, such as CuffLinks.com, Blinds.com and eTickets.com. They also include free services, such as online advertising, affiliate offers, office supplies and more! These offers are reserved exclusively for purchasers of this book; it's our way of saying thank you!

Follow the link below to receive the latest digital premiums or go to: GetRichClick.com/DigitalPremiums

Think about it: By using just one of these digital premiums, you will pay for the cost of this book! Now that's the *Get Rich Click* mindset!

I sent you an e-mail and forwarded a copy to
your PDA, cell phone and home computer.
I also faxed a copy to your office assistant and laptop.
Then I snail-mailed hard copies to you on paper, floppy and CD.
But in case you didn't receive it, I'll just tell you what it said . . .

This could be the FIRST interactive book ever!

1. WHAT IS THIS?

If you haven't seen them in your favorite newspaper or magazine, it's called a Quick Response Code or a "QR" code. In short, lets just say, it's like a "barcode" – but better! The difference is that a "QR CODE" will take you *instantly* to a web page when scanned by a smartphone. It's one of the latest cool technologies that helps bridge the virtual world and the physical world.

2. Why Are They in the Book?

Get Rich Click is the ultimate source for the latest information, advice and tips on how to make money online. The problem is, there are SO MANY new ideas, tips, tricks and ways people are making money using the Internet, we thought this would be a great way to bring you the latest updated information on how others are making money online. One of the best new technologies that allows us to make this book "come alive" and enhance the readers experience is to use QR codes throughout the book.

3. How Will They Benefit Me?

It's our favorite saying . . ."Learn More, Earn More.™" The Internet changes fast and we are committed to bringing you the most up-to-date information possible.

4. How Can I Use the QR Code – Now?

It's an APP on your smartphone. There are many FREE APPs available via iTunes, the Blackberry App World and the Android Marketplace if you search for "QR code" so you can download the APP that will read the above image. Download one now and try the QR code above.

Note:

- If you have an iPhone, you can go to GetRichClick.com/iphone
- If you have a Blackberry, you can go to GetRichClick.com/blackberry
- If you have an Android phone, you can go to GetRichClick.com/android

1

The *Get Rich Click* Mindset

Change creates opportunity! When one door closes, another opens.

Whenever there's major change in any market or industry, some people make a lot of money – and others lose money. What makes the difference? The winners have three weapons that give them a strong competitive advantage:

Information

Knowledge

Understanding

In the last 18-24 months, simple, easy-to-use "tools" have emerged allowing ANYONE or ANY BUSINESS to easily and quickly play the "get rich on the Internet" game that was previously enjoyed by "the geeks" of the world. NOW is the time! It's your turn to *Get Rich Click!*"

The changes now occurring are long term, dramatic . . . and getting faster! More money than ever before is now changing hands, and the pace will be speeding up over the next few years. This pace is driven by the Internet, and it's happening in every business in the world today, regardless of the industry. The doors are wide open! A LOT OF CASH awaits those that learn, understand, and play in the new economy.

My goal for *Get Rich Click* is to show you how thousands of people – aged 7 to 77 – are making money, and how I, too, have managed to create, grow, sell and still own more than my fair share of "Internet based" businesses. All of them are profitable in their respective markets. Some make a few thousand dollars a month, some make a few hundred grand a year and a few make millions of dollars every twelve months!

Making money is exactly like war. It is a *very* competitive environment. The winner of a war is the side with the best information, knowledge and understanding of the terrain they're on and the opposition they're facing.

Just as in a war, your business needs "intel" in order to succeed and make money. You need to know everything you can about:

- **The Buyers**
- **The Sellers**
- **The Products**
- **The Services**
- **The Competition**
- **The Supply Chain**
- **The Distribution Channel**
- **The Methods others used to win**
- **The Methods others used that failed**
- **The financial methods used as leverage to grow faster**
- **The most efficient ways to buy, sell, create, outsource and network**

My father was a professor who taught MBA students. He knew success was all about knowledge. He used to say, "I simply give them more knowledge so, hopefully, they make fewer mistakes. THEY WILL MAKE MISTAKES, but with the information I give them before they get into the game, they will make their mistakes sooner, learn from their mistakes, and move ahead."

The Minefield Game

I heard about this game at a recent conference I attended. Two teams are challenged to simply get across a path of 30 marked steps. Five of the 30 steps are "mines" – when stepped on, they light up. The player has to go back to the beginning and start over. The goal of the game is to see which team can cross the minefield the fastest.

Let's imagine how this game might look . . .

Both teams start out the same way, not knowing which steps were "mines." The first player from Team #1 moves ever so slowly on the first step, then the second step, and so on until he hits one of the hidden "mines" under step #5. He must now start over, knowing next time to avoid step #5. The next player from Team #1 now crosses the first 4 steps, and then gently steps over the fifth one. This cautious approach continues until the player hits the next "mine" at step #12. Then the next team member begins, knowing to avoid the two previously mined steps.

It seems simple enough. But Team #2 approaches the game very differently. The first person RUNS across the steps until hitting the mine on step #5. The next person then RUNS across the first four steps, jumps the fifth one, and RUNS until hitting the mine under step #12. The next team member RUNS past the first four steps, jumps over #5 and #12, until they hit the next mine as soon as possible.

Needless to say, Team #2 won. The difference was that Team #2 knew they had to **"FAIL FAST!"** They knew that they would hit the mines, but if they learned from those mistakes fast enough, they would win the competition.

The analogy is clear. In the supercompetitive world we live in, learning from others' successes as well as from their failures is an essential element of success. Otherwise you're doomed to relive the problems others incurred in the past.

As my dad said, we will all have failures along the way. It's failing fast, learning from that failure, and getting back in the game that makes the difference between winners and losers.

We live in a new world of "intellectual property" – where the Internet and "mindshare" (like owning the right domain name) are the new real estate. Whether or not we're playing a Minefield game, we are definitely playing "The **Mind** Field Game" in the age of the Internet.

– Marc Ostrofsky

Don't be fooled. Business *is* war – and just like in war, you need "intelligence" to win, collect your cash and create the wealth you deserve. Fortunately, so much of this can be accomplished by using the Internet for gathering information and learning – quickly – the blueprints for success in any business or industry.

Continuous learning
is the central key to success!

The Internet is creating winners and losers every day – BIG winners, and companies that don't "get it" and go out of business in a relatively short time frame. You can get on the train or watch it pass you by! Stop watching the rest of us prosper with this wonderful new toy and start LEARNING about the thousands of ways young and old are making more money and saving more money by using the Internet.

The Internet FORCES change. Using the Internet, I learn something new, exciting and tremendously innovative EACH AND EVERY DAY. Actually, finding new online "niches" to make $50 or $500 a day has become my obsession. (I will share those with you via my blog and my website – GetRichClick.com.)

I'm tired of people saying "it's too late" to start making money on the Internet – or my favorite: "Someone else is already doing that online." How ridiculous! They are doing it over and over because by doing it they KEEP MAKING MONEY! The truth is, the excuses are actually showing that those people are afraid. They are afraid of change. They are afraid to get into the game for fear that they will fail.

Right now we're only in the bottom of the first inning of how the Internet is changing history. There are tens of thousands if not hundreds of thousands of individuals – JUST LIKE YOU – that will get rich beyond belief in the coming years!

Get this into your head! For your business to stay in business and grow in the new digital economy, you will HAVE TO PLAY smarter, to be better, to be more efficient, to network, to let others manufacture the products you sell, to let others manage the product fulfillment, even to let others handle the customer service – while you are the one that makes the sale!

I'll have much more to say about this in the chapters that follow. For now, take my word for it:

If you keep doing what you've always done,
you'll keep getting what you've always gotten!
But if you're ready for change . . .
you've come to the right place!

Success starts with an idea. Next comes a plan to realize that idea. That's the proper mindset for any business venture.

An idea for a business venture is like an acorn. For the person who really understands it – that's you – the idea includes both what it is now (a nut) and also what it will be (an oak tree). That may seem simple enough when we're talking about acorns and oaks, but it takes a special kind of person to really see a profitable business when it's in a very early stage.

That kind of vision doesn't exist in everybody. Not everyone is born with it. But even if you weren't, you can develop it starting now. Just be aware that every good idea was fragile and unproven at the start. Many really great ideas seemed positively ridiculous. Train yourself, therefore, to endow ideas (especially your own) with a significant amount of confidence at the beginning.

Ideas are good until proven otherwise!

Ideas are fragile and need to be handled accordingly. A nurturing approach to ideas is essential for any Internet-based business or any business that uses the Internet even in a supporting role. With that in mind, here are some points that will help:

- **Be an original thinker. If "it's never been done that way before," you might actually have a winning idea.**
- **There's more than one kind of originality. Can you come up with creative twists on already existing ideas?**
- **Think about selling as you go. Successful online entrepreneurs plan, set goals, measure and sell. Be a good doer, not just a good planner.**
- **Convert prospects to paying customers. Having followers or even fans is great, but you need to enable them to exchange their cash for your product or service.**
- **You should also empower them to inform others who need your product or service.**
- **Once you have a paying customer, learn how to serve that customer on an ongoing basis. Shoot for an ongoing relationship.**
- **Be sure to thank your customers for their business. Then turn thank-you opportunities into cash-generating sales.**
- **Are you testing new ways of putting your ideas into action? If something works, tweak it to see if you can get even better results.**
- **Can you replicate your success? Is your idea "scalable"?**
- **Are you relentless in your pursuit of profits? The top line is important but the bottom line is what you put in your pocket.**

On the Internet, what exists today
will exist differently tomorrow.

No matter what product or service you see working today, there is a competitor, who thinks he or she can do it better. I call it Technology Leapfrogging™ .

No matter what a firm comes up with, another firm will do it plus one. The next firm will do it plus two. Then the market will decide who succeeds.

Disintermediation: A New Word for an Old Idea

It means "eliminate the middleman." Through the Internet, a company can deal directly with customers instead of funneling supply through distributors, wholesalers or brokers. Buyers quickly see how disintermediation translates into lower prices and more efficient service. And the companies get more sales.

The Internet is the most powerful agent
of disintermediation in history.

Disintermediation is vastly simplified by the Internet, but it comes easier to some companies than others. Certain industries take to it naturally, like computer supplies, travel agencies, bookstores, brokerage services and jewelry sales. But industries such as food and beverage, real estate and automobile are still learning. Meanwhile, furniture sales, pet supplies and home food delivery have so far been unsuccessful with Internet disintermediation.

Consider the purchase of airline tickets. In the past, travel agents provided necessary value in the supply chain. They were interpretive intermediaries. They had access to fares, times, connections, special offers, the travel experiences of others – everything related to airport travel. Today, individual airlines have a website offering much the same functionality, effectively eliminating the job the travel agent used to do. The Internet and these online travel sites disintermediated the whole travel business, especially airline ticket sales.

One classic success story is Amazon.com, the largest bookseller on the Internet. Amazon's customers connect to and order from the source of the product, eliminating the delays and costs of distribution channels. Amazon realized early on that buyers didn't need help with the selection process or other forms of ongoing support. Traditional intermediaries were replaced with a direct ordering process.

Supply Chain (with intermediaries)

VENDOR'S PRODUCT MARK-UP LADDER

Supplier $20
▼
Manufacturer $40
▼
Wholesaler $60
▼
Distributor $75
▼
Retailer $125
▼
Customer $250

Internet Modified Supply Chain (disintermediated)

Supplier $20
▼
Manufacturer $40
▼
Customer $80

Amazon has even applied disintermediation to the physical nature of books themselves.

The Kindle is a tablet device that removes the need for pages and covers, and even eliminates the manufacturing process as a whole. No printers. No presses. No middlemen. No distributors. All this means higher profits with few moving parts! With the Kindle, it's even possible to shop, order and download books using cell phone technology. That is major disintermediation!

CLICK TIP ▷ Amazon has been called a disruptive force in the publishing industry, contributing to the demise of traditional bookselling practices. But many independent booksellers and small publishers have stayed in business and done well. They've developed their own direct Internet sales approaches and have successfully implemented their own websites.

Reintermediation

Disintermediation is not one-size-fits-all. For some businesses, especially those focused on mass production, cutting out the middlemen can actually create higher costs. Now they were serving a smaller customer base (or customers who ordered in small quantities), often with more complaints and a multitude of other issues. The number of orders might have increased but so did the problems.

Reintermediation is a reintroduction of middlemen. This is what Levi Strauss had to do after the unsuccessful launch of a multimillion-dollar online operation to sell jeans directly to consumers. The company realized disintermediation meant that instead of keeping a few large chain retailers happy, they had to satisfy millions of customers – each of whom might buy one pair of jeans.

Levi Strauss decided to keep the focus on product quality. They let their retail partners handle the quality of the customer's buying experience.

How Much Is That Diamond in the Window?

Most small jewelry stores in this country are family owned and family-operated. They provide hands-on service, are well known in their communities, and sometimes have served clients over several generations.

Ask any of them how they're doing right now and you'll hear, "The store is very quiet. It's getting tough to stay afloat." Then ask these same people what they're doing on the Internet and the answer is even more predictable: "Nothing," or, "Not much," or, "We have a website but it doesn't do any business."

People with this mindset still think the world is flat. They have inventory on hand, staff, a retail shop, rent and a host of other "overhead costs." In contrast, an online jeweler has a photo of a diamond and a price that is often 25 to 50 percent less than the brick-and-mortar retailer. When online jewelers sell diamonds from a website, it is only AFTER they make the sale and collect the money that they buy the diamonds from a wholesaler and have them drop shipped directly to the retail customers.

Think about what that means. Retailers who have inventory of $500,000 in diamonds are at a huge disadvantage. Their money is tied up in inventory, rents, advertising, etc. Which business model do you think will survive?

CLICK TIP ▷ I'm sometimes asked to invest in web-based businesses that have all the right components but haven't accounted for cash flow. The entrepreneurs tell me, "I'll make it up in ad sales or subscriptions from all my web visitors." Sorry, that's not good enough anymore. You must have an income other than "ad sales" unless you have an immense volume of traffic coming to your site. If ad sales are your only income stream, don't bother to solicit the "smart money." The smart money won't invest unless you have millions of unique visitors already coming to your site and can sustain those visitors and create growth with very little additional capital.

Assume both firms made the sale of a $10,000 diamond ring. Diamond Seller "A" already owned the diamond so they made a 50% profit or $5000 profit on the sale. Diamond Seller "B" sold someone else's stone and made only 25% or $2500. The vast majority of profits for Diamond Seller "A" were essentially eaten up in their overhead. If you expect a lot of sales and are willing to take the gamble of having all of the overhead in Option "A" each and every month, year in and year out, you might make more money because there are no new variable costs to speak of for Diamond Seller "A" when making additional sales.

$10,000 Diamond Sold

Costs & Expenses

	Diamond Seller A (Physical Sale in the Store)	Diamond Seller B (Internet Sale)
Inventory	$500,000	None
Rent	$2,500/month	$250/at home
Utilities	$350	$100
Salaries	$10,000	$2,000
Insurance	$1,500	$250
Theft	$500	$0
Misc. Expenses	$1,500	$250
Monthly Overhead	$16,350	$2,850

Business Models: Anything New under the Sun?

Not long ago the term business model was not exactly on the tip of everyone's tongue. Then, in the early to mid-1990s, business model became a catchphrase that described how a company makes money or saves money.

For example, suppose a company needs a design for a logo or business card. The company can create an online contest for graphic artists to compete for the gig. The success of that business model means that graphic artists and other service providers need to adapt or suffer serious consequences.

Is this a new business model or a very old one in a new medium and on a different scale? Hundreds of years ago Renaissance artists competed for the chance to paint the ceilings of cathedrals. Even today, there are contests among architects for the design of major projects like the Vietnam War Memorial in Washington, D.C.

The Internet produces new business models and also reinvents traditional business models.

With regard to "new" business models, the people supplying answers and support are often the first to make money. That means you can *Get Rich Click* by assisting other people in taking advantage of online opportunities. You become a resource instead of looking for the next "big" idea yourself.

The Picks-and-Shovels Business Model

The standard business model of the 1849 Gold Rush was to mine gold and then exchange it for currency. For most, the dream didn't pan out. The real winning business model in the Gold Rush was selling picks and shovels to the miners!

The same scenario exists today on the electronic frontier. Internet "prospectors" need tools to make money. They need online support in every way, shape and form. Providing that support can be a winning strategy on the Internet. Online business models are still evolving. New and different products and services pop up every day. This gives rise to supporting products and services. A business can make substantial profit by helping others execute their plans for making money.

Whenever one or more components of a company's business model changes, new business models are created for supporting companies. The changes might involve niches served, new marketing angles or improved value propositions. One business model can also combine with another to form a completely new approach to business.

That's where you come in. Look at the services that supported the gold miners, and the new opportunities you can access by supplying 21st-century "picks and shovels."

New and Innovative Ways to Make Money:

GetRichClick.com/MakeMoney

Gold Mining Versus Internet Mining

Gold Mining

Blue jeans

Laborers

Housing

Food and Water

Land title services

Picks

Shovels

Transportation services

Internet Mining

Advertising placement

Advertising services

Affiliate programs

Affiliate recruitment

Customer satisfaction measurement

Data analysis

Directory services

Domain name registration

E-liquidators (popular right after the first dot-com bubble burst)

E-mail marketing

Handling transactions

Hardware

Human resources management

Information

Lead generation

Market research

Online banking

Online marketing consultation

Online tracking services

Processing payments

Sales content management

Software

Teaching others

Traffic generation

Training

Web hosting providers

Website design services

Website Analytics

A Picks-and-Shovels Success Story

Scott Plantowsky was known in Houston as the furniture rental guy you always saw on TV commercials. The business was simple and elegant: rent out furniture, pay for those assets in a short time frame and use the cash flow to grow the business.

Scott sold that company and then founded BindView Development, a tech firm in the security and systems management industry, with his friend Eric Pulaski. After taking that firm public and putting a few pennies in his pocket, Scott made many investments with his partners that ranged from condo development to medical devices.

But what he really wanted was something like his furniture rental business: rent the product, recoup the costs and use the rest of the income for growth.

Scott partnered with former business associates and invested in a company called Softlayer. The firm rents computing power, storage and bandwidth to its customers by the month. There are no collection issues – they can simply turn off a server if the monthly rental is not paid. They provide a wide variety of configurations that are simply and easily customized for the customer.

Softlayer's "secret weapon" is that almost every aspect of the business is automated. They can offer dozens of servers to customers in just a few hours and allow customers to run whatever system they choose. Everything can be accessed via public or private networks. In the first 36 months of business, the firm grew to nearly 20,000 servers in 3 data centers with over 5,500 customers in more than 110 countries!

The data on the Internet says sales are over $100 million in January of 2010. Softlayer customers range from Facebook and Salesforce to many of the largest social networking service providers, web hosting companies and data storage firms that host multiplayer games over the Internet. Their infrastructure was designed for unlimited scalability and should expand along with the growth of the Internet itself. (As this book was going to press, we heard that the company was sold for $400 million+.)

CLICK TIP Often the website owner with the biggest footprint and biggest vision will win the ultimate war. For example, I used a site that would send me an e-mail when a friend had a birthday. Now Facebook does the same thing. I subscribed to another site that allowed me and my friends to share photos. Now Facebook does the same thing. Sites like Reunion.com or Classmates.com are very well done, but Facebook now does the same thing for free. Think about creating proprietary software or a system in your new business that requires a larger firm to buy versus create your next competitor.

Another Success: LaundryView.com

This is my current favorite entrepreneurial website. It's such a good idea in the age of the Internet. I learned of LaundryView.com when my daughter and I went to visit a college in Boston. The site was pitched "as a major benefit" of attending this particular school for higher education! According to the site:

LaundryView.com is an Internet application that allows you to monitor the status of washers and dryers in connected laundry rooms through a web browser. LaundryView.com was developed in response to requests for greater control over laundry activities. Since many people tend to do their laundry during similar time periods, it results in busy laundry rooms. LaundryView's mission is to help you save time by providing information about the current state of laundry room equipment wherever you have access to a browser or e-mail messages.

Only a college student frustrated with always wondering whether his or her laundry was done yet could have come up with this. The application is owned and operated by a public company.

CLICK TIP Go to Guru.com or Elance.com and look at how inexpensive freelance help is around the globe in the category of search engine optimization. Maybe consider how inexpensively artists work to create a logo for a business or a website. Research these firms and individuals, and then offer search engine optimization services, logo creation services or website creation services as a business.

In *Get Rich Click* style, you now have "services" you can sell . . . and employees that can do the work . . . cheaply! You have just created an instant company for yourself with little or no overhead. The benefit of this business model is that you have an unlimited amount of freelance talent out there to help you. The hard part is getting, finding and signing up the client. Doing the work itself is quickly becoming a commodity.

Insights from Zappos.com Founder Tony Hsieh

I have met many brilliant technology and Internet pioneers, including Bill Gates, Michael Dell, 1-800-Flowers.com founder Jim McCann and Venture Capital guru John Doerr who financed Google, Amazon, Sun Microsystems and many others we all know and use daily. I love to meet and learn from the smartest people I can find. Many of these folks I met at the TED conference (TED.com) and "the-eg" conference (the-eg.com), which stands for "the entertainment gathering."

But I have never met anyone like Tony Hsieh, the founder of Zappos. He is truly a brilliant, down-to-earth guy who is easy to talk to about anything. No one would ever know he's worth close to $1 billion. I had the opportunity to become friends with Tony after taking a tour of his facility. It turns out CuffLinks.com supplies Zappos with their cuff links – so that was a plus.

After we met, Tony invited my wife, Beverle, and me to his home in Las Vegas on July 4. We spent time talking about Zappos and I asked him to give me some insights for the readers of *Get Rich Click*.

Little did I know that Tony was just about to announce the sale of his firm to Amazon.com for a whopping $1 billion!

Yet, talking with Tony (and his follow-up e-mails to me) was like talking to an old friend. An amazing guy who doesn't seem to have let his financial status change who he is inside. Rare indeed!

So, here are some insights direct from Tony for *Get Rich Click*. While they may seem fairly simple, making them happen is another level of business operations that few can pull off successfully.

1. Zappos is committed to WOWing every customer.

2. Customer Service that is just what the customer wants:

- 24/7 1-800 number on every page

- Free shipping

- Free return shipping

- 365-day return policy

- Fast, accurate fulfillment

- Most customers are "surprised" – upgraded to overnight shipping

- Create WOW

- Friendly, helpful "above and beyond" customer service

- Occasionally direct customers to competitors' websites

3. Zappos delivers happiness to employees and customers.

4. Their motto is:

**"People may not remember
exactly what you did or what you said,
but they will always remember
how you made them feel."**

A few days before the book went to press, Tony sent this list to include in *Get Rich Click*.

Zappos' Ten Lessons in building a successful business on the Internet:

1. **The e-commerce business is built on repeat customers.**

2. **Word of mouth really works online.**

3. **Don't compete on price.**

4. **Make sure your website inventory is 100% accurate.**

5. **Centrally locate your distribution.**

6. **Customer service is an *investment* and *not* an expense.**

7. **Start small. Stay focused.**

8. **Don't be secretive. Don't worry about your competitors.**

9. **You need to actively manage your company culture.**

10. **Be wary of so-called experts.**

And finally, if given the opportunity to visit Zappos, do so. The corporate culture of working in a truly fun, innovative, creative and exciting environment was nothing short of shocking. Everywhere we turned, people were laughing, joking, ringing bells in their offices and decorating their "cubicles" to any number of 1000+ different themes.

I have *never* seen so many happy people working in one place. Could that be why Jeff Bezos snapped up Zappos for over $1 billion?

Putting Your Ideas into Action

Having a *Get Rich Click* mindset means thinking differently. CHANGE = OPPORTUNITY for someone in the game. True Internet entrepreneurs look way beyond their last online transaction or the most recent commission check.

Their websites become part of their lifestyles. They live and breathe everything Internet: their clients, their affiliates, their products and services. Having that mindset makes a huge difference in what you can do to reach your goals.

Be aware of how the online medium will change the way you work, live, plan and communicate. Below are some steps you can take to put these ideas into action.

- The Internet is a communication medium. Consider it a supplement and extension of non-Internet marketing. It's not a replacement.
- If you use a website to make money on the Internet, your website should have a specific purpose. Having a website just because "everyone else does" is not a good reason. Goals for your website must be part of your overall business model.
- Make your website as interactive as possible. That means both initiating communication with your clients and responding to their initiatives.
- Define the target audience you want to reach and address those people in a way that will make them want to respond. "Meet them where they are."
- Learn as much as you can about your prospect and target market: What do they want? What do they need? What do they read? Where do they go? With whom do they interact? What are they paying others for their products and services?
- Set specific and measurable goals for every aspect of your business activity.
- Make it easy to do business with you, easy to buy from you, easy to respond to you and even easy to complain to you.
- Watch what other successful businesses and entrepreneurs do. If it works for them it may work for you. If it doesn't work for them, understand why and see if the same conditions apply to you and your business. Pay attention, understand, analyze. Implement or don't implement accordingly. Effectiveness on the Internet is not a one-size-fits-all proposition. Every business is different.
- Learn your craft and learn it well. For our purposes, this applies to making money on the Internet. Reading this book is a valuable step toward achieving that goal, but the undertaking requires time, energy and concentration. To learn more and to stay in touch with other Internet entrepreneurs just like yourself, visit GetRichClick.com.

2

E-commerce and Reverse E-commerce: Sell It, Then Buy It!

In college I wanted to sell jewelry to the sororities at the University of Texas at Austin. Those young ladies loved jewelry and had the money to pay for it. The trouble was, I didn't have any jewelry to sell.

No jewelry? That didn't stop me. I found a wholesale jeweler who accepted my dad's credit card. The jeweler loaned me $3,500 worth of jewelry (at his wholesale price) for 24 hours. Then I set up a "store" at the sorority house for an afternoon.

I sold $1000 in jewelry (my cost) for $2000. After I paid the wholesaler for the $1000 worth of jewelry I sold and returned the other $2500 worth of jewelry, I had $1000 profit for the afternoon.

I had borrowed the product, sold it and paid for it with the money I made from the sale!

This was my first step into what I call "reverse e-commerce." The model is honest, legal and smart – especially in a marketing medium like the Internet.

In the traditional business world, most people think of stores as places where businesses sell items they have on hand. The business purchases the item, displays it, then sells it.

But that was then.
This is now!

Making Money with No Money: Reverse E-commerce in Action

For many people, "selling-then-buying" is an unheard-of business model. But on the Internet it's one of the best and most profitable ways to operate. A small but growing group of online entrepreneurs already employs this model with great effect.

Why don't you hear much about these success stories? It's because the entrepreneurs involved are guarding their secrets, insights and competitive advantages. If you had the Golden Goose, you'd do the same thing!

Yes, making money is great. Making money with no money is even better. What's best of all is making money with no money while eliminating the roadblocks that reduce your profits. The roadblocks include spending money on inventory that may or may not sell, taking possession and ownership of that inventory and using valuable space to store all that stuff.

Selling something you don't own, then later buying it to fulfill the order, is a way to make money with no money. The concept sounds almost illegal or unethical, doesn't it? But in reality it's neither – and you can do it. This is a "no-risk" approach that you can start capitalizing on right now!

Actually, stock market and securities investors use this concept every day. They sell stock at one price, and then attempt to buy the stock at a price lower than they sold it for – pocketing the difference. It's called short selling. Selling a stock high, then buying it low.

Applying this practice on the Internet is just as smart and actually easier to

profit from. And . . .you don't need money to do it!

7 Different E-commerce Business Models to Choose From

Over many generations, fortunes in the business world were made through buying and selling products in physical stores. Internet fortunes have been made buying and selling products online. While some Internet fortunes employed the traditional business model, many more (and bigger!) opportunities await the online entrepeneur.

Here are seven different ways to buy and sell products and services on the Internet and profit through e-commerce:

1. Make your own product and sell it yourself.

2. Make your own product, and find a third party to sell it and fulfill the orders.

3. Make your own product, find a third party to sell it, and you fulfill the orders.

4. Buy someone else's product, then sell it to the end consumer.

5. Buy someone else's product, then sell it to a reseller (third party) with a lower profit margin per product, so they can resell it for a profit.

6. Sell someone else's product without buying it, collect the money, then have the product manufacturer manage the fulfillment.

7. Sell someone else's product without buying it, then let the manufacturer handle collection and fulfillment. In this model, you typically collect a commission for the sale that is less than you would make with the other six options above. However, you benefit by not having to purchase or store inventory, or maintain staff to manage fulfillment. (See Chapter 6 for more on this concept.)

For any product, there are four areas that require effort: making the product, selling it, collecting the money and fulfilling the orders. You can handle any or all of these activities yourself, or you can outsource them (I like to make certain my firms oversee the money portion in any option we choose). Depending on the product and how you "delegate" these four activities, you can make a substantial income with minimal effort. Remember: you will have a competitive edge in business (and in life) when you play up your strengths and hire or outsource your weaknesses!

E-commerce Business Model Dynamics

From brick-and-mortar to Internet back to brick-and-mortar

Here is what is happening with e-commerce business models today:

• **BRICK-AND-MORTAR USING THE** Internet: Some brick-and-mortar companies have started using the Internet as another method for lowering costs as part of a new business model. For instance, you can now order dinner from a number of restaurants or groceries from most local supermarkets so your order is ready to pick up at one of their physical locations.

• **CLOSE ALL BRICK-AND-MORTAR LOCATIONS:** Some former brick-and-mortar firms, like Blinds.com, were so enthusiastic with the financial benefits of the Internet, they closed their physical shops and went 100 percent Internet.

• **CREATE NEW BRICK-AND-MORTAR STORES:** Some businesses, like Dell and 1-800-FLOWERS, started out exclusively online and subsequently added brick-and-mortar locations to expand their original Internet-only business model.

For More Information, go to GetRichClick.com

The Freedom of No Inventory

Let's look at a real example of how reverse e-commerce works. I invested in a window blinds company that I thought had real potential as an online venture. When I invested, the company consisted of two "retail" operations. First, there were two physical stores called Laura's Draperies, in Houston, and one online website selling window blinds and window treatments at nobrianerBlinds.com.

The website actually made more money than both retail locations. It had little or no overhead and minimal risk. Meanwhile, the retail location had to cover rent, utility bills, payroll and insurance, as well as maintain on-site inventory.

Working with owner Jay Steinfeld, I saw a clear scenario for growth and big money. Today the company does over $75 million annually in online sales.

We manage the website, sell the product, take the order, handle customer service and put the money in the bank.

Then we send the order electronically to the manufacturer, who makes the custom blinds and drop ships the order directly to the customer. We pay the manufacturer 30 or 45 days later. Blinds.com also has an affiliate program where anyone can sign up to sell Blinds.com blinds and get a commission.

Here's the underlying strategy that makes this basic business model so incredibly successful. Blinds.com has no physical inventory and no product on hand. Nothing is purchased before it is sold. There is no guesswork about what we need to maintain in stock, and *money isn't spent to purchase the product until after the sale is made*. The Blinds.com website is very user friendly. Customers purchase the products, the business places the order with one of many preferred suppliers, and then each supplier drop ships the item to the customer. We'll have more to say about Blinds.com later in this chapter.

Many big online retail sites operate along these lines. Do you think Amazon has a warehouse containing the tens of millions of books and other items? Well, Amazon does have warehouses stocking the current best sellers. But what really makes Amazon is the reverse e-commerce business model.

They sell an item, take your money, then send the order to another firm that stocks the item. This firm then drop ships the product directly to you. So Amazon has far less money tied up in stock and warehouse space. If the item doesn't sell, Amazon has no leftover inventory. This is how Amazon can offer products at a discount and still make a profit.

"Sell It Before You Buy It": How to Do It Step by Step

You can "sell before you buy" with virtually no limits! Do you need products to sell or ideas to get you started? Here are some suggestions:

10 Steps to a Successful "Reverse E-commerce" Business

1. Go down to your own version of "Harwin Street." That's a location in Houston, Texas, where importers sell large and small quantities of products at wholesale prices. Most cities have a Harwin Street. New York has Canal Street; Los Angeles has a few streets downtown; San Francisco has a handful of them in or around Chinatown. If your city doesn't have a concentrated location for importers, check out your local flea market or a major city that has a shipping port where items flow into the United States.

2. Take some digital photos of 20, 30 or 50 products you think might sell well online. These could be watches, statues, automotive products or articles of clothing. This is a test to see what will sell.

3. Make sure to note the costs and how much inventory the importer or wholesaler has available.

4. Write advertising copy to accompany your photos to try and sell your newly found "virtual inventory."

5. Post them on eBay or any other online sales outlet (Craigslist, online classifieds, USAds).

6. See which products sell and which don't.

7. Collect the money.

8. Fulfill the sale.

9. Repeat steps 4-7 for the products that sell.

10. Go back out and find more products to test for sale.

Then, repeat the same process, often with the very same copy and photo you just used. Remember, the most successful sellers sell and resell and resell again – often from the very same photo. As long as there is inventory to sell, why not keep selling if the customers keep buying?

You can also take a picture of something in your home, in a friend's home, in a wholesaler's warehouse, in a used car lot or from anyone who wants to sell more of what he's already selling. The ideas are endless.

CLICK TIP ▶ **Suppose your friend has a car for sale. Make an agreement, preferably in writing, that if you can sell his car you keep all the money above his asking price. Then take a picture of the car and sell it (with your profit or markup included) via the Internet. Your friend is happy because he has money for his car. The customer is happy because he got the car he wanted. You're happy because you're pocketing your profit. You can do this with any product, any supplier or any importer who has inventory he or she wants to move.**

USA SuperSale.com – Selling Then Buying

Many people believe that there are very few opportunities left to make money on eBay. Gary Casper, owner of USASuperSale.com, proves them "flat" wrong!

Casper had the entrepreneurial bug, but hadn't found the right products to sell – until he met my college roommate David Fleishman, who had warehouses full of after-market auto parts. During their first conversation, Gary learned David had a surplus of automobile floor mats, which he asked if he could try to sell on eBay. Gary took photos of a few mats and immediately sold them at a substantial profit. So, Gary ramped up his marketing even before the actual mats were in his possession.

At first, to fulfill an order, Gary picked up each mat from his supplier. Soon, he was making trips to the wholesale supplier daily – often more than once a day – so Gary decided to purchase mats in bulk.

Maintaining inventory carried a higher risk, but that inventory was turning over at a rate of 200 mats per month. Within months, he had to rent warehouse space to store the mats he was selling on eBay. Able to store larger quantities, he invested in other wholesale products from his supplier, selling them mostly on eBay.

Eight months later, Gary tested automotive tail lights and again, they sold quickly and for a substantial profit. So he invested more and became known as a tail light and floor mat company. Then, Gary and Cheryl, his wife and business partner, tested selling another product, brake hardware, and subsequently added this, too. Volume was turning, and profits were soaring, but Gary's inventory model still carried increased costs and risk.

Hoping to take his eBay business to a new level, he launched his own e-commerce website, USASuperSale.com, profitably selling all of the same products he has on eBay. Because Gary's eBay and e-commerce sales are cash sales, he carries no receivables, which contributes to his overall profits.

As Gary consistently investigates new opportunities to prepare for the day the floor mat business slows down, he judges three levels of risk: no inventory, moderate inventory and massive inventory. As a result, Gary started to use a drop-shipping model for products where he makes less money per sale but reduces his risk because he doesn't have these products as inventory. Only when a product takes off and shows strong promise of ongoing popularity does Gary warehouse it in order to increase his profit per sale.

Scan the QR code or go to GetRichClick.com/gary to see his website in action.

In the world of the Internet,
no one ever knows if you, a friend
or a third party actually owned
the product you have listed for sale!

Customers don't care whether a product comes from your warehouse or someone else's. They only care that the product is as you've represented it, and that the transaction unfolds as promised.

Using this business model isn't just about making money—you are also being paid to learn. You learn what sells, what doesn't and how much profit you can get from each product. You find out which items are popular, how many people are bidding on your products and much more.

Get Rich Click means learning from your experiences and the experiences of others. Learn what clients want, what they're willing to pay and what your competitors are doing. Study the successes of others and be sure to . . .

Learn from others' mistakes!

The Online Retail Market

Online sales for 2010 were over $155 billion and they are expected to double by 2014. And online retail accounts for only 6 percent of total retail sales. Leading the way in online sales were travel, computer hardware and software, autos and auto parts, followed by apparel, accessories and footwear.

Vertical search – searching a market by a specific business category – is ripe for growth. This includes the computer category, software, video games, baby products and toys. Growth rates for pet supply, cosmetics and fragrance categories are expected to exceed 30 percent, surpassing all other growth rates.

CASE STUDY:
Shopster.com . . . or How to Sell over
1,000,000 Items and Own None of Them

Until recently, creating an "etail" business involved substantial up-front costs. But thanks to Shopster (shopster.com) and other similar sites (see Resources at the back of this book), budding web entrepreneurs or seasoned etail pros can sell any of over 1,000,000 items from Shopster's warehouse.

There's an unlimited upside with an e-commerce business of this type, and virtually no risk. Shopster handles all the hard stuff: product inventory, customer service, product delivery and shipping charges, fraud protection and your storefront hosting. You market your store and own your customers for as long as you can keep them coming back; it's a true e-commerce solution with an online storefront operating under your own website address. NOTE: You want to "own" your own customer, meaning that if you take the order and a firm like Shopster.com fulfills it, you need an agreement that they can't sell or resell to that customer. That customer is YOURS and you need to know and understand that the only person in this "supply chain" that can resell to that customer is you. If a supplier of yours EVER goes "around you" and sells to them again, never use them and find another supplier.

There is no simpler or easier way to start and run a new e-commerce business. Shopster is an all-in-one solution that gives you control of price, products, look and feel, all for a minimal monthly fee.

CASE STUDY:
BikeTiresDirect.com . . . or Rolling, Rolling, Rolling

If I had to pick my favorite *Get Rich Click* story in this book, it would be the story of Zachary and Nathan Doctor, two brothers who started a business in their dad's garage when Zachary was 10 years old and Nathan was 12. Their online bike tire business now generates $8 million in annual sales.

The Doctor boys were your average preteens. They went to school, played sports and found all kinds of ways to have fun. They also lived in an entrepreneurial family and did what the typical kids of entrepreneurial parents do, from setting up lemonade stands to finding other ways to make a few bucks. Their dad is Lou Doctor, a successful executive living in Silicon Valley. He runs a boutique investment banking firm called Arbor Advisors.

Lou Doctor enjoys cycling. His sons also adopted the sport early on. All three learned that in the world of cycling, special bike tires are the equipment of choice. You must have the right tires for the right application, from paved road to mountain path.

One day in 2002 Lou and his bike club ordered tires online from a specialty firm in the United Kingdom. To get the best price, they had to order in quantities of 10 tires per type. When they received their first order, Lou and his bike club were not thrilled. The tires were an odd color. No one in the bike club wanted them on their bikes.

Lou Doctor struck a deal with his sons. He gave the boys the tires and suggested they try to sell them on eBay. They could sell them for whatever price they wanted, but he needed $30 a tire to cover his costs. Above that, the boys could keep anything they got above that as profit. The sons went into action. They snapped digital photos of the ugly-colored tires, posted them for sale on eBay and waited.

Not only did the boys sell them in quick order, but they sold them for $35 each. Lou got his $300 investment back and the boys pocketed $50 for their efforts. The boys asked their dad to order 10 extra tires next time.

The same thing happened. The boys sold the 10 extra tires and again made a tidy profit.

Zachary and Nathan wanted more! They were making money and having fun at the same time. Soon there were more orders, more sales, more customers and more profits. They went from ordering 10 tires to ordering 50 and as many as 500 at a time from the retailer in the United Kingdom, who eventually gave them discounts for large-volume purchases.

Then the boys opened an eBay store. They got up each day at 5:00 a.m. and pulled the items, packed the orders, filled out the shipping labels and got to school at 7:30 a.m. When they came home, they went to work printing out the orders and getting them ready for fulfillment. Every day at 6:00 p.m., they took the packages to the local post office, where they became known for pulling bins of boxes and placing them directly on the back of the post office truck before it left for the distribution center.

It wasn't long before the brothers launched BikeTiresDirect.com, their own e-commerce website. The business kept growing – and in the *Get Rich Click* spirit, Zachary and Nathan pursued online marketing, learning how to buy the right Keyword combinations to get higher rankings in the search engines. They attribute much of their success to buying traffic via Keywords . . . *thousands* of Keywords and Keyword combinations that increase the number of "free" hits they get on Google, Yahoo and other search engines.

Thanks to the Doctor family, their tire supplier became the largest supplier of specialty bike tires in the United Kingdom. Today Zach is 20 and Nathan is 22. They have less time to work at the company, but they still help with buying Keywords and work during the summers. The company, with over $9.5 million in sales annually, now sells everything for the serious cyclist. And it's still growing.

Order Delivery Time in Five Minutes

Customers in virtually every country in the world order from BikeTiresDirect. Occasionally an order comes from a Silicon Valley customer. For fun, Lou Doctor would drive his kids to the customer's home, ring the bell and deliver the order – allowing the boys to meet and get to know some of their customers.

One day, they received an order from someone who lived only a few streets from their home. They quickly fulfilled the order, jumped in the car and drove to the customer's home, arriving five minutes after the order had been placed. When the customer answered the door, 10-year-old Zachary and 12-year-old Nathan were standing there, order in hand. Needless to say, the boys had a new customer for life. Word-of-mouth referrals from the delighted customer generated even more business for BikeTiresDirect.

eBay: The Easiest Way to Begin!

In 1995, to help his girlfriend buy and sell PEZ dispensers, Pierre Omidyar created eBay.com in his San Jose living room. Since then, guided by the vision of former president and CEO Meg Whitman, eBay has become a true cultural phenomenon, by far the largest person-to-person trading community on the Internet.

Using an auction format, sellers list items and buyers bid on them. Each eBay item has its own auction; buyers can choose the price they are willing to pay by bidding on the item or they can purchase those items listed as "Buy It Now." It's the equivalent of an online garage sale, yard sale, flea market or estate auction, presented through a business model that fulfills eBay's vision of connecting people. On any given day, 113 million concurrent listings are available through auction-style and fixed-priced events, representing the activity of 86.3 million active members worldwide.

eBay generates revenue with:
- seller listing fees
- charges for additional listing options and enhancements like bold type
- customization options (colors, borders and other highlight features) for auction presentations
- sales fees, generally ranging between 1.25 and 5 percent of the closing auction price

CLICK TIP ▶ **eBay has become the largest site on the Internet for buying and selling used cars, motorcycles and auto parts. Making Money with eBay is very easy to do. To make serious money, in *Get Rich Click* fashion, you need to find ways to "scale" and automate parts of the sales and fulfillment process. Examples include taking one product photo and using it over and over; finding suppliers that have the necessary inventory in stock and sell that same product over and over or cutting a deal with the manufacturer or supplier to "drop ship" the orders on your behalf – eliminating all of the time constraints of fulfillment on your end.**

One of the holy grails of making money on the Internet is attracting lots of visitors to a website. Driving traffic is an important way to generate online income. Because of eBay's popularity and growth, site traffic has skyrocketed to over 1 billion page views per day. So if you choose to sell using eBay, you minimize your traffic hurdle. The site has a worldwide customer base of nearly 100 million active customers, a global presence in 39 markets and in 2008 it traded 60 billion dollars in merchandise.

To get started making money on the Internet with eBay, you need access to a computer with an Internet connection, a registered eBay account (which is free) and a way to collect money. You can wait for a check or money order to arrive in the mail, but having an online collection method encourages customer spending.

To facilitate payments, eBay purchased PayPal in 2002, and this has become the standard payment option for eBay auctions. PayPal allows customers to register a bank account, credit card or debit card against which they can charge their purchases. Customers can also keep funds in the PayPal account. The fact that customers can pay (especially by credit card) without sharing their financial information with sellers has dramatically increased eBay's sales.

eBay Fun Facts

- eBay users trade more than $2,000 in goods and services on the site every second.
- In 2006, a luxury 405-foot yacht (sold by a company called 4Yacht) closed on eBay for $85 million. And that was just the deposit, its full cost was $168 million.
- eBay engineers have to add about 10 terabytes of new storage every week to cover new transactions.
- eBay has such high margins partly because it has no factories or inventory, and because its customers do the work.

Source: eBay, JennyHow and BlingIt.us

Many successful eBay businesses today practice reverse e-commerce as well as the drop-shipping business model. You find a company that will supply and drop ship high-quality, name-brand products that you sell first, then order from the supplier. These companies offer thousands of products they can drop ship to eBay buyers. Most suppliers do not require you to pay the wholesale cost of the item until a sale is made.

Other Ways to Make Money on eBay

The conventional sequence for making money on eBay is to list an item for auction and sell to a winning bidder. While this method works, there are others:

- **Create an eBay store.** An eBay store lets eBay sellers display all the items they sell "in one place . . . or under one virtual roof." Some stores sell niche items, and all their auctions are for similar products. Other stores are more like general stores. If someone clicks on your auction item and likes what you are selling, they can easily access your store site from that auction and other items you sell online.

- **Help other people sell their items.** You can do this with one of the new drop-off franchise retail stores, (AuctionDrop, QuikDrop and iSoldit), or you could do it as an independent consultant. The *Get Rich Click* principle at work here is: learn it and help others do it for a fee or a percentage of what you sell for them on eBay.

- **Teach others how to buy and sell on eBay.** If you like to offer others guidance, check out the eBay Education Specialist certification program available from eBay.

- **Buy "photo-less" items on eBay,** photograph them and relist them for sale, with a photograph. Items with photos sell on average for 20 percent more than those without photos, allowing you to mark up the item you bought and plan to relist with a product image.

- **Find poorly listed items, buy them, reword the descriptions, rewrite the sales copy and titles and relist them at a higher price.**

- **Buy and relist auction items that have a more desirable ending time.** Some items may "end" at 1:30 a.m. and hence sell for less than they would had they closed at 1:30 p.m. Watch auction closing prices and times to see if you can discern a pattern. Buy items from auctions that end low at off-peak times, and relist them to close higher at peak times. Business items, for example, sell best when the auctions end during typical business hours.

- **Buy lots, collections or groupings of items.** Relist and resell items individually. The profit from selling items individually will usually be higher than selling the items as a lot or in a bundle.

> **Sometimes people will pay more for an item on eBay than the normal "retail" price. Why? It's new, it's fun, it's different and they don't have to leave their home to get it.**

eBay Pricing Experiment

Call it a deal, call it a scheme, call it a strategy. Whatever you call it, it's a good example of the *Get Rich Click* principle of understanding how market dynamics work.

Ryan Black and Giff Nielsen, best friends and schoolmates, were always out to make a deal. Whether it was trading tuna sandwiches for tater tots during lunch at school or reselling lost golf balls to wayward golfers, these two had the entrepreneurial bug.

Fast-forward to eBay. Ryan and Giff's entrepreneurial fever reached a new pitch one day during their sophomore year in college. While checking the status of some hunting equipment Ryan had listed on eBay, they witnessed an unusual phenomenon: people were actually paying MORE than the retail price for items they were selling. They decided to test five more auctions of the same item – listing and selling each before they had actually purchased it.

When those five eBay auctions ended, buyers once again had paid more than the retail price. The two found the items at an online store, purchased them and drop shipped them to the various buyers. This phenomenon doesn't happen for every product on eBay, but it is another example of understanding markets and adapting to them – or leveraging your attack – in *Get Rich Click* fashion.

Ryan and Giff continued to repeat this process with a variety of goods during their college years, producing a more than adequate supplemental source of income!

CASE STUDY
Blinds.com ... or Traditional Marketing in an Online World

When you think of e-commerce in its simplest form, you think of a store (website), a product (or service), merchandising (online marketing), a way to take orders (a shopping cart) and a way to take money (a merchant processor). That's it!

But you still have to provide value. You still have to offer something different from the competition, and you still have to increase your visibility to potential buyers. You need to stake out a niche and carry out all the marketing fundamentals, exactly as you would a traditional brick-and-mortar retail store.

Jay Steinfeld, founder, owner and CEO of Blinds.com, took all these factors into consideration in 1994, during the dot-com boom. With little technological savvy, Jay entered the online world. He had an idea, he had $1,500, he had retail experience running a drapery store and he had some guts. He launched a simple, one-page website.

At the time, shopping carts and online merchant processors were not commonplace on the Internet. Jay spent time and money getting his company listed high in the most popular search engines. He solicited links for his site and soon had over 1,000 inbound and reciprocal links. He made sure the right online ordering system was on his site. With these elements in place, he rode the fast track to success.

Jay implemented and managed the right fundamentals for his online retail business, much as a brick-and-mortar retail store would:
- Serve a unique niche market
- Make it easy to buy
- Create and maintain a presence with your target market
- Ally yourself with others
- Offer something unique or better than what is currently available in the marketplace

Jay knew online success depended on making the buying process easy. Emphasizing functionality over aesthetics, Blinds.com was listed as one of the top 200 in *Internet Retailer* Top 500 (even ahead of Nike), and *Internet Retailer* identified it as the tenth fastest-growing e-commerce company.

Part of Blinds.com's success depends on things brick-and-mortar retail operations don't or can't do:

A. Blinds.com carries no physical inventory. They operate on a just-in-time, made-to-order manufacturing business model.

B. Customers pay for orders online, prior to the custom blinds being made so Blinds.com has no accounts receivables.

C. Blinds are drop shipped from a variety of suppliers.

Blinds.com started its online life as nobrainerBlinds.com. Four years later, Jay changed the name to Blinds.com. He found the most popular domain name in the blinds business and purchased it. This was an exceptional strategic move that gave his company a competitive edge. It also helped search engine rankings, especially when prospects typed in "blinds" as a direct navigation term. At the time, the domain name resale market was just evolving and heating up. Jay spent well into six figures for the Blinds.com domain name, but it was a strategic move that has paid for itself many times over.

How well is this model working for Blinds.com? Typically a Walmart superstore will do an estimated $600 to $700 in business per square foot of space. Blinds.com has a small office and area for order processing that generates close to $8,000 per square foot.

What's next for Blinds.com? Jay Steinfeld realized his firm wasn't a blinds company. It was a direct marketing company. With his processes, procedures, methods and marketing, he discovered he had a formula for extending that model to other complex, customizable products for consumers. His newest venture, under the umbrella of Global Custom Commerce, will offer a variety of products online. These products are unrelated to blinds and may not even be related to the home at all. Scale and a reproducible business model are the keys.

Putting Your Ideas into Action

- Get the best domain name(s) you can that define your products or services.
- Get good, high-quality links pointing to your site.
- Understand how to increase Internet traffic – both free traffic, (known as organic traffic) and paid traffic.
- Master "niche marketing." Don't try to sell everything. Be the best with your own product or category.
- Make it easy for customers to do business with your site.
- Sell before you buy. You don't need inventory.
- Customers pay for all sales up front and in full.
- All orders are drop shipped by the manufacturer after the custom blinds are made at any one of their suppliers around the U.S.

3
SEARCHing for Gold

You've just been invited to appear before your largest prospect's board of directors. You're going to discuss your target market, your offerings, your competition and other topics critical to your business. The meeting is in two days.

A few years ago, preparing for this meeting would have involved phone calls, visits to the library, interviews and other time-consuming research. Impossible in two days!

But today the Internet puts millions of pages of information at your fingertips. This information can give you a competitive edge. When you know how to search for it, you'll be in a much better position to create a profitable business.

Search Engines: Understanding Them Is the Real Key to Success

Given the huge volume of data on the Internet, people turn to search engines when they are looking for information. So search engine marketing is critically important to online businesses. You can spend every penny you have on a website, but it will all be for nothing if nobody knows your site is there.

CLICK TIP ▷ Search engines will "blacklist" sites that violate their rules. The most common violation is Keyword spamming – adding Keywords to your titles and tags that have nothing to do with your site's content (and yes, search engines can tell). Other offenses can include Keyword crowding, Keyword repetition and Keyword drowning. Learn what these terms and concepts mean, and don't do them! Blacklisting can seriously reduce your traffic, which affects your income, which affects the value of your assets. I saw a website's income plummet from $12,500 a month to $1,500 a month. You can get your website off the blacklist, but it's difficult.

How the Search Engines Really Work

Search engines use electronic devices (called "spiders," "bots," or robots) to scan the Internet for information from all public websites. After the search engine has cataloged this information, someone entering a word or phrase (a "query") can call up a ranked list of all the relevant search results.

Relevance is a search engine's holy grail. People want results that are closely connected to their queries. Different search engines use different criteria and rules to determine relevance. For example, some engines use the number of links pointing to a particular website as a gauge of its popularity. Others use the domain name. For example, CuffLinks.com would be more popular than abcufflinks.com.

Every search engine has developed formulas – and the formulas are constantly changing – to evaluate the relevance of any web page's content to a search query. Search engine companies tend to keep their formulas for this process secret.

Here's an explanation of this from Google, the most popular search engine. Stop reading if you get a headache:

> *The software behind our search technology conducts a series of simultaneous calculations requiring only a fraction of a second. Traditional search engines rely heavily on how often a word appears on a web page. We use more than 200 signals, including our patented PageRank™ algorithm, to examine the entire link structure of the web and determine which pages are most important. We then conduct hypertext-matching analysis to determine which pages are relevant to the specific search being conducted. By combining overall importance and query-specific relevance, we're able to put the most relevant and reliable results first. (Corporate Information, Google)*

Organic Search

Most Internet users are not inclined to wade through pages and pages of search results. So the goal for businesses is not merely to be listed, but to place in the first few pages of results – ideally, on the first page.

In the past you could pay for higher placements in query results that applied to your site. There are still a few search engines that will do this. But Google changed the playing field when it designed an egalitarian model that produced ranked, relevant results from all available sites, not just those that paid for the privilege. As a result search engine optimization and search engine marketing soon became critical areas businesses needed to address to improve visibility and drive traffic.

At the present time search results come in two flavors: organic and paid. Paid results appear in a pale-colored box across the top and run part-way down the right side of the page. Organic results fill the majority of the page, usually include more description and have a link near the end of the text.

When you optimize your pages for organic search, your goal is to move your pages higher in the list of search results. Search engine optimization should be a part of your marketing program. It does take time to achieve improved rankings this way, but the work will pay off in the long run. Basic optimization strategies include cultivating incoming links and presenting quality content (especially text) that incorporates important Keywords.

While it's difficult to track how much website owners are making from organic search engine marketing, many people are making a living from the business leads they get through organic results. There are many companies that offer optimization services, and it can definitely be worth your while to invest in their expertise.

On-Page and Off-Page Factors That Affect Ranking

Many factors contribute to getting higher search-engine rankings. "On-page" factors are those associated with your site's web pages. "Off-page" factors are ways to affect your ranking that don't appear on an actual web page.

ON-PAGE FACTORS INCLUDE:

1. **Strong Keywords.** Determine the best Keywords and Keyword phrases for your market, products and the people searching for your products and services.

2. **Design.** Know how to design a page that is search-engine friendly. This is part art, part science and extremely important. I recall an entire website that was designed in a type of software that makes website design easy. The site looked great, but the search engines couldn't "read" any words on the page. The result: the beautiful site was invisible to the search engines.

3. **Create words.** Put words on your page that are the exact same as the top search engine queries people type into the search engines when they are looking for what you provide. It's also a good idea to use synonyms for these words.

4. Each page on the site must be original content. Don't copy text from a supplier. If you take the product description directly from a supplier, your page will be the same as every other firm that uses the same text. You won't place any higher in the rankings, and the duplication may work against you.

5. Freshness of the content. Keep your content up-to-date. Be on top of your market so you can continually revise Keywords and copy.

6. Usability. Make certain your site is user-friendly. Categorization schemes based on hyperlinked text are excellent ways to improve rankings and help your visitors quickly find what they are looking for.

7. Direct navigation. How much direct navigation traffic does the site get? A domain name built on one of your primary Keywords is like gold.

8. Metatags. Each page of your site needs a unique "metatag" to tell the search engines about that page. Make sure you understand how to use metatags properly.

9. Stickiness. Look at website metrics that let you know how long a visitor stays on a page and on your site overall. Do people stay on your site for 8 seconds or 15 minutes? If users stay on a site longer, the site is generally doing a better job meeting their needs. Sites that aren't sticky generally fail to present targeted, persuasive copy (and copy does affect your ranking). When visitors stay on a page longer, search engines give the page a higher importance rating.

10. Site submissions. In general, you are better off waiting until the spiders naturally crawl your site. There are techniques to speed up the process (see Chapter 5). When search engines do allow you to submit your site, the process can take time. Submitting your site may make sense if you have made major changes to your site, but be very careful not to submit frequently. Understand the specific requirements of each search engine and submit your web address accordingly.

OFF-PAGE FACTORS INCLUDE:

1. Links. Frequently reevaluate the inbound and outbound links to your site and answer these questions:
- How many links point to your site?
- Are they quality links?
- How old are the links?
- What is the content at the other end of those links?
- Were they "free" links or did you pay for them?
- Do you "reciprocate" these links?
- Do the links take the prospect directly to the page they want or to the homepage?

2. Directory listings. Services such as Open Directory Project (DMOZ) and Yahoo! are respected directory listings. When these directories include a link to your site, it has a bearing on how the search engines rank your site. Submitting each page on your site separately (each with its own set of Keywords) to a directory can also help raise your rankings.

Paid Search

Internet users submit hundreds of millions of inquiries into search engines and don't pay a dime – but the search industry takes those free searches and turns them into gold. They do it by offering advertising to those who want to reach targeted buyers.

Here's how it works. Businesses enroll in a search engine's advertising program and create Pay-Per-Click ads that are Keyword-driven. They choose words or phrases that are relevant to their businesses. An auto repair shop in Chicago might choose "Chicago car mechanic." The ads appear when search engine users type in those words. When someone clicks on the ad, the business pays the search engine for that click, whether the prospect buys anything or not.

Advertisers don't pay a flat fee for ad placement. Instead, they bid how much they are willing to pay when a search engine user clicks on one of their ads. The highest bid wins placement at the top of the Pay-Per-Click list. Advertisers pay the per-click amount they bid only when a user clicks on the ad.

This is a revolution in marketing. This model puts advertisers in closer touch with the people who are predisposed to purchase their products or services. Those people have expressed their interest (and their intent) through the Keywords they entered in their search query. As a result, businesses waste fewer advertising dollars. Search-based advertising has attracted thousands of small businesses and entrepreneurs that haven't spent money on advertising in the past.

Advertising and Local Search

Local search allows users to designate a geographical locality when they search for Keywords and phrases. The local-search search engine then restricts results to the location the user specified.

Some of the larger local search sites are:
- Yahoo! Local (local.yahoo.com)
- Windows Live Local (maps.live.com)
- Google Maps (formerly Google Local) (maps.google.com)
- Superpages (superpages.com)

Like their traditional counterparts, these search engines compete for traffic and ad revenue. Traditional local media are adding local search capabilities to their sites so they can share in the local search traffic and ad revenues in the local markets they serve.

If you want to increase your visibility in these search engines, make sure you embed location information in your website. If you don't, local search will not locate you.

The Opportunity

The number of small businesses in the United States totals about 25 million. Because most of these have a local trading territory, relatively few advertise online. Online advertising reaches the masses of the Internet world, whether they are local or not. As more and more of their customers migrate to the Internet, small businesses will need to consider some form of online advertising.

Your awareness that this growth is coming makes for a huge *Get Rich Click* opportunity. Learn as much as you can about local advertising and marketing via the Internet. Then help firms accomplish the transition from radio, television and billboard marketing to Internet-based marketing.

CLICK TIP "Geo-targeted" domain names are gaining a huge following. Names like NewYork.com, Dallas.com or Bahamas.com have become instant profit centers. For that reason, these domain names have become the ultimate Internet real estate investment.

7 Tips for KEYWORDS

If you want to truly understand the good, the bad and the ugly of search engines, I strongly recommend you read this. Keywords for a website need to be specific to the site or page on the site, relevant, applicable and clearly associated with the content on your page.

1. Understand how search engines allow you to use Keywords (i.e., placement, color).

2. Understand how many times you can use a Keyword on a page (frequency, density, distribution, etc.).

3. If you use redirection technology, it should facilitate and improve the user experience. Know this is almost always considered a trick and can lead to a search engine blacklisting your site.

4. If you use redirection technology, it should always display a page where the body content contains the appropriate Keywords (no bait and switch).

5. If you use redirection technology, you may not alter the web address (redirect), affect the browser back button (cause a loop) or display page information that is not the property of the site owner (or is not allowed by agreement) without sound technical justification (i.e., language redirects).

6. Do not submit pages to the search engines too frequently.

7. For more Keyword tips, go to GetRichClick.com/Keywords.

Direct Navigation Traffic

There are **ONLY** three ways to reach a website:

1. Click on a link from another website.

2. Click on a link in search engine results.

3. Enter the specific domain name or URL into the browser address bar . . . known as direct navigation.

Many people bypass search engines altogether and still find what they're looking for online. These Internet surfers are using direct navigation.

In direct navigation, users type exactly what they are looking for in the browser's web address field. This could be the exact domain name or web address.

Millions of people do this, emphasizing the need for on- and offline marketing and branding. As much as 8–14 percent of Internet traffic comes from direct navigation.

Direct navigation traffic is by far the most highly targeted form of web traffic available. If your firm is lucky enough to own the proper domain name for its industry, not only will you get this highly targeted "type-in" traffic, but you will keep you competitors from obtaining those leads as well.

When you choose your domain name, remember this quote from the former CEO of McDonald's: "We are in the real estate business. The only reason we sell hamburgers is because they are the greatest producer of revenue from which our tenants can pay us rent."

Real estate is a great road to wealth. "Domain names and Websites are Internet Real Estate.™" – Marc Ostrofsky

Entering a generic web address often directs the browser to a page populated with relevant ads that generate commissions for the site owner when visitors click on them. Many times these ads provide the relevant content the searcher is looking for.

Several organizations have estimated that traffic to unused, generic domain name sites, also known as "parked domains," drives 10 percent of the Pay-Per-Click market. Conversion rates from click to purchase for direct navigation are almost double those for search engines.

CASE STUDY:

Jobster and Recruiting.com

In mid-2006, a recruiting company called Jobster acquired Recruiting.com. Recruiting.com is more than a domain name. It's a recruiting blog with multiple writers and over 1,400 visits a day, mostly from people interested in what is going on in the world of recruiting. The site has strong content and ideas, and creates a vibrant community.

The key here is that Jobster acquired a branded domain name that has the potential of direct navigation traffic as well.

According to Keyword searches, the term "recruiting" has a monthly search volume of 400,000 inquiries. That represents a significant amount of traffic, even if Recruiting.com is getting only a portion of it. Because Jobster now gets direct navigation traffic, they are saving money they otherwise would have had to spend on paid search and search engine optimization to get the same traffic. Owning a direct navigation domain name lessens the need for Pay-Per-Click and optimization, which not only saves money, but increases the return on the investment of maintaining that domain.

Making Money with Direct Navigation

The best thing you can do to bring traffic to your website is to control as many natural, direct-navigation, typed-in domain names as possible, provided they are related to your niche market or industry. Traffic generated in this way comes directly to you and will never be dependent on the ever-changing search engines.

Here are three ideas that'll help you quickly generate dollars using direct navigation:

1. Redirect ALL of your generic domain names to your primary domain name website. Barnes and Noble does this with books.com.

2. Use a generic domain name site as a vertical portal that redirects to your company's products or to your main site. Johnson and Johnson does this with Baby.com.

3. Create a new "brand" with a generic domain name. Beer.com has done this on their site with the tag line "the official beer of the Internet." Other owners of generic names are following suit and should do well (until corporate America figures out the value of these assets and starts to buy them up).

Investing in a direct navigation generic domain name can yield a good if not great return on your investment. It will depend on the quality of the domain name, how you market and promote it, how you attract traffic and how you convert the traffic into actual clicks and sales. Generate enough traffic and sales, and you build equity. In the *Get Rich Click* world, cashing in on this equity will increase your income significantly.

The purchase of a highly targeted, marketable, generic domain name can deliver more high-quality, targeted visitors at a lower cost than Pay-Per-Click advertising.

10 Great Reasons to Own a Generic Domain Name

1. You get the best targeted traffic possible, better than Pay-Per-Click or link traffic. If a person is typing in the very word your firm represents, they are more likely to be a buyer.
2. You keep your competitors from getting this targeted traffic.
3. You can get traffic you never expected.
4. The domain is considered "Internet real estate." You can "write off" the cost of this business asset (but ask your CPA or lawyer for advice first).
5. You can increase your search engine ranking with a great domain name.
6. You can get "accidental" traffic that might otherwise have gone to your competitors.
7. You own "mindshare." That, too, will bring traffic to your business.
8. There is great public relations value in owning a one- or two-word generic domain name that is the name of your industry or business. When stories are written about an industry, topic, product or service, the media often look up these firms by the generic word or web address.
9. Your firm saves money on not having to buy as much Pay-Per-Click advertising.
10. No one else can ever own it – as long as you pay your annual fee!

Taking advantage of direct navigation by investing in domain names can be a viable *Get Rich Click* strategy. However, investment in direct navigation can be expensive. It might entail a significant financial investment, as it did when we purchased the Blinds.com domain name. Sometimes this investment is beyond the reach of many of us, and sometimes a whole business is built around the buying and selling of these domain names (see Chapter 7 and GetRichClick.com).

Direct navigation won't replace search engines, but as more and more people type searches directly into their browsers, investing in additional domain names may prove prudent. That may include investing in domain names with new suffixes. Dot-com names are still the most popular and are expected to remain "the gold standard" for domains. But new suffixes like .biz, .info and others called "cc.TLDs" offered by specific countries like .eu (European Union), .cn (China) and .es (Spain) may also provide opportunities to make money from direct navigation traffic.

Vertical Search Is the Next Big Market

Vertical search is search narrowly defined around a central topic, industry, niche, format, genre or location. Vertical search engines or websites that offer vertical search for a given topic can focus on travel, health and medicine, shopping, law, government, blogs or even geographical areas and municipalities.

Vertical search is a growing tier in the search industry. Because search engines are tremendously successful at generating advertising revenue, vertical search engines have an opportunity to target users specifically interested in that domain's industry category, product, service or industry.

Eighty percent of vertical search engines fall into the four primary categories of retail, travel, financial services and media/entertainment. Other types of vertical search engines include:

● **Pay-Per-Click**	● **Computing**
● **Children**	● **Science**
● **Country-specific**	● **Shopping sites**
● **Image search**	● **Mailing lists**
● **Audio and Video**	● **Domain names**

Traditional horizontal search engines cannot always identify the target audience, niche or vertical industry of a page or site. Vertical search engines address this issue by the nature of their design. They identify sites according to more specific criteria and sometimes even by human input.

Visit SearchEngineWatch.com to learn more about vertical search.

Benefits of Vertical Search Engine Marketing

Vertical search engines that match your business, service or products with a target market offer you a higher conversion rate than traditional search engines. Because they have already qualified their interest by coming to a search engine with a specific focus, searchers will be more receptive to targeted advertising. Pay-Per-Click campaigns with a vertical search engine result in higher click-through rates and higher conversion rates. When optimizing your site and your overall marketing efforts, consider these vertical engines, and develop a presence and position with each one.

A GOODE physical business and a GREAT piece of the pie . . .

If you like BBQ, Texas is the place. And if you want the best BBQ in Texas, you go to Goode Company BBQ in Houston. Goode Company is a family-owned and family-operated chain of restaurants that started as one small eatery and has since grown into a multimillion dollar restaurant conglomerate! Included in Goode's many delicious options are a seafood restaurant, a hamburger and Mexican food taqueria and a saloon-themed music hall called the Armadillo Palace.

Recently, the Goode family has ventured into the virtual world by selling a host of their homemade delicacies online, ranging from savory BBQ sauce, to sweet pecan pralines and their signature, world-famous, five-pound pecan pie. They're even experimenting with taking Internet orders for BBQ meats for overnight delivery anywhere in the country – bringing a taste of Texas to citizens in all 50 states!

"We started with one store, and over time grew into 7 locations, now serving more than 10,000 people a week," explains Levi Goode, president of the company and son of founder Jim Goode. "We moved into direct mail a few years back and that evolved into selling on the web. Now we do millions of dollars of revenue online, and based on the growth and profit margin of our Internet sales, I could easily see the online component of our business out-selling some of our retail locations in a few years."

Goode, who has a degree in culinary arts and assumed his current leadership position after spending years working in every aspect of the family business, clearly has a firm grasp of the new economy: "It's obvious that the Internet is a game changer – for us and for almost any other business or entrepreneur. My goodness, we produce BBQ and Pecan Pies. If we sell on the Internet, anyone can. Oh," Goode adds, "and if you don't want to sell your own products, you can sell ours!" He's apparently not joking. The company is planning to create an affiliate program that should be available very soon. Imagine, even if all you've ever known is New York cheesecake and Philadelphia cheesesteak, now you can enjoy – and profit from – genuine Texas BBQ and pecan pie!

Scan the QR code or go to GetRichClick.com/levi to watch Levi's interview.

**Our new website is eggsalad-armpit.com.
All of the good names were already taken!**

Vortals: The Vertical Portal

Danny Sullivan, the guru who founded a fantastic website called SearchEngineWatch.com, wrote the following:

For those times when you want to find more than just web pages and websites, some of the specialty search engines will prove useful. Also called topical search engines, vertical search engines, or vortals, they'll help you search through specific types of listings in different areas.

- **Answers searching**
- **Computer search engines**
- **Domain searching**
- **Financial search engines**
- **Government search**
- **Invisible web**
- **Legal search engines**
- **Mailing lists**
- **Medical search engines**
- **Newsgroup search**
- **Science search engines**
- **Shopping search**
- **Travel search engines**
- **WAP search engines**
- **Other specialty services**

Here's a *Get Rich Click* money-making idea. Build a better mousetrap. Some firms simply aggregate sites or data from other sites by compiling information, products or services and make that data easier to read, easier to navigate, more presentable, more efficient or better organized for the particular target market. [Note: If you want to play with this business model, please be sure to ask your copyright attorney about the legal ramifications before proceeding.]

Price and Product Comparison Sites

Comparison sites save people's time. They offer many types of products from many providers. Moneysupermarket.com is a good example. Here users can find multiple providers for products and services related to money, insurance, travel, mobile plans, broadband providers, general shopping and more. Moneysupermarket.com allows customers to compare the marketplace prices for products and services.

A comparison site owner earns commissions on the sale of products or services from the comparison site. Comparison sites have a reputation for pushing the products and services on which they earn the highest commissions, compromising the objectivity of comparison. As you might expect, some do this, some don't.

Merchants sign up with a comparison site and make their product inventory available for the comparison site's search engine by Keyword. The merchants pay when visitors click on their items or domain name. Sometimes merchants can pay for a privileged position in the comparison site results listing or on the actual website itself. Paid positioning is usually identified as a sponsored link, a featured link or a featured merchant.

Other popular shopping comparison sites include:
- **PriceGrabber.com**
- **ShopWiki.com**
- **Shopzilla.com (formerly bizrate.com)**
- **Shopping.com (now owned by eBay)**
- **LowerMyBills.com**
- **Smarter.com**
- **Become.com**
- **Edeals.com**
- **Product Search (google.com/products, Google's comparison site, formerly Froogle)**
- **NexTag.com**

If you have information
that has value to others,
the Internet allows you to
easily package, sell or resell
that information.

CASE STUDY:

Mpire.com

Mpire.com found a way to compile, collect and distribute information related to eBay products and auctions (they have since expanded to include a wide variety of online retailers). Mpire then packaged the information and made it available online to shoppers and businesses through their Researcher application (mpire.com/products/researcher.html). Researcher is available as a "widget" and as a "plug in" on your computer and allows you to:

● Find out how likely an item is to sell on eBay, which helps you evaluate an item's resale potential

● Learn the average selling price of an item for sale on eBay

● See how many matching items have been sold on eBay, which tells you whether your product is one in a million or one of millions like it

● Find information related to factors that include top Keywords, best day and time to sell an item and average starting price

This information is precisely the sort of invaluable intelligence you need to make informed buying and selling decisions and manage a business and gain a competitive advantage over others.

Social Media Marketing Guide

101 Social Media Sites to Help Market Your Business or Yourself Online

Copyright by SEOmoz.org

GetRichClick.com/social

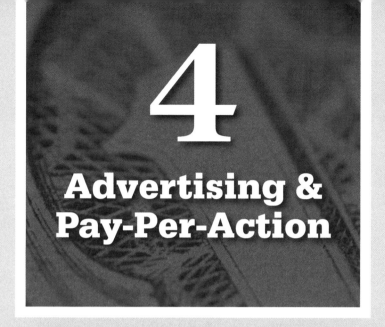

4
Advertising & Pay-Per-Action

In recent years new words like "podcast" and "bling" have made their way into the dictionaries. One of the most important new words to enter the language is "google." The Merriam Webster Collegiate Dictionary made "google" an official verb and noun in 2006. It's impressive when a company name or a branded product (think "kleenex") enters mainstream use. And Google has certainly been impressive.

Get Rich Click
with a Broader View of Google

In mid-2008, Google provided results for over 235 million searches daily. That's a huge source of potential traffic to your website. Thanks to Google's efforts to make their search model profitable, you have the opportunity to direct some of this traffic your way.

Every online entrepreneur and business should consider paid search advertising as a strategy for making significant income. If you are still unaware of these opportunities and think of Google as just a search engine, we are about to change that.

The umbrella platform for all Google's paid advertising, including Google AdSense, is Google AdWords. Google has created a suite of free business tools for users – powerful programs like Google Analytics and Google website Optimizer.

Why would Google invest resources in developing sophisticated tools like these and then offer them for free? It's because Google's goal is for you to realize the value of optimization and monetization, so you'll sign up for their paid AdWords service.

Welcome to the world of Google Ads, those little ads you see on the right-hand side of so many websites selling anything and everything!

Google AdSense: The Beginning of the "Internet Advertising" Gold Rush!

When Google first developed its AdSense program in 2003, web publishers heralded it as a monetization revolution. Today Google AdSense is one of the most popular site "monetizers" in the world today. No matter what your online business model, Google AdSense offers you a powerful, proven way to increase your earnings.

AdSense is a great way for businesses, entrepreneurs and website owners to generate steady income, publicize and market any product or service to a targeted audience.

To start using AdSense, you simply enroll. You must have a launched website with a valid web address and content that meets Google's "acceptable" guidelines. You must also have a valid name and address for receiving payments. You then customize how you would like your ads to appear, add a block of html code to your site and you're off and running.

Google uses its AdWords advertiser database to match highly relevant ads to your site's content and feeds these ads to your site. You do not need to maintain relationships with advertisers, select ads or even pay for them; Google manages it all. Advertisers "pay" (it's actually a bidding process) for placing their ads in the AdWords database, but you pay nothing. Using AdSense is free.

In essence, Google is renting your website for billboard space. This increases ad exposure for Google's advertisers. And because advertisers pay Google every time a visitor clicks on one of their ads, it's in Google's interest to make sure the ads that appear on your site are highly relevant.

AdSense operates on a Pay-Per-Click model; Google pays you "rent" every time a visitor clicks on one of the AdSense links. Each click translates into pennies or dollars a day for you. The more clicks, the more money you make.

CLICK TIP Caution! Never, never – and I mean never – click on your own site's ad links in Google AdSense or any other Pay-Per-Click program. That's known as "click fraud," and the penalties can be severe.

If you want to make money, you can, and should, participate in AdSense. It truly is one of the easier ways to make money, especially since Google does most of the work for you. It's too good to pass up for the small effort that is involved. The only time it might not make sense to use AdSense is when ads compete with your own products and services (although AdSense does provide filtering to minimize these conflicts).

Using AdSense isn't completely effortless. You still have to create and maintain a site, fill it with content people find interesting, generate traffic and enroll with Google. But if you do these things – especially if you focus on driving traffic – you can make significant income in *Get Rich Click* fashion.

How much money can you earn using AdSense? The answer depends on how much advertisers pay Google for the Keyword ads that comprise AdWords. A per-click commission can range from a few cents to several dollars, which can translate into hundreds, even thousands a day, week or month depending on traffic volume at your site. Remember that targeted traffic will "out-click" or have a higher value than generic traffic.

7 Steps to Start Making Money with Google AdSense

1. Sign up for a Google AdSense Account at GetRichClick.com/adsense.

2. Place the html code that Google supplies into the coding for your website. This allows AdSense to feed relevant ads to your site.

3. Monitor clicks with the software Google supplies.

4. Tweak and refine content and Keywords to get ads that are as targeted and relevant as possible. This increases the likelihood visitors to your site will click on the ads.

5. Drive targeted traffic to your site.

6. Review your content and Keywords periodically to improve the quality of your traffic so that you make more money.

7. Receive commission checks from Google.

How to Refine Your Site's Use of Google AdSense

● Keep your content to one main topic per web page.
● Help the ads stand out with colors, positioning, borders, bold type and white space.
● Continually test ad placement and appearance (you can use Google website Optimizer to test these factors – it's free).
● Add more content related to the primary Keyword phrase.

- Create more Keyword-focused pages.
- Increase click-through rate. Use a simple design for your site with lots of white space. Don't make the appearance cluttered. Display the AdSense ads prominently. According to Google, ads in the skyscraper format on the right side of the page work best. Focus on one topic per web page. This allows Google to place the most relevant ads, which will increase your click-through rate.
- Increase the value of clicks. Create pages and topics to encourage AdSense to feed ads with more expensive Keywords or use Keywords that pay you $.75 per click vs., say, $.50 a click.

Google AdWords: There's Gold in the Words!

AdWords is the backbone of Google's paid advertising programs. All the advertising Google provides through its various search platforms (like Product Search, Google Maps, Google Finance) and AdSense come from AdWords.

Advertisers "buy" ads based on Keywords, and AdWords places those ads, as "Sponsored Links," on the Google search engine on sites that use AdSense. Advertisers can also choose to show their ads through Google's network partners, including AOL Search, Ask.com and Netscape.

To begin using Google AdWords, you need to establish an AdWords account. You provide a credit card and pay a small activation fee. You don't pay to have Google display your ad; you pay only when someone clicks on your ad. You can specify exactly how much you are willing to spend; you can set an overall budget maximum and a per-click fee maximum. AdWords has no minimum or maximum spending requirements.

AdWords offers a Starter Edition and a Standard Edition:

- **Starter.** Advertise a single product or service with simplified options. Recommended for those who are new to Internet advertising. Move up to the Standard Edition at any time.

- **Standard.** Use our full range of AdWords features and functionality: advanced bidding options, multiple campaigns, conversion tracking and more. Recommended for experienced Internet advertisers and medium- or large-sized businesses. (Google AdWords)

An AdWords campaign is built on one or more ads using one or more Keywords. Keywords trigger the ad; when a user types the Keyword into the search engine, Google calls up the ad.

Usually an ad is composed of three lines of text. The first line of text is your ad title; it's the dominant element in your ad and contains the link users click on. You get 25 characters (including spaces) to capture the attention of your audience. The next two lines are for descriptive copy; each line contains a maximum of 35 characters. The last line of the ad is the web address to which the ad links, so users know where the click will take them (this line is not linked).

Creating the copy for these ads is both art and science. You have very little space in which you can communicate how you can meet the user's needs, so compose carefully. The better you understand your customers, the more successful your ads will be. Test the performance of your ads to determine which combination of words works best for them (and you).

Choosing your Keywords is critical to the success of your advertising campaign. So Keyword research is essential. The AdWords interface provides a way for you to get Keywords related to the ones you think are important. Depending on the cost of the Keyword, these may be more cost effective to use. When you set your cost-per-click – how much you will pay Google each time someone clicks on your ad – you are essentially bidding for your Keyword.

Pay-Per-Click advertising is one of the best ways to generate high-quality traffic to your website. Because it lets the advertiser control expenses by setting maximums for each click, AdWords is the most popular platform for Pay-Per-Click advertising for small businesses.

As Google explains:

• Your ad will compete with ads from other advertisers who also have set their own prices. Your success will be based on how much you bid, the quality of your ad, how many other people want to advertise on the same Keywords and other factors.

• Very popular topics and Keywords (such as "real estate" or "hotels") can cost more because so many other people also want to advertise on them. If you set very low prices on those popular Keywords, your ad may appear only rarely or not at all. If you set higher bids on very specific Keywords, your ad is likely to appear more often, and in higher positions yielding more clicks, at the price you want. (Google AdWords)

The Importance of Keywords in Online Advertising

Keywords are an expression of intention. They indicate the nature of the problem users are trying to resolve. From a business's perspective, these Keywords can indicate targeted traffic with an intention to buy.

Constructing Keyword lists is an "ongoing and never-ending" brainstorming exercise. New products, services, trends and concepts — any and every Keyword or set of Keywords that you can think of to bring prospective clients to your site should be written down and used on the site to attract more eyeballs to your site. Think of every word or phrase related to your company, your industry and to the products or services you sell. Brainstorming has no rules, so don't fence yourself in. You can edit or pare down your list after your brainstorming session is done. Play random association games with your Keyword list. Ask others what comes to their minds when they think about what you do. Look at sites for those doing business similar to yours.

CLICK TIP ▶ Using AdWords is a good strategy for getting a new site to appear more quickly in the search engines. Far fewer search engines today have for-fee listing services. Inclusion in the Google search engine is free. Nevertheless, it can take time for the search spiders to find you.

Algorithms determine how frequently search spiders crawl sites to locate them and update information. How often this happens depends on a number of factors, and it's inevitable spiders can miss your site.

Virtually every product, benefit, brand and Keyword are matched together to come up with that list of words. If you can anticipate the right set of words a potential customer might type in and use them on your site in ways that get you higher rankings in the search engines (see Chapter 5), you get the lead that might have gone to a competitor . . . at NO COST to you!

Remember, there are only three ways to get to a website:
- Using a search engine
- Via a "link" from another site or domain
- By direct navigation (typing the domain name directly into the toolbar)

The majority of Internet users rely on search engines to research and locate the things they want to buy. Compiling a large list of suitable Keywords helps you create ads for paid searches that will reach your target audience. Because there's stiff competition for many popular Keywords, targeting secondary Keywords is often a better strategy.

How many Keywords and phrases do you need? BikeTiresDirect.com has over 15,000 Keyword combinations for its site while others have 50,000+ Keyword combinations!

Determining the Value of Keywords

Research every possible Keyword, brand name, benefit, slogan, slang – anything and everything that someone might type into a browser that could bring you a client. Then determine how often people search for the Keywords you have chosen and determine who else is using those words in their Internet marketing. You can learn more about Keywords at GetRichClick.com.

***Get Rich Click* Resource:** Here are some Internet tools to find out what Keywords users are searching on:

- Google offers a version of its Keyword tool; it can help you identify Keywords, synonyms and their popularity (GetRichClick.com/Keywordtools).
- Google Analytics (google.com/analytics) contains a feature called "Keyword Campaign Comparison" for use with AdWords.
- Google Sandbox Tool (GetRichClick.com/Keywordtools) is designed for use in an AdWords campaign and covers data on Keyword popularity on Google.
- Wordtracker (GetRichClick.com/Keywordtools) is the biggest and possibly most respected Keyword research tool. They have other related tools and fee-based services.
- KeywordDiscovery (GetRichClick.com/Keywordtools) is Wordtracker's rival, offering a database of search terms over a yearly seasonal trend analysis, as opposed to Wordtracker's 90-day trend window. Like Wordtracker, they offer other related services that track misspellings, phonetic matches, Keyword translation and Keyword permutations.
- Yahoo! Small Business (GetRichClick.com/Keywordtools) offers a paid search, a contextual ad program and tool support for online advertising.

If you understand that Keywords reflect the intention of a search, then you are in a position to offer potential customers exactly what they hope to find.

- The user who queries "DVD player" is probably just beginning to research a buying decision.
- Someone who types in "Sony DVD player" is probably narrowing down their choices.
- Someone who enters "Sony DVD DVP-NC800H/B" is probably getting ready to make the purchase.

Imagine if a competitor to Sony puts their ads on the side of the page when people are typing in these SONY Keywords. How smart is that?

Consumers communicate their intentions through their Keywords. Keywords are the code. Break the code and the reward is yours in the form of online profits.

***Get Rich Click* Resource:** Keyword analysis is critical to any Pay-Per-Click campaign. The more popular Keywords for a certain product, genre or industry usually are associated with higher bid prices. The lesser-known or lesser-used Keywords have lower bid prices.

For a list of Google AdSense top-paying Keywords showing highest cost per click for a given word, average cost for one click of the Keyword and the best-paying Keywords, take a look at adsensepay.com.

Get Rich Click Money-Making Idea

1. Using an application like Keyword Elite, compile high-paying AdSense Keyword lists for certain niches, vertical markets and related Keywords. Then sell your "research" online to those needing it or to those developing niche websites containing content revolving around high-paying Keywords for Google AdSense. Keyword Elite is available at GetRichClick.com/Keywordtools.

2. Display the actual Keyword lists you compile from Keyword Elite on your high-paying Keyword list website and attract search engine traffic and visitors.

Make a Fortune with "Internet Advertising Arbitrage™"

This amazing money-making method uses Keywords, and the information that you research from the tools discussed here is known as Internet Advertising Arbitrage™. Although the business model is changing daily and the market to make huge profits has changed in recent years, it is a very viable online business; you can improve your effectiveness with optimal page design, ad placement and optimized bidding strategies.

Here is how it works:

1. Using a Keyword tool (see above), identify low cost-per-click Keywords in a niche market, then check the relative value of the words within the niche market using a bidding Keyword tool.

2. Create AdWords campaigns using the lower-priced Keywords, and direct the visitor to a landing page where you have placed ads that pay higher than the words you bid on with the following method:

- Develop a well-optimized web page for higher-valued Keywords.
- Publish your web page to your website or as a separate page and run the respective Pay-Per-Click advertising campaign for it.
- Write a targeted ad and run an AdWords campaign. (NOTE: Ads on Facebook can run as low as $.02 a click.)

The AdWords ad directs visitors to your web page containing the higher-priced ads (that you receive a commission on).

3. The visitor now clicks on the ads that pay more than the ones you bought for your AdWords campaign, and your profit is the difference between the two.

Suppose you bought the Keyword "gold watch" from a small search engine or another website for $.10 per click. You can then direct that $.10 per click traffic to your own website and make $.25, $.50, maybe as much as $1.00 each time a user clicks on your ad.

I have known large firms to make as much as $1,000,000 in a very short time using this money-making strategy. I was part owner of one of them . . . it REALLY does work but is getting harder and harder as more people learn about this concept.

This market and the "spread" on the "cost per click" from one search engine to income you can get from being paid by another client or search engine has diminished recently, but you can make money if you study this market opportunity. *However, you must understand how to play the game or you could lose your money fast. And be sure to read the rules and regulations of any Pay-Per-Click advertising agreement. Make sure they allow this type of "advertising arbitrage" or buying/selling and redirecting traffic (clicks).*

Get Rich Click Money-Making Idea

Many new businesses are looking for a suitable domain name. Using one of the free Keyword suggestion tools and a little imagination, you can go into the domain naming business.

It might surprise you what a busy entrepreneur, pulled in several directions at once, might pay for a service of this type. It's one fewer thing they have to deal with directly, and it frees up their time to do what they do best.

My team is having trouble thinking outside the box.
We can't agree on the size of the box, what materials
the box should be constructed from, a reasonable
budget for the box, or our first choice of box venders.

Providing "LEADs" to Financial Independence

We've all heard a thousand times that lead generation is the key to any business – after all, without potential buyers, what good is a product? But who knew you could get paid for just about every single lead you generate? Apparently, Malaika Schmidt and Amy Sheridan did.

Malaika and Amy's company, Blue Phoenix Media, runs a slew of websites that connect students with potential colleges and schools (both online and on-the-ground) based upon the particular background of each student.

Here's how it works: Students go the site, enter their geographic information, age, gender, income bracket and education level. In turn, the site produces a list of appropriate programs. Then the competing schools reach out to the students directly. But in exchange for the "introduction," the schools pay Blue Phoenix $20 to $50 for every lead passed along from the website to the school . . . to the tune of approximately $4 million a year!

Sheridan and Schmidt started Blue Phoenix after working for a company with a similar business model. Instead of moving on to just another job, they started CollegeConduit.com, designed to connect college students with schools. Then they expanded by doing what Sheridan calls "verticalizing" by major. Meaning, they launched nearly 20 sister sites, each of which focuses on a specific major. There's a site for nursing schools, criminal justice programs, another for culinary arts institutions, etc.

Today, Blue Phoenix Media, which Schmidt and Sheridan started with only $5,000, is a full-fledged marketing and consulting firm with 10 employees that enables the women to earn as much as $5,000 an hour by generating leads.

For these two self-trained women, their innovation hasn't stopped at CollegeConduit .com or their other school sites. Blue Phoenix Media has also launched Blue Phoenix Network, an affiliate network that uses online advertising to drive high volumes of traffic – and lead generation – for a wider variety of clients. In essence, their experience in lead generation has helped transform Sheridan and Schmidt into "client acquisition" experts.

Malaika and Amy admit that their own education in business isn't one they could have received in one of the classroom programs offered on their sites. "You just can't take a course in how to do this stuff in college," said Sheridan. The two learned their online marketing skills and the value of lead generation through real-life immersion.

"It's not as easy as it may seem. If you stay the course and learn the value of a good 'lead' to a car dealer, a college or, say, an insurance agent, there is a lot of money to be made in the online lead generation business," Sheridan added.

Scan the QR code or go to GetRichClick.com/amy to watch Amy and Malaika's video.

15 Ways to Create Strong Keywords:

1. Think of an idea you want to write about.
2. Go to KeywordSpy.com or Wordtracker.com and find out how often people type in the Keywords associated with your idea.
3. Go to GetRichClick.com/keywordtools to find out the costs to buy those Keywords from various search engines.
4. Evaluate the return potential.
5. Choose as many good Keywords as you can.
6. Read popular magazines and newspaper headlines for GREAT Keywords.
7. Create an eBook on the topic – full of the various Keywords you have chosen.
8. Buy the domain name and hosting.
9. Develop a simple website.
10. Hook it to a shopping cart and merchant processor.
11. Publish the website.
12. Buy Pay-Per-Click advertising from various search engines.
13. Launch your marketing campaign; buy the appropriate Keywords.
14. Tell your friends on Facebook and Twitter to visit the site.
15. Watch for an increase in bank deposits.

Pay-Per-Call

The term "pay-per-call" was first introduced to the market with "976" telephone numbers, then quickly became the standard 1-900 telephone numbers. Callers were charged, say, $2.99 a minute to talk to an astrologer. On the Internet, pay-per-call is identical to Pay-Per-Click – but when users click the associated link or ad, the click generates a telephone call to the advertiser. The caller (or clicker) is charged nothing; the firms charge advertisers or website owners on a per-call basis for each call they generate.

Ingenio (paypercall.ingenio.com), owned by AT&T, reports some calls earning between $10 and $12 per click or call. Here's how the process works:

Consumers search for merchants or service providers in a designated geographic area. Then, relevant pay-per-call ads appear in search results. When your business's ads appear in search results, consumers can reach you via the toll-free numbers that Ingenio provides in your pay-per-call ads. These toll-free numbers forward calls directly to your business number as well as track calls for billing and reporting purposes. You set a maximum price per call that you are willing to pay for a call from a potential customer. (Ingenio)

Higher conversion rates are an advantage of pay-per-call. Many companies break even or even generate a profit even on the first run of a campaign.

When people go online, they tend to operate in a more introverted mode; they surf and research quietly and privately. Making a call usually takes place when the person is closer to making a buying decision. The key is to have a logical selling process, including follow up if a sale isn't made on the first call.

Pay-Per-Call on a Local Basis

Local news organizations can supply mobile device users with content that contains local advertising (sold at a premium). Mobile content providers can realize the benefits of being in a local search database and advertising on a pay-per-call basis. It often makes better sense for an advertiser to get local calls than to advertise nationally or globally through paid search.

Pay-per-call is not restricted to local advertisers. Many of the pay-per-call search engines allow advertisers with a national presence to create ads with local telephone numbers.

The cable television industry and the directory industry have made limited-use toll-free numbers to track and bill for leads for years. With the ascendancy of Pay-Per-Click advertising, it was inevitable that businesses would create an advertising medium for the millions who rely on the phone to generate leads and close sales.

It's not clear yet whether pay-per-call will substitute for a portion of the Pay-Per-Click advertising market or how businesses will adopt and use both. The advantage of making contact by phone often depends on whether a business is selling a service or a product. Service providers may prefer pay-per-call campaigns, while those selling actual products may find Pay-Per-Click campaigns more effective.

One advantage of pay-per-call advertising is that it expands the number of companies that can use online advertising. A business does not need to maintain an online presence to take advantage of pay-per-call advertising. Pay-per-call can help grow a business by driving phone leads directly from the Internet, so offline businesses can reap the same benefits as online businesses.

Advertisers create their pay-per-call ad just as they would a Pay-Per-Click ad and bid the maximum they are willing to pay when a user clicks on the call. Relevant pay-per-call ads appear in search results in the same contextual, Keyword-based way Pay-Per-Click ads do, but instead of entering a link to a web address, the advertiser enters the phone number that will receive the call as a result of the click.

CASE STUDY:

Ingenio, Web-to-Phone Pioneer

In 1999, Ingenio cofounder and e-commerce executive Scott Faber was riding in a New York City cab, eavesdropping on the driver's animated cell phone conversation, when he was struck with an idea. What would happen if you combine the vast searching capabilities of the Internet with the powerful person-to-person interaction of the telephone? Shortly thereafter, Ingenio's unique platform was born, and has since pioneered a variety of applications that combine the communications power and ubiquity of both the Internet and the phone to create new opportunities for online buyers and sellers.

The company's technology powers the leading Live Advice™ Directories product and the Ingenio Pay-per-Call® Network. Ingenio Pay-per-Call is the industry's first and only paid search-based advertising system that allows any advertiser to capitalize on the popularity of Internet search and drive targeted phone leads – rather than clicks – to their business. (Ingenio)

Ingenio.com is now owned by AT&T. This is an ad from their website:

Online Advertising and "Pay-Per-Action" – The Perfect Way to Conduct Business!

Every online advertising model is essentially a pay-per-action (or cost-per-action) model. Pay-per-action or pay-per-performance are simply catch all terms for the options devised by clever marketers.

Pay-per-action models are usually straightforward. Whenever a site visitor clicks on an ad and performs a specified action, the advertiser pays the owner of the site. This pay-for-performance marketing model allows advertisers to focus on their campaign strategy, product offering and creative execution. They can be confident that their media dollars spent will be 100% cost-effective.

Pay-Per-Action or Pay-Per-Performance: 30 Ways to Get Paid!

In writing this book, I did *extensive* research into the ways creative marketing professionals are charging for a variety of services. Many pay-per-action models are available in the world of online advertising. In the list below, the owner of a website is considered the "publisher" and the person wanting the sale or lead is the "advertiser." Here are some of them:

1. **Pay-Per-Sale (or cost-per-sale)**. An advertiser pays the publisher each time a user makes a purchase. Also known as pay-per-conversion.

2. **Pay-Per-Click (or cost-per-click)**. Of all the terms in this list, PPC is the one you will hear about most often. An advertiser pays the publisher every time a visitor clicks on the advertiser's ad – whether they buy the product or not. It doesn't matter how many times the ad appears on the site, the publisher only gets paid when a user clicks on the link displayed.

3. Pay-Per-Lead (or cost-per-lead). The advertiser pays the publisher for every visitor who signs up as a lead, typically by filling out a form or creating an account. Some firms sell this "lead" to multiple vendors and get paid each time they sell the same lead.

4. Pay-Per-Call. An advertiser pays the publisher every time a user "places a call" by clicking on the ad link (see above).

5. Pay-Per-Post. PayPerPost.com created this brilliant concept. PayPerPost delivers online "word of mouth" marketing, brand building and traffic generation by paying people to "post" their thoughts, opinions and reviews on blogs, social networks and websites. They get individuals to write about websites, products, services, companies or whatever the client company is willing to pay for.

6. Pay-Per-Impression (or cost-per-impression). This payment option is used for Internet marketing campaigns and is typically based on a "cost per 1000 impressions" or CMP. The advertiser pays the publisher for the number of times the advertiser's banner ads, text links, e-mail spam or opt-in e-mail advertising appears on the publisher's site. (One appearance is one impression.) The publisher receives payment regardless of whether anyone clicks on the ad.

7. Pay-Per-Time (or cost-per-time). An advertiser pays the publisher or hosting service based on how much time is spent on the site. Charges can be in minutes, hours, days, weeks, months or years. Gamers and web conferencing services often use this model. Pay-per-time models are often paired with pay-per-impression; the ad can appear an unlimited number of times over the term of the contract. Some contracts allow for a guaranteed minimum number of impressions.

8. Pay-Per-Download. An advertiser pays the publisher a commission every time the content is downloaded. This can be an audio file, video file, word document, a game, software or any other type of digital content.

9. Pay-Per-Install. An advertiser or client pays the publisher a commission when the digital content is installed by the client onto their laptop, PC or server. In some cases, a sample of the product is downloaded, used and tested by the client. When the final product is actually installed by the end user or client, a fee is then paid to the publisher or marketing agency for their work.

10. Pay-Per-Read. This model is often used by e-mail marketing agencies. An advertiser pays the publisher each time a user opens the advertiser's e-mails, takes their surveys or even play their games. (See MyPoints.com in Chapter 8.)

11. Pay-Per-Subscription™. An advertiser pays the publisher when a user purchases a subscription to a newsletter, magazine, newspaper, website or any other fee-based content. The product being purchased can be online or offline. The subscription may also be a onetime or recurring purchase.

12. Pay-Per-Inclusion. This is a payment technique typically used by search engines to have a firm's URL included in their search engine. Some websites also charge in this manner to include a link or web address on their site.

13. Pay-Per-Placement. Firms need stories, video, audio, photos and other digital assets placed on other websites to get more distribution. Some public relations firms are finding it's a better business model to charge a client in this manner. If the firm gets the client's content placed onto another firm's website, they're paid for their work. If they don't, they make no money.

14. Pay-Per-PR. Similar to pay-per-placement, this is a payment system used by some public relations firms to get your business. They only charge you if they get the publicity you seek.

15. Pay-Per-Link. As mentioned in other pages of *Get Rich Click*, inbound and outbound links are a major driver of traffic to a website. There are many firms on the market that charge you to help add links to your site from another site or from your site to another site. It helps build traffic to your site and the more links you have pointing to your site, the higher your listing on various search engines.

16. Pay-Per-Application. The client only pays when an application is filled out. This is often used by affiliate marketers on credit-card and subscription-based applications. Advertisers pay the publisher based on how many applications are filled out.

17. Pay-Per-Applicant. This payment system is used by the Yahoo/Hotjobs! in which the client pays for the job applicants that pass a specific test or questionnaire. After the application is filled out, those applicants that received a passing grade are sent on to the advertiser who then pays a per-applicant fee.

18. Pay-Per-Play. This model is typically used by gamers that charge a user each time they play the publisher's game.

19. Pay-Per-Word. In the world of the Internet, content is king. While writers, editors and journalists have been charging on a "per word" basis for many years, this payment model is becoming more acceptable as most websites are looking for additional content to put on their site.

20. Pay-Per-Listen. This is an interesting model for audio downloads being tested and used by satellite radio, audio books, public speakers and webinars. PayPerListen.com says it "delivers an extensive selection of audiobooks in an electronically downloadable format at approximately 75-80% less than the cost of typical CDs." This market will grow as more and more people realize they can use the Internet to read, watch and listen to information.

21. Pay-Per-View. Most of us know this term from watching a special event, boxing match or a movie on our local cable system. But pay-per-view is also being used as a way publishers charge advertisers to run their story or video online. One site has an offering similar to this called "Pay-per-episode."

22. Pay-Per-Ringtone. MobileMarketer.com reported that firms are now offering ring tones on a per-download fee.

23. Pay-Per-Text. DMnews.com reports that a new service has launched in Europe called pay-per-text. Firms are being charged on a per-text basis to market short messages to cell phones and even e-mail accounts. In Britain, the leading directory assistance firm will sell the service enabling advertisers to buy space within tens of millions of text messages sent to directory assistance users that are sent along with the phone number they requested. Expect this market to EXPLODE as firms such as Hertz rent-a-car can send a message for a discounted car when anyone asks for the phone number to Avis or National.

24. Pay-Per-Fax. This is an online service that allows you to send and receive faxes from your computer at a per-page or per-fax price. It is also a pricing scheme for outbound faxing services used in marketing a product or service via fax.

25. Pay-Per-Ad. This model is basically the same as the pay-per-impression model. A publisher is paid by an advertiser each time their ad is shown on a given website or network of websites. The advertiser is charged per ad or per impression and not per action. This is a great marketing option for firms that are trying to build a brand image and get the word out because the per impression ad costs are considerably less than the per-click fees.

26. Pay-Per-Seat. This model is typically used by application service providers (ASPs) that charge a "per seat" user license, royalty or fee to use their software. The more users (or seats) in the firm that uses the product, the more fees that must be paid to the software developer or publisher.

27. Pay-Per-Server. All websites need servers to host their data. The problem occurs when your site grows faster (or slower) than you can plan for. This business model is being used by hosting firms so that the client only pays for the number of servers they need to use.

28. Pay-Per-Response. Marketers are clever. They come up with many different ways to charge for the same product. A response could be defined in any manner between the publisher and the advertiser but might be defined this way: "A prospect, lead or sale is generated when someone clicks a link, completes an online form or calls a specific telephone number to request more information about your type of product, service or business."

29. Pay-Per-Article. *The Financial Times* is planning to introduce a "pay-per-article" business model for accessing articles online and is reviewing whether any content on FT.com will remain free to access. This model will certainly grow over the years as "micro" payments are easier to charge to the end user and when sites are forced to charge for their content . . . even a newspaper that charges the reader one article at a time.

30. Pay-Per-Tweet. I saw this one as the book was going to press. Companies are paying individuals and small public relations firms to tweet on their behalf. The firms are paid "per tweet" so that each time they tweet about the firm's products or services, they are paid or compensated in some way.

How a Third Party Can Lead to a Second Home

Harvey Manger-Weil — a former street musician — was looking for a job that would let him be creative and never, ever force him to work in a real office.

In 2003, Manger-Weil launched a consulting firm showing others how to start businesses. He began advertising on Google Ads, but his efforts produced few leads and sales. But rather than throwing his hands up Manger-Weil noticed the competing advertisers who were earning enough to maintain their ads. Apparently, they were making money — but how?

He realized that these successful advertisers were members of the ClickBank network affiliates program — which allows a third party (you) to sell digital products created by others — and be paid commissions on sales. Manger-Weil was amazed that people were making money by selling other people's products, so he decided to try his hand.

Even when online advertising was cheap, and competition was slim, Manger-Weil knew he had to differentiate himself. He began using third-party, "objective" reviews to vouch for the products he sold. These are the same type of reviews used in infomercials and other testimonial-based products.

"I thought to myself, what could I do to add more credibility to my sales story, and I realized that if someone other than the provider was saying this was good, that would do it," Manger-Weil explained.

Soon after, the money "suddenly started coming in." In fact, Manger-Weil made $5,000 in one week from a single product! "I remember thinking: Is this going to last a week? Is it going to last a month?"

His success has lasted for years, and he and his wife went from worrying about making their house payments to owning two homes outright. According to Manger-Weil, his success, and the peace of mind it brings, has "all come from ClickBank money."

Manger-Weil still relies on ClickBank while also finding new ways to use the Internet for business. He now runs College Wizards, an online SAT and college prep service offered internationally via Skype that allows Manger-Weil to teach clients well beyond his geographic market.

If there's one thing Manger-Weil learned about successful Internet business, it's that, "you have to come up with the next new idea and run it as well as you can until too many people catch up . . . and then you need to come up with the next new idea."

Scan the QR code or go to GetRichClick.com/harvey to watch Harvey's interview.

Putting Your Ideas into Action

- Understand Pay-Per-Click, Pay-Per-Lead and over 30 other ways to make money on the Internet. Which way is best for you and your website?

- Learn and understand EVERYTHING YOU CAN on Google Adsense and Google Adwords. They are amazing ways to make money from the Internet.

- Use Keyword Tools to help find the highest-paying Keywords and the Keywords that will get you the most traffic to your website.

- Visit some Keyword search sites and become familiar with them. Try searching for some words that interest you. Then see how you can tweak them to generate more searches.

- Understand Keywords and create as many Keywords as possible for every page of your website.

For More Information, go to GetRichClick.com/KeywordTools.

GLASBERGEN

I just read the book *Get Rich Click*.
Is this the slot where the money comes out?

5

100+ Ways to Optimize Your Website for Search and Improve Traffic

If nobody can find you,
nobody can do business with you.
This is true in Waterloo, Iowa,
and it's true in New York City.
It's definitely true on the Internet.

To make money online, you *must* be visible to people who want your products or services. You need targeted traffic, and as much of it as you can get. Driving traffic is absolutely one of the most important functions of Internet marketing. The key to driving traffic can be stated in just three words: *search engine optimization*!

When you work to optimize your site, be careful how much you change at one time. Test in a manner that lets you know which changes give you the biggest benefits. If you make four changes and one of those changes benefits you but three count against you, you haven't optimized, and you can't identify what works for you. In short, you must carefully and intelligently make sure your site is search engine optimized to its full potential.

You can do this in two basic ways:

The first involves the use of techniques that allow search engines to crawl and index your site efficiently. These are largely coding-based, technical challenges.

The second involves tactics for improving your search engine rankings. These usually fall within the scope of your business and marketing strategies.

Some of the things you're doing to optimize your rankings may actually be hurting you. So in this chapter we'll look at many of the best search engine tactics.

Some of these tactics are quite technical. If you're not "up to speed" with something, try consulting a friend who has more knowledge. Find out more at GetRichClick.com.

Below, you'll find a list of practical steps you can take to make your Internet presence as visible as possible. The list is organized into six sections:

- **Content Applications**

- **Keyword Applications**

- **Inbound and Outbound Links**

- **Domain Names, Links and Site Submissions**

- **Understanding and Benefiting from Indexing and Ranking**

- **Link-Building: The Real Currency of the Internet**

Before moving on to the list, let's review some basics of how search engines work. The raw data for search engines is gathered by electronic "spiders" crawling across the web. The search engines then index the data to facilitate fast, accurate information retrieval when someone performs a search. This means you must pay attention not only to ranking, but also to the indexing that precedes it.

The details of how search engines operate change almost daily. The ideas below are suggestions that our research has shown help in search engine rankings. Because of the pace of change in search engine technology, I can't guarantee that the information below is the same for each search engine, or for any given time in the future. The points are listed here as one element to help guide you. While you can do a great amount of work on your own, there are also benefits to finding a search engine optimization firm to help.

The list below is a compilation of many different SEO techniques. I freely admit that I am NOT an SEO expert. We have shown it to several of the top SEO professionals for review. NO technique is absolute or guaranteed to work 100%. Old SEO ideas may change, new ones will be added. These are all ideas, techniques and thoughts from our group of experts on ways we THINK we can help you in your quest to SEO a given site.

Content Applications

1. Unique content that is relevant and different to that on another site gives you a big boost.

2. Make sure you incorporate a call to action such as "call now" on your web pages. They're good for optimization and increase conversion.

3. Keeping your content fresh and adding new content to your site improves your ranking. Making small changes to your existing content is not nearly as effective as adding new content. For this reason, a blog linked to a business website often gets higher rankings than the business site itself.

4. If you'd like to improve your importance and credibility, convince your CEO to blog. This strategy can benefit your optimization efforts in many ways, the least of which is good PR. (There is an opportunity here for firms that need someone else to blog "on behalf" of the CEO or another executive.)

5. Some believe Keywords presented in font sizes larger than surrounding text rank higher. Therefore larger headings and larger captions can be beneficial.

6. Bolding and italics emphasize important words and phrases. But overdoing this can count against you with some search engines.

7. Old copy on your site doesn't work as well for you as recent copy does. Change your copy often and don't allow other firms or resellers of your products to use the same copy on their sites.

8. Consider distributing page content over several pages (if this makes sense in the context of your site). I'm told shorter pages get higher rankings over longer pages.

Keyword Applications

9. Place Keywords in heading tags. In your code, they look like this: <H1>, <H2>, etc. These placements rank higher. You also need to include these Keywords elsewhere in your content.

10. Rather than optimizing a page for multiple Keywords, focus on optimizing for one Keyword per page.

11. Include Keywords in text at the beginning of your pages. Placement counts, though not as much as anchor text, title tag or headings. The beginning of a document does not necessarily mean the first paragraph – for instance if you use tables, the first paragraph of text might be in the second half of the table.

12. Place Keywords in <alt> tags. Spiders can't read images, but they do read their textual descriptions in the <alt> tag, so if you have images on your page, fill in the <alt> tag with some Keywords about the reference images. Since searches for images often include the word "image" or "picture," it helps to add these to your tags. The same is true for videos.

13. Place Keywords in metatags. This used to be far more important when optimizing for Google. However, if you are optimizing for Yahoo! or MSN, you'll want to do this. It isn't going to undermine your optimization efforts for Google.

14. Because context matters, keep Keywords together when you use them. Separating them with content reduces their value.

15. Keyword phrases. You can also optimize for phrases searchers enter in their queries, for example, "conversion rate marketing." If searchers query the phrase less frequently (you may consider it an important phrase, but searchers may not), it may make better sense to optimize for individual words.

16. Secondary Keywords can often be more valuable to you than primary Keywords, especially when competition for the primary Keywords is fierce and everyone else is optimizing for them. "Lexus SUV Houston, Texas" will get you traffic that is better targeted than is "Lexus Texas."

17. Be sure to optimize your RSS feed with a Keyword-rich description.

Inbound and Outbound Links

"Link" is short for "hyperlink." A hyperlink is a reference or a navigation element that, when you click on it, takes you to a point within your website or anywhere else on the Internet. Most commonly, links are blue, underlined bits of text. The text is called anchor text; the address the link points to is the anchor.

18. The anchor text of your internal links matters, but not so much as the anchor text of your inbound links.

19. When you write copy for anchor text, consider linking longer phrases and questions. Lots of searches enter phrases as queries: "How to hang window blinds." If you use this phrase, it can help to link all of it. Building pages around these phrases helps, too.

20. Pay attention to the text surrounding the anchor text. The context of a link is an indication of its relevance; irrelevant text clues spiders to spamming.

21. When you specify the anchor (the destination) for your anchor text, include a name in the code; it allows you to stress what's important in the phrase. If you do not know how to include the name in the code, ask someone who does.

22. Provide links to the profiles you maintain on social media sites. Connections with social media and practicing social marketing improve your competitiveness in searches. Also, using your business name on your Twitter account is an excellent way to boost your rankings and improve your exposure.

23. Want to speed up the "spider" process on your brand-new site? Get an inbound link from a quality site.

24. Sometimes website designers use an image or a graphic for the link; this tactic is far less effective than linking text. If you absolutely must use an image as a link, you absolutely must make sure to use an <alt> tag.

CLICK TIP To get your website a higher ranking on a search engine, you want inbound links from other sites that have a high ranking. Sites are ranked 0 to 10 with 10 being the highest ranking page. One inbound link to your site from a site with a ranking of 10 has much more value to your site than 10 inbound links with a number 1 ranking. For more information, go to GetRichClick.com/linkranking.

Domain Names, Links and Site Submissions

25. Be careful with redirects for www and non-www domains. Decide which you want to use and 301 redirect the other to it. In other words, if domain.com is your preference, then domain.com should redirect to it. 301 redirects are considered "permanent," and are more search engine friendly.

26. You'd like your web addresses and filenames to include Keywords. This is especially important for rankings in Yahoo! and MSN.

27. Use a dedicated server for your site rather than a server that hosts multiple websites. It minimizes the risk your site will be affected by problem sites that may share your server. You also tend to get more inbound links if your site doesn't "time out."

28. Things like broken links, errors and password-protected areas make for a site that search engines cannot index.

29. Spiders love complete, up-to-date sitemaps. You can present yours in basic .html or use Google's sitemap format.

30. Spiders love large sites, so in general, the bigger the website, the better the ranking. Having a substantial site with excellent content is also a great way to get more traffic. However, take care to create ways visitors can easily navigate a large site.

31. The age of your site, overall, suggests it is respected and credible. This works in your favor.

32. When your site fits into a topical theme, you get a boost for all the pages related to this theme.

33. Try to locate your files in your root directory. This gives you a better boost than placing them in lower levels.

SEO

34. Have separate domain names for each site related to your business. That is, instead of putting several of your business sites under one domain, give them different names. This may boost your overall rankings in the search engines.

35. Include your site in local-search search engines. This can help boost your ranking in organic search. Be sure to include your location in your anchor text: "Our office in Brooklyn," not "our office."

36. Register the domain name for 5 or 10 years so you don't need to do it yearly. Also, have your domain registrar "lock down" your domain names so they are not stolen.

CLICK TIP ▶ Locking down your domain names is *very* important. My business partner and I had a $250,000 domain stolen and sold on eBay for $110,000 to a professional basketball player. We didn't even know that had happened until several months later. The laws DO NOT PROTECT SUCH THEFT. As of this writing, we do not have the asset back in our hands although the New Jersey Cyber Crimes unit working with the FBI has now arrested our thief. We expect the thief to get jail time in this precedent-setting case. More about this on the *Get Rich Click* website.

Understanding and Benefiting from Indexing and Ranking

37. Search engines want natural language content. Don't overstuff your text with Keywords. It won't work. Search engines look at how many times a term appears in your content. If it is abnormally high, this may count against you. Shoot for 3 to 7 percent for major Keywords, 1 to 2 percent for minor. Keyword density of over 10 percent may be suspicious and looks more like "Keyword stuffing" than naturally written text. Search engines can blacklist you for this.

38. If you are on a shared server, do a blacklist check to be sure you're not on a proxy with a spammer or banned site. Their negative notoriety could affect your own rankings. To find blacklisted sites, visit urlblacklist.com.

39. Be aware when you register a domain by using services that block domain ownership information, search engines may see you as a potential spammer.

40. Don't overoptimize your Keywords, and especially don't optimize for Keywords that have nothing to do with your business. This can constitute Keyword spamming; it will definitely undermine your rankings and you may be blacklisted.

41. Don't use the same title or metatag for all your pages. It's a good idea to make your metatags unique.

42. Keep your outbound links under 100 per page. Overpopulating with outbound links can lower your search engine ranking.

43. Overdoing linking can lower your ranking, especially if you have lots of inbound or outbound links with the same site. It looks suspiciously like link-buying and spamming. Even if you aren't penalized, only a few of these links will count.

44. Outbound links to link farms and other suspicious sites may count against you. Be very careful of linking to "bad neighbors."

45. When three or more sites link in a loop (linking from A to B to C and then linking back to A) or in an even more complex way, you could be penalized for behavior that looks like reciprocal link trading.

46. If you create a link that is so small a visitor can't even see it – for example, one pixel – you are heavily penalized for trying to manipulate the search engines.

47. Separating your content based on IP or browser type on one web address confuses the search engines, because they can't figure out that actual topic of the page or the site. Doing this may have marketing value, but it's a problem for search engine optimization.

48. A search engine won't ban you for poor coding and bad design, but it may not be able to index your site. That hurts you a lot.

49. If you use copyrighted material without permission or violate the law, you can get blacklisted. (You also could get sued.)

50. When "Internet spiders" discover that you have created invisible text (text specially written for a spider and not a human) you can bet the search engines will penalize your site if not blacklist it!

DID YOU KNOW in the early days of the Internet, some website coders wrote Keywords all over the first page of a website using WHITE text on a WHITE background? Hence the human eye didn't see this "Keyword spamming" technique. Since these sites were being looked at by humans but indexed by computers, these sites were often indexed very high by the computers. This trick was short lived but those techies keep finding interesting ways to "beat the system."

51. "Cloaking" your pages, so that spiders see one optimized page and your visitors see a different version of that page, will get you blacklisted when caught.

52. Creating "doorways," or pages that are meant to trick spiders into thinking you have a relevant site, is another way to get blacklisted.

53. Duplicate content can be a problem. You get a penalty for placing the same content on multiple pages on your site. Because article repositories and mirror sites have their advantages, when copies of your content appear on other sites, you may be penalized for duplicates. If you keep duplicate content on your own site, rewrite it. If you will have duplicate content residing on another site, make sure to publish it on your site first to identify yourself as the originator.

54. According to LinkMetro.com, the number-one ranked website on Google for the search term "web hosting," there are over 15 million websites linking to it. If you are a competitor to this business, your firm may need hundreds if not thousands of inbound links to your site to crack into the top 10 page rankings in the larger search engines. Each industry has different metrics relative to the websites in that given marketplace.

55. Spiders can have a difficult time figuring out Javascript, and if your coding is very messy, it can hurt you.

Use images judiciously. A page that is all images and no text is a terrible optimization tactic.

56. Search engines also can't see podcasts, audio files or videos. Include a transcript or good descriptive copy so these elements can get indexed properly.

57. Spiders don't handle frames. If you don't absolutely need them, don't use them. They will hurt your ranking.

58. Some search engine spiders don't index "Flash-" based content. While Google does, it is rare to see flash content index well. You need to provide a textual description in addition.

59. Flash is often invisible to search engines. For this reason many web designers don't use Flash when creating websites.

60. If your hosting company is unreliable (down more than 2 or 3 percent of the time), you should find another firm to host your site. Spiders can't crawl your site if it's down, and you are basically "out of business" when this happens.

61. Dynamic and overly long (more than 100-character) web addresses can be a problem. Spiders prefer static web addresses.

62. If a search engine has banned part of your site, spiders won't come as frequently to crawl the parts of your site that aren't banned.

63. Be careful how you redirect traffic. Redirects can hurt, especially when the target page doesn't open. When they immediately take a visitor to a different page, they can hurt you a lot.

64. If you are using a test domain to test your site, keep it invisible using a robots.txt file; if it's public, it will confuse the spiders.

Link-Building: The Real Currency of the Internet

Wikipedia calls links "the currency of the world wide web." Everyone's experience on the Internet depends on "the click." Every action starts with a click on a link. Search engines also determine placements in organic results based on links – both inbound links TO your site and FROM your site to other sites. When you work at optimizing your site, pay close attention to your links, those on your site and those that point to your site. Quality content on your site and quality links make search engine spiders happy.

65. Build a network of quality inbound links. If the inbound link uses one of your Keyword phrases as an anchor, that's even better.

66. Cultivate links from sites similar to yours. These are high-quality votes for your site.

67. High-ranking incoming links are the priority of any linking strategy. The goal is to link to good sites with good content.

CLICK TIP ⟩⟩ I recall a story when Internet marketing first got started a few years back where a smart advertising executive cut a deal with the *San Jose Mercury News* website. He *purchased* a small box on the homepage of that top-ranked site. He then resold links from that box to advertisers (other websites). The beauty of this idea was twofold. Great traffic to the advertisers' website and increased site ranking for the site as they were getting an outbound link from a top-rated website. *Very* smart marketing indeed.

68. If the page that links to your site is a bigger site and has only a few outbound links overall, then the link they point to your site is given higher weighting. In this case, fewer is better for those that receive the outbound link.

69. The age of your inbound links matters. Older links get better ratings; having lots of new links suggests you've simply purchased them.

70. Inbound links from directories are good, as long as the directory is reputable. Directories like the DMOZ and Yahoo! Directory give you a good boost. Submit your site to these directories. You can also consider paid submissions to quality directories.

71. The origin of your inbound links does make a difference; sites with higher page ranks are more reputable. Because it's also harder to get inbound links from these sites, they influence your importance. Links from .edu and .gov sites generally give you a higher ranking than those from sites with other extensions. Quality should significantly outweigh quantity in your inbound linking strategy.

72. Consider whether to use inbound links from the same IP address. Google says this doesn't matter, but Yahoo! and MSN may ignore them.

73. Trade links. In a reciprocal link, you link to them and they link to you. Use caution when trading reciprocal links, however; trade on a small scale with relevant businesses and associates that can send you traffic. Avoid link trading hubs and networks.

74. Search on Keywords related to your site. Find sites with high rankings, and target these high fliers for link-building.

75. You can embed links in content anywhere. This includes online discussion forums. Signatures are great places to put your link. If you are offering a valuable contribution, you build your credibility and authority; people will read what you have to say, spread the word and link to you.

76. Write articles and circulate eBooks with embedded links in the content.

77. Trade articles with other quality websites.

78. Look into syndicating articles at EzineArticles, GoArticles and iSnare. Article sites actually rank highly and tend to send highly qualified traffic. You can also submit articles to industry news sites and to companies with "in the news" pages.

79. Send out well-crafted press releases. In addition to submitting to PRWeb and PRLeap, e-mail them to selected journalists and bloggers. Pay attention to who picks up your articles and press releases so you can offer them exclusives.

80. Publish interviews of important people in your industry.

81. Comment on blogs that are related to your industry to encourage direct traffic and establish your credibility.

82. People love to link to tips lists and these lists can become documents of authority in your industry. Publish lists and articles to your blog or include them in customer-oriented content.

83. Publish a list of specialists and experts in your industry.

84. The quality, readability and proper use of grammar in your content matters if you want credible authorities to link to you. Help build credibility and trust further with an easy-to-understand privacy policy and a well-crafted "About Us" page.

85. Encourage your visitors to link to you; simply ask them. If they like what they see on your site, your humbly worded request might convince them.

86. Approach your manufacturers, retailers or other business partners and ask if they will link to you.

87. Perform and publish surveys and studies that attract attention. Salary.com published a study on how underpaid mothers were and got lots of high-quality links from it.

88. Produce a topical directory about your field of interest; link to your own important content where possible.

89. Pay attention to sites like Digg, Del.icio.us, Buzz, Twitter and so forth. Tag and submit stories. This can lead readers to your blog and encourage linking that transfers some authority to your page.

90. Provide RSS feeds to your content so readers can syndicate you. If you provide great information, they may link back to you.

91. Join your local Better Business Bureau and look into your Chamber of Commerce. If it makes sense, submit your link to associated state and federal resource agencies. See whether your local libraries will list your site on theirs.

92. Leverage offline and online relationships with noncompeting businesses in your industry.

93. Be part of the Internet "Buzz" and get free links back to your site. Go to Google Groups, Yahoo Answers or better yet, an interactive blog about your area of expertise. Get involved and help people get answers to their questions and put a link into your answer that points back to your website.

94. Set up a Squidoo page. Develop quality content in the area of your expertise and link to useful information (as well as back to your site).

95. Consider whether it might make sense to create an article about your company for Wikipedia or some of the topic-focused wikis.

GLASBERGEN

Someday all the *good* domain names will be taken. That's when I'll make a fortune selling nuhnuh.com, fleenwup.net, prukboogle.org, boopluffle.com, zitzat.net, weeniewaffle.com, hoofeenoofee.org, wupfuzz.net . . .

96. Write thoughtful reviews of products you offer on your site. Review content generally ranks well for those sites that have established authority.

97. Participate in Amazon's community. Create a list of top related products – when you mention your background, include your link. Reviewing related products on Amazon can also direct traffic and get you some links.

98. You can contribute reviews for related products to a number of respected sites. Target shopping search engines, like ePinions. This helps build your authority in your industry and increases your exposure.

99. Review related sites on Alexa to draw in relevant traffic streams.

100. Incorporate Technorati tags in your blog posts when you can (this affects your rankings in Yahoo! and MSN more than it does in Google).

101. Research blog directories, choose the ones that seem advantageous and submit your blog to their listings.

102. You can rent links. Text Link Ads has a good reputation as a link broker. You can also ask a site directly, even though it may not be in the business of renting links.

103. Get involved in charities. Many charities link back to their sponsors. If you donate a portion of your eBay profit to charity, charities often link to both you and your auctions.

104. Get involved in conferences. Conference sites link back to their participants and sponsors. Conferences, seminars and workshops are also great ways to build your offline relationships, which you can translate to online influence.

105. Have a contest (contests are great link bait).

106. Encourage feedback by offering free samples.

107. Build a cool online tool people will want to link to – dashboards and calculators have lots of appeal.

108. Design and offer open-source templates for document preparation, web design, blogs and such. Be sure to include a "Designed by You" link in the template.

109. Produce a plug-in for Firefox. Include a download and support page for the plug-in on your site (check out DownloadHelper or ScribeFire).

110. If it's appropriate, include a picture gallery on your site where you tell stories about important people in your industry and display pictures (make sure you have the person's permission to use his or her image).

111. Be sure to submit your site URL to the Vertical search engines.

If all the link-building possibilities seem a bit too much for you to manage, you can always outsource link-building. In the *Get Rich Click* mindset, turn to others to fill the gaps in your own expertise – it will pay off!

112. Google has made a website's "speed" a factor in search engine rankings. They want to "return faster sites" to the user – "but not at the expense of relevance of the data on the page." There are two parts to this section of the Google Algorithm puzzle. First, "how fast a page responds to Googlebot." Second would be "the speed of the 'load time' as measured by the Google Toolbar."

"Conversion Rate" Marketing

The purpose of driving traffic to your online business is to get customers. Once a prospect lands on your site, you still have to convert that prospect into a buyer. You might be able to drive 100,000 visitors to your site, but your efforts aren't worth much if your site can't monetize their clicks. This is where conversion rate marketing steps in.

The conversion rate experts are my good friends Bryan and Jeffrey Eisenberg. They are the undisputed gurus on search engine optimization for conversion and wrote the following:

> *Conversion rate is the number of folks who visit your site within a specified time period divided by the number of folks who actually do something productive on your site (like buy or register or subscribe). These days, a conversion rate of 2–4% is considered average, below 2% is shabby and 5% or more is really quite amazing.*
>
> *Let's assume you spend $10,000 in advertising to drive 5,000 people to your site, and your conversion rate is 2 percent. This means that 100 transactions cost you $10,000, or $100 per transaction. Now let's assume your conversion rate rises to 4 percent. The same $10,000 buys you 200 transactions at a cost of $50 per transaction. An 8 percent rate gives you 400 transactions at a cost of $25 per transaction.*
>
> *It all seems so simple. Higher conversion rates mean more money coming in and less money spent to attract a customer. (GrokDot-com)*

Dollars spent	Visitors	Pay-per-click price	Cost per visitor	Conversation rate
$10,000	5,000	$2.00	2% = 100 Sales	$100
$10,000	5,000	$2.00	4% = 200 Sales	$50
$10,000	5,000	$2.00	8% = 400 Sales	$25
$10,000	10,000	$1.00	8% = 800 Sales	$12.50

If you can get twice the number of visitors for the same amount of money and maintain the same conversion rate, you get twice the number of sales at one-half of the cost per sale. Of course, the final objective, regardless of which variable you change in the above chart, is to get the lowest possible cost per sale.

When you consider that even small improvements in your conversion rate translate into dramatic increases in income, you begin to understand that investing time in trying to convert the traffic you drive is well worth your effort. Conversion rate marketing has a big effect on your profitability. Search on "conversion rate marketing" to start incorporating this practice in your marketing strategies. If your firm closes 2 percent and makes $100,000 in profit

Split Testing: Vital to Increasing Your Bottom Line!

It was an unexpected $7 check from an affiliate and vendor network called ClickBank that made Miles Baker realize the beauty of passive income. It was the first time he understood that he could become wealthy by referring other people's products online.

Before that fateful check arrived, Baker was certainly *not* finding wealth by selling hot tubs or offering computer technical support services. So, he began learning how to make money on the Internet.

He tried a few different angles, from selling on eBay to posting classified ads that referred vendor products. Nothing seemed to be working, at least not until he received that $7 check from ClickBank.

That money, it turned out, was from an ad he had posted two years previously, an ad that referred affiliates to the ClickBank network itself! In fact, when Baker received the check, he had to do research to figure out which ad had earned the check.

"I just knew I had gotten $7 and I was making hardly any money at the time," said Baker. "It kind of got my mind thinking, 'Wow, if I can make money by not doing anything, what if I really put my effort into this?'"

He began selling informational products, ranging from how to build a resume to how to find movies online.

He later became a product vendor on ClickBank, selling PC repair software and other products. It was an important step, since it allowed him to sit back and let other people sell his products, rather than the other way around.

To increase his success, Baker got organized, and learned to build contact lists for each vertical market he served. He then narrowed his focus to computer and IT-related products.

Over time he also began split testing, posting different versions of the same website, using different colors, layouts, fonts, etc. to see which site attracts the most clicks and is likely to make the most money.

Baker's strategies have paid off. In fact, his websites generate annual six-figure sales. To this day, he relies on ClickBank, which he calls his "main marketing partner," for his income.

With just two employees, he works 20 to 30 hours a week, spending the rest of his time with his wife and four-year-old son – a lifestyle his previous job never would have allowed.

Scan the QR code or go to GetRichClick.com/miles to watch Miles' interview.

and you want to get to $200,000, you would have to ask yourself – do we spend more on marketing or spend more money on research to learn a better way to convert those leads and shoot for a 4 percent closing rate? The beauty here is that the 4 percent closing rate continues while the marketing dollars must be spent month after month.

Good website practice and optimizing for conversion usually makes for good search engine optimization. These work together to ensure you drive quality traffic and can persuade that traffic to help you meet your business goals.

16 Great Ways to Attract More Traffic

Just because you've put up a website doesn't mean you'll get any visitors to walk through the virtual door. The more tactics you use to announce the fact you're out there doing business, the more traffic you will attract. The more traffic you attract, the sooner you will be able to accomplish your business goals. Below is a list of ways – not directly related to search engine optimization – through which you can improve your site's visibility and increase traffic:

1. **Article writing**. Write a short, relevant article on your subject of expertise and post it to many of the online article websites. To find these, type "article submission" into any search engine. Your contact information and an inbound link to your website appears at the bottom of your submission. Search engines pick up this link, and your site rises in popularity in search engines.

2. **Newsletter publishing**. Keeping in constant touch with your potential customers through an online newsletter will bring you traffic. Providing word-of-mouth viral links in your newsletter can bring you more traffic. You can also announce that you provide (and link to) more free information on your website.

3. **Online networking**. Include your website address in your signature when you post to online networking sites or online forums and bulletin boards so interested people can visit your site.

4. **Blogs**. Posting information of value – especially information that will start word-of-mouth marketing – to visitors will increase traffic. People are always looking for information, whether it's about personal experiences, product reviews, recommendations, news about you, your products and services, your company or industry. Well-maintained blogs give visitors a reason to return. As you post compelling content, visitors will want to see what's next from you.

5. **Post to other blogs**. Find other credible bloggers in your niche, then comment regularly (and intelligently) on their posts. Most blogging platforms allow those who comment to include a web address. You can also find blogs that have a stable of contributors – see if you can become a regular contributor.

6. **E-mail signature listing**. List your web address at the close of every e-mail you send. People are familiar with signatures as a source for contact information, and software makes it easy to automatically add a signature to every e-mail you send. Think of how many e-mails you send; each is an opportunity to generate traffic.

7. Inviting visitors to return. Give visitors a reason to return to your website. Offer e-mail updates, alerts and special offers to keep your visitors coming back on a regular basis.

8. Online public relations. There are many sites online where you can post press releases. Include your contact and site information, and interested readers will click through. Search engines will also find that link.

9. Traffic exchanges. These are similar to link exchanges. You spend time on another person's website. As you view these sites, you earn credits you can use to display your site (impressions) to other people. Search on "traffic exchange" to learn more about this tactic.

10. Offline marketing. Publish your web address anywhere and everywhere you can – cards, letterhead, envelopes, print ads, signage and brochures.

11. Marketing hook. Offer things like a free ebook, free entry into a contest, a free subscription to an online newsletter or e-course, free admission to online seminars or free content for reprints.

12. Word-of-mouth traffic. Word of mouth is extremely effective, so much so, it has spawned its own association, WOMMA or Word of Mouth Marketing Association (womma.org), dedicated to online word-of-mouth strategies. Offer your site visitors an opportunity to share what they discover on your site with others. Providing a customer opinion platform for your products and services can bring you testimonial benefits.

13. eBay. List items for sale on eBay, and in the description of the item, mention your website. Use this as a way to get more customers to your site.

14. Facebook, LinkedIn and other social networking sites. Use these sites to promote your product, service or website – but be careful not to be too direct. Social networking site users hate when people use these sites as a platform to sell.

15. Consider using LinkedIn. This is a business version of Facebook (though they are not related in any way) where businesses and professionals can network and do business with one another.

16. Domain name. Try to find a domain name that describes what your business is and what users can find on your website.

Putting Your Ideas into Action

- Create a Google AdWords ad directing people to a landing page other than the home page of your site. The landing page should relate to your overall site content, but it doesn't have to.

- On the landing page, have links to affiliates that you have signed up with. Then earn a commission from all the clicks that result in sales to those affiliates.

- Understand everything that you can about search engine marketing and search engine optimization.

- Read and Reread the 16 ways to attract more traffic . . . It is probably the most important page in this entire book.

For More Information, go to GetRichClick.com.

6

Actionable Info from SEOmoz.org

While researching the data to include in the pages of *Get Rich Click*, I came across a specific website that is just simply amazing. Called SEOmoz.org, this site has so much important, well-written and "ACTIONABLE" data that two things immediately happened.

1. I contacted them and asked for permission to include portions of their site into the pages of *Get Rich Click*. I got permission from a very helpful woman there named Sarah Bird.

2. I decided to devote THIS ENTIRE CHAPTER to the folks at SEOmoz.org because they have so much amazing information there, it was an obvious choice on my part. So, below is information from SEOmoz.org.

Beginner's Guide to SEO

by Rand Fishkin of SEOmoz.org

How Search Engines Operate

Search engines have a short list of critical operations that allows them to provide relevant web results when searchers use their system to find information.

1. Crawling the Web

Search engines run automated programs, called "bots" or "spiders" that use the hyperlink structure of the web to "crawl" the pages and documents that make up the World Wide Web. Estimates are that of the approximately 20 billion existing pages, search engines have crawled between 8 and 10 billion.

2. Indexing Documents

Once a page has been crawled, it's contents can be "indexed" – stored in a giant database of documents that makes up a search engine's "index." This index needs to be tightly managed, so that requests that must search and sort billions of documents can be completed in fractions of a second.

3. Processing Queries

When a request for information comes into the search engine (hundreds of millions do each day), the engine retrieves from its index all the documents that match the query. A match is determined if the terms or phrase is found on the page in the manner specified by the user. For example, a search for car and driver magazine at Google returns 8.25 million results, but a search for the same phrase in quotes ("car and driver magazine") returns only 166 thousand results. In the first system, commonly called "Findall" mode, Google returned all documents that had the terms "car" "driver" and "magazine" (they ignore the term "and" because it's not useful to narrowing the results), while in the second search, only those pages with the exact phrase "car and driver magazine" were returned. Other advanced operators (Google has a list of 11) can change which results a search engine will consider a match for a given query.

4. Ranking Results

Once the search engine has determined which results are a match for the query, the engine's algorithm (a mathematical equation commonly used for sorting) runs calculations on each of the results to determine which is most relevant to the given query. They sort these on the results pages in order from most relevant to least so that users can make a choice about which to select.

Although a search engine's operations are not particularly lengthy, systems like Google, Yahoo!, AskJeeves and MSN are among the most complex, processing-intensive computers in the world, managing millions of calculations each second and funneling demands for information to an enormous group of users.

Speed Bumps and Walls

Certain types of navigation may hinder or entirely prevent search engines from reaching your website's content. As search engine spiders crawl the web, they rely on the architecture of hyperlinks to find new documents and revisit those that may have changed. In the analogy of speed bumps and walls, complex links and deep site structures with little unique content may serve as "bumps." Data that cannot be accessed by spiderable links qualify as "walls."

Possible "Speed Bumps" for SE Spiders:

- Spiders may be reluctant to crawl complex URLs; for example something such as url.com/page.php?id=4&CK=34rr&User=%Tom%. URLs like this often result in errors with nonhuman visitors.

- Pages with more than 100 unique links to other pages on the site (spiders may not follow each one).
- Pages buried more than three clicks/links from the home page of a website (unless there are many other external links pointing to the site, spiders will often ignore deep pages).
- Pages requiring a "Session ID" or cookie to enable navigation (spiders may not be able to retain these elements as a browser user can).
- Pages that are split into "frames" can hinder crawling and cause confusion about which pages to rank in the results.

The key to ensuring that a site's contents are fully crawlable is to provide direct HTML links to each page you want the search engine spiders to index. Remember that if a page cannot be accessed from the home page (where most spiders are likely to start their crawl) it is likely that it will not be indexed by the search engines. A sitemap is a tremendous help for this purpose.

Measuring Relevance and Popularity

Modern commercial search engines rely on the science of information retrieval (IR). That science has existed since the middle of the 20th century, when retrieval systems powered computers in libraries, research facilities and government labs. Early in the development of search systems, IR scientists realized that two critical components made up the majority of search functionality:

Relevance: The degree to which the content of the documents returned in a search matched the user's query intention and terms. The relevance of a document increases if the terms or phrase queried by the user occurs multiple times and shows up in the title of the work or in important headlines or subheaders.

Popularity: The relative importance, measured via citation (the act of one work referencing another, as often occurs in academic and business documents) of a given document that matches the user's query. The popularity of a given document increases with every other document that references it.

Keywords and Queries

Search engines rely on the terms queried by users to determine which results to put through their algorithms. But, rather than simply recognizing and retrieving exact matches for query terms, search engines use their knowledge of semantics (the science of language) to construct intelligent matching for queries. An example might be a search for loan providers that also returned results that did not contain that specific phrase, but instead had the term lenders.

The engines collect data based on the frequency of use of terms and the co-occurrence of words and phrases throughout the web. If certain terms or phrases are often found together on pages or sites, search engines can construct intelligent theories about their relationships. Mining semantic data through the incredible corpus that is the Internet has given search engines some of the most accurate data about word ontologies and the connections between words ever assembled artificially. This immense knowledge of language and its usage gives them the ability to determine which pages in a site are topically related, what the topic of a page or site is, how the link structure of the web divides into topical communities and much, much more.

Search engines' growing artificial intelligence on the subject of language means that queries will increasingly return more intelligent, evolved results. This heavy investment in the field of natural language processing (NLP) will help to achieve greater understanding of the meaning and intent behind their users' queries. Over the long term, users can expect the results of this work to produce increased relevancy in the SERPs (Search Engine Results Pages) and more accurate guesses from the engines as to the intent of a user's queries.

Paid Placement and Secondary Sources in the Results

The search engine results pages contain not only listings of documents found to be relevant to the user's query, but other content, including paid advertisements and secondary source results. Google, for example, serves up ads from its well known AdWords program (which currently fuels more than 99 percent of Google's revenues) as well as secondary content from its local search, product search (called Froogle) and image search results.

The sites/pages ranking in the "organic" search results receive the lion's share of searcher eyeballs and clicks – between 60–70 percent depending on factors such as the prominence of ads, relevance of secondary content, etc. The practice of optimization for the paid search results is called SEM or Search Engine Marketing while optimizing to rank in the secondary results requires unique, advanced methods of targeting specific searches in arenas such as local search, product search, image search and others. While all of these practices are a valuable part of any online marketing campaign, they are beyond the scope of this guide. Our sole focus remains on the "organic" results, although links at the bottom of this paper can help direct you to resources on other subjects.

How to Conduct Keyword Research

Keyword research is critical to the process of SEO. Without this component, your efforts to rank well in the major search engines may be misdirected to the wrong terms and phrases, resulting in rankings that no one will ever see. The process of Keyword research involves several phases:

1. Brainstorming: Thinking of what your customers/potential visitors would be likely to type in to search engines in an attempt to find the information/ services your site offers (including alternate spellings, wordings, synonyms, etc).

2. Surveying Customers: Surveying past or potential customers is a great way to expand your Keyword list to include as many terms and phrases as possible. It can also give you a good idea of what's likely to be the biggest traffic drivers and produce the highest conversion rates.

3. Applying Data from KW Research Tools: Several tools online (including Wordtracker & KeyWordSpy – both described below) offer information about the number of times users perform specific searches. Using these tools can offer concrete data about trends in KW selection.

4. Term Selection: The next step is to create a matrix or chart that analyzes the terms you believe are valuable and compares traffic, relevancy and the likelihood of conversions for each. This will allow you to make the best-informed decisions about which terms to target. SEOmoz's KW Difficulty Tool can also aid in choosing terms that will be achievable for the site.

5. Performance Testing and Analytics: After Keyword selection and implementation of targeting, analytics programs (like Indextools and ClickTracks) that measure web traffic, activity and conversions can be used to further refine Keyword selection.

Building a Traffic-Worthy Site

One of the most important (and often overlooked) subjects in SEO is building a site deserving of top rankings at the search engines. A site that ranks #1 for a set of terms in a competitive industry or market segment must be able to justify its value, or risk losing out to competitors who offer more. Search engines' goals are to rank the best, most usable, functional and informative sites first. By intertwining your site's content and performance with these goals, you can help to ensure its long-term prospects in the search engine rankings.

Usability

Usability represents the ease-of-use inherent in your site's design, navigation, architecture and functionality. The idea behind the practice is to make your site intuitive so that visitors will have the best possible experience on the site. A whole host of features figure into usability, including:

- **Design:** The graphical elements and layout of website have a strong influence on how easily usable the site is. Standards like blue, underlined links, top and side menu bars, logos in the top, left-hand corner may seem like rules that can be bent, but adherence to these elements (with which web users are already familiar) will help to make a site usable. Design also encompasses important topics like visibility and contrast. Separation of unique sections like navigation, advertising, content, search bars, etc., is also critical as users follow design cues to help them understand a page's content. A final consideration would also take into account the importance of ensuring that critical elements in a site's design (like menus, logos, colors and layout) were used consistently throughout the site.

- **Information Architecture:** The organizational hierarchy of a site can also strongly affect usability. Topics and categorization impact the ease with which a user can find the information they need on your site. While an intuitive, intelligently designed structure will seamlessly guide the user to their goals, a complex, obfuscated hierarchy can make finding information on a site disturbingly frustrating.

- **Navigation:** A navigation system that guides users easily through both top-level and deep pages and makes a high percentage of the site easily accessible is critical to good usability. Navigation is one of a website's primary functions. It provides users with obvious navigation systems: breadcrumbs, alt tags for image links, and well-written anchor text that clearly describes what the user will get if they click a link. Navigation standards like these can drastically improve usability.

- **Functionality:** To create compelling usability, ensure that tools, scripts, images, links, etc., all function as they are intended and don't provide errors to nonstandard browsers, alternative operating systems or uninformed users (who often don't know what/where to click).

- **Accessibility:** Accessibility refers primarily to the technical ability of users to access and move through your site, as well as the ability of the site to serve disabled or impaired users. For SEO purposes, the most important aspects are limiting code errors to a minimum and fixing broken links, making sure that content is accessible and visible in all browsers and without special actions.

- **Content:** The usability of content itself is often overlooked, but its importance cannot be overstated. The descriptive nature of headlines, the accuracy of information and the quality of content all factor highly into a site's likelihood to retain visitors and gain links.

Overall, usability is about gearing a site toward potential users. Success in this arena garners increased conversion rates, a higher chance that other sites will link to yours and a better relationship with your users (fewer complaints, lower instance of problems, etc.). For improving your knowledge of usability and best practices, I recommend Steve Krug's exceptional book, *Don't Make Me Think*, possibly the best $30 you can spend to improve your website.

Link "Bait"

When attempting to create the most link-worthy content, thinking outside the box and creating a document, tool or service that's truly revolutionary can provide a necessary boost.

Even on corporate image or branding sites for small companies, a single, exciting piece of content that gets picked up en masse by your web community is worth a small fortune in public relations and exposure.

Better still, the links you earn with an exciting release stay with your site for a long time, providing search visibility long after the event itself has been forgotten.

With content that generates links becoming such a valuable commodity, creating solely for the purpose of gaining links has become a popular practice. In order to capitalize on this phenomenon, it's necessary to brainstorm.

Below are some initial ideas that can help you build the content you need to generate great links.

● **Free Tools:** Automated tools that query data sources, combine information or conduct useful calculations are eminently link worthy. Think along the lines of mortgage calculators and site-checking tools, then expand into your particular area of business/operation.

● **Web 2.0 Applications:** Although the term Web 2.0 is more of a buzzword than a technicality, applications that fit the feature set described by the O'Reilly document do get a fantastic number of links from the web community and followers of this trend. Think mashups, maps, communities, sharing, tagging, RSS and blogs.

● **Collaborative Work Documents:** Working in concert with others is a good way to produce content more quickly and with generally higher quality. If you can get high-profile insiders or several known persons in an industry to collaborate, your chances for developing "link-bait" substantially increase.

● **Exposés of Nefarious Deeds:** Writing a journalistic-style exposé detailing the misdeeds of others (be they organizations, websites, individuals or companies) can generate a lot of links and traffic if done in a professional manner (and before anyone else). Make sure you're very careful with these types of actions, however, as the backlash can be worse than the benefit if your actions provoke the wrong type of response.

● **Top 10 Lists:** Numbered lists of tips, links, resources and rankings can be a great way to generate buzz. These lists often promote discussion and thus referencing.

● **Industry-Related Humor:** Even the most serious of industries can use a bit of humor now and again. As with exposés, be cautious not to offend (although that, too, can merit mentions) – use your knowledge of stereotypes and history inside your market to get topical laughs and the links will be yours.

● **Reviews of Events:** Industry gatherings, from pubcrawls to conferences to speeches and seminars, can all garner great links with a well-done review. Write professionally, as a journalist, and attempt to use as many full names as possible. It's also wise to link out to all the folks you mention, as they will see the links in their referral logs and come check you out.

● **Interviews with Well-Known Insiders:** Anyone inside an industry whose name frequently appears in that industry's internal press is a great candidate for an interview. Even if it's a few short questions over e-mail, a revealing interview can be a great source of links and esteemed professionals are likely to answer requests even from smaller sources as they can benefit from the attention, too.

● **Surveys or Collections of Data:** Offering large collections of industry data culled from polling individuals, an online survey or simply researching and aggregating data can provide a very link-worthy resource.

● **Film or Animation:** Particularly in industries where video clips or animations are rare (i.e. Geology, not Movie Reviews), a high-quality, entertaining or informative video or animation can get more than a few folks interested.

- **Charts, Graphs or Spreadsheets:** These standard business graphics should certainly include analysis and dissection, but can provide a good source of links if promoted and built properly.

- **High-Profile Criticism:** Similar to the exposé system, well-written critiques of popular products, companies, sites or individuals in a sector have the ability to pull in quite a few links from folks who agree and disagree.

- **Contests, Giveaways and Competitions:** Giving away prizes or public awards (even if they're just website graphics) can get a lot of online folks interested and linking.

- **Trend-Spotting:** Identifying a story ahead of the crowd is commonly called "scooping" in journalism. Do this online, and all (or many) blog posts on the subject will reference your site as the first to "call it."

- **Advice from Multiple Experts:** If you're creating an article that offers advice, pulling opinions from the well known experts in the industry is a great way to make sure links flow your way. The experts themselves will often be inclined to link.

There are dozens of other great ways to get bloggers, writers and website editors in your field to add links to your site. Imagine yourself as an industry blogger, seeking to cover the most exciting, unique trends and pages in the sector. If this individual stumbled across your content, would they be likely to write about it? If the answer is yes, it qualifies as link-bait.

Link-Building Based on Competitive Analysis

Looking at the links obtained by your top competitors and pursuing methods of your own to get listed on those sites/pages is an excellent way to stay competitive in the link-building race. It's also a good way to get natural traffic; as these are the links and sites that send your competitors their traffic, they will also bring visitors to your site. The methodology for investigating a competitor's links is fairly straightforward, although more complex methods can be used by the advanced researcher.

The best source of linkage data is Yahoo!. Google purposely does not report accurate link data with their link: command and MSN's rankings of links can often show less valuable and effective links at the top. Yahoo!, however, currently shows the greatest accuracy in numbers of links, and also sorts well, typically placing more valuable links near the top of the results.

At Yahoo!, the following searches can be used to find links:

1. Linkdomain:url.com

This command will show you all the pages that link to any page hosted at the domain url.com.

2. Link:url.com/page.html

This command will show only pages linked directly to the specified page.

3. **Linkdomain:url.com word**

This search will show all pages with the term "word" that link to pages hosted at the URL. You can use this to find topical linking pages that may be providing benefit for specific areas.

4. **Linkdomain:url.com -term**

Use the - sign to indicate that pages that include a particular term should be excluded from the search, for example, all links that point to a site that don't contain your company name (i.e. linkdomain:seobook.com -seomoz). Note that searches can contain multiple - signs and terms if you require very specific information (or wish to exclude lots of noisy data).

5. **Linkdomain:url.com -site:url.com**

In addition to the - sign as a term remover, you can remove sites from the results as well. This can be especially valuable if one large site links to the target site on every page, and you wish to see the links that don't include that site. It can also be valuable to remove the site itself, (i.e., linkdomain:seomoz.org -site:seomoz.org), so as not to see results from internal pages.

Competitive analysis also includes using the top search results themselves as sources for links. If a site or page ranks particularly well for many related searches, a link from that site can send a healthy number of interested surfers to you. Rankings in the SERPs is also an excellent way to determine the value of a link, so if a page ranks highly for the term or phrase you're targeting, a link from that page is sure to provide great assistance in achieving top placement.

Measuring Success:
Website and Ranking Metrics to Watch

One of the most valuable sources for data, analysis and refinement in an SEO campaign is in the statistics available via website tracking and measuring programs. A good analytics program can provide an incredible amount of data that can be used to track your visitors and make decisions about who to target in the future and how to do it.

Below is a short list of the most valuable elements in visitor tracking:

• **Campaign Tracking:** The ability to put specific URLs or referrer strings onto ads, e-mails or links and track their success.

• **Action Tracking:** The ability to track certain actions on a site such as form submission, newsletter signups, add-to-cart buttons, checkout or transaction completions and tying them together with campaigns and Keyword tracking so you know what ads, links, terms and campaigns are bringing you the best visitors.

• **Search Engine Referral Tracking:** Seeing which search engines sent which visitors over time and tracking the terms and phrases they used to reach your site. Combined with action tracking, this can help you determine which terms are most valuable to target.

- **Referring URLs & Domain Tracking:** This allows you to see what URLs and domains are responsible for sending you traffic. By tracking these individually, you can see where your most valuable links are coming from.
- **First-Time Vs. Return Visitors:** Find out what percentage of your visitors are coming back each day/week/month. This can help you to figure out how "sticky" and consistently interesting your site is.
- **Entry Pages:** Which pages are attracting the most visitors and which are converting them. You can also see pages that have a very high rate of loss – those pages that don't do a good job pulling people into the site.
- **Visitor Demographics:** Where are your visitors coming from, what browsers are they using, what time do they visit? All these questions and many more can be answered with demographics.
- **Click Path Analysis:** What paths do your visitors follow when they get to your site? This data can help you make more logical streams of pages for visitors to use as they navigate your site.
- **Popular Pages:** Which get the most visitors and which are neglected? Use this data to help improve low popularity pages and emulate highly trafficked ones.
- **Page Views Per Session:** This data can tell you how many pages each visitor to your site is viewing – another metric used to measure "stickiness."

Applying the information you learn from your visitor tracking is a science unto its own. Experience and common sense should help to discover which terms, visitors, referrers and demographics are most valuable to your site, enabling you to make the best possible decisions about how and where to target.

I can't say enough about how many great articles appear on SEOmoz.org. What I can do is suggest a few others you will want to read:

1. **Social Media Marketing Guide: 101 Social Media Sites to Help Market Your Business or Yourself Online**
seomoz.org/article/social-media-marketing-tactics#101-social-media-sites
2. **The Internet Marketing Handbook** by Danny Dover
seomoz.org/dp/the-Internet-marketing-handbook
3. **The Beginner's Checklist for Learning SEO** by Danny Dover
seomoz.org/blog/the-beginners-checklist-for-learning-seo
4. **SEO TOOLS** seomoz.org/tools

7

Partner Up with Affiliate Marketing

Suppose a website called ABC.com pays website XYZ.com a commission for each visitor or new client XYZ sends to the ABC website. This process is known as an "affiliate" relationship.

XYZ has no investment in ABC's product or service. ABC doesn't pay XYZ unless the referred party takes the agreed-upon action on ABC. This might be making a purchase or just registering the referred party's e-mail address. Some firms will pay for a lead while others pay only for an actual sale.

Essentially, affiliate marketing means paying the owner of one website to direct traffic to another website for a fee or a percentage of the sale that is made. In the *Get Rich Click* spirit of making money while investing little or no money of your own, affiliate programs are one of the very best ways to profit from the Internet.

Affiliate marketing benefits both the affiliate and the merchant. As an affiliate, you can generate income from traffic to your website. If you choose your affiliations well, you also increase the value to your site visitors. Meanwhile, merchants get more traffic to their sites. Because this traffic arrives through a referral, it's predisposed to make a purchase. Assuming the customer is satisfied, affiliate marketing can be a win/win/win business model for everyone involved.

Businesses find affiliate marketing attractive because most programs use a "pay for performance" model. Compare this to traditional forms of advertising. Creating a television ad and buying the air time for it is expensive – and there is no guarantee the ad will be a success. In online affiliate marketing, businesses pay only for results.

For example, Amazon Associates, the affiliate marketing program of Amazon.com, has marketed Amazon.com across millions of websites since July 1996. Through this program, Amazon has acquired millions of customers without incurring the expenses associated with traditional branding campaigns or maintaining a dedicated sales force. Amazon Associates is among the largest and most successful online affiliate programs.

Amazon.com's main site is made up of millions of pages. As an Amazon Associate, you can create an e-mail campaign that points people to any one of those pages and include your affiliate code as an embedded link. Whenever a recipient clicks through and buys that Amazon product, you earn a commission.

CASE STUDY:

Blinds.com

If you enroll as an affiliate of Blinds.com, you can resell their products and get paid a 5 to 7 percent commission. If the lead you supplied makes a $400 sale, Blinds.com handles the entire transaction – receiving, manufacturing and fulfillment – and then sends you a commission check for $20 or more. All you do is send Blinds.com a site visitor. Blinds.com does all the work.

Which sites make great candidates to be a Blinds.com affiliate? Any site that sells products and services like carpets, tiles, paints or interior design to new homeowners or those who remodel homes, apartments and office buildings.

There are two ways to get involved in affiliate marketing with Blinds.com:

1. Suppose you have a business selling wallpaper, floor tile, paint or carpet. Or perhaps you are an interior designer, sell real estate or build houses. Your business has web traffic for buyers of home decorating and remodeling products or services. There is a good chance those same buyers may want to buy window blinds, drapes or shutters. Your firm can put up an affiliate link to the Blinds.com site and they take care of the rest.

2. Blinds.com did have an affiliate who took this a step further. He bought a domain name with the word "blinds" in it. He set up a website to sell window blinds, submitted the website to the search engines, worked to optimize his site, built links to other sites he owned and then sent Blinds.com the leads. The best part of the story? This affiliate took all his product photos from the Blinds.com site! Blinds.com management had no idea he was doing this until they looked at his site and saw the photos that were the exact same as the Blinds.com photos. Another firm might hire a lawyer to stop such a practice, but he was a great affiliate and was making Blinds.com a lot of money!

10 Steps to Making Money with Affiliate Marketing

1. Buy a domain name that includes the specific Keyword for the product.

2. Set up an affiliate relationship with one or more firms in that field.

3. Create a simple website for the products.

4. You can obtain the photos you need from the firm for which you are selling, but be sure to ask permission first.

5. Create new copy for your website. Don't use the same copy your partner uses; it can hurt your search engine rankings as well as other firms that have this copy on their sites.

6. Submit your website to the search engines.

7. Build links to and from your site with other related sites.

8. Create links to your new site from your Facebook and MySpace accounts. Consider asking your friends to list your site on their Facebook and MySpace accounts.

9. Write about your products on other sites, blogs, and social networks such as Twitter and Facebook to get more traffic.

10. Optimize your site to improve your search engine rankings and increase traffic (see Chapter 5 and GetRichClick.com).

Affiliate programs are the fastest-growing area of e-commerce. They're easy to set up and take little or no money to get started.

How Affiliate Marketing Programs Work

Most affiliate programs are free to join. When you enter an affiliate relationship with a merchant, you agree to place links on your site to the merchant's site. The merchant agrees to pay you a commission for the traffic you send.

Merchants offering affiliate programs pay in three basic ways:

• **Pay-Per-Sale (or cost-per-sale)**. When you send the merchant a customer who subsequently makes a purchase, the merchant pays you. Your commission may be a percentage of the sale or a fixed amount for the sale. Amazon's Associates Program is an example of this arrangement.

• **Pay-Per-Click (or cost-per-click)**. The merchant pays you for every click on the link directing the visitor to the merchant's site. The referred visitor does not need to purchase anything for you to get your commission.

• **Pay-Per-Lead (or cost-per-lead)**. You send the merchant a visitor who subsequently signs up as a lead. This means the visitor completes an online form on the merchant's site. The merchant may then pass the lead to the sales department or sell the lead information to another company.

The Riches ARE in the Niches . . .
$5 Million a Year Selling Cuff Links Online!

The Internet is the ultimate machine for marketing "niche" products. Ravi Ratan figured this out early on.

Working in his family's mulitgenerational custom-clothing business, Ravi decided to register CuffLinks.com. For years, the domain sat dormant, until one day Ravi figured he might as well try to sell on the site. So, Ratan went out and bought products at a local retailer and put them on CuffLinks.com. They all sold. Quickly. He bought more, and once again, they all sold. A 21st-century entrepreneur had been born!

These days, Ravi Ratan runs a $5 million-a-year business selling cuff links online. He's the largest retail seller of cuff links in the world and sells more than most of his online competitors – combined! In addition to designing and manufacturing his own incredibly creative ones – such as a pair that include usable flash drives (featured in *GQ* and *Maxim* magazines) – Ravi sells name-brand products from other fashion designers, and has managed to obtain authorized distribution rights from the NFL, NBA, MLB and a host of NCAA schools.

In a very smart move, Ratan set up the firm so that he sells at every level of the sales channel. What started as an "online only" site has morphed into a small powerhouse selling retail, wholesale, custom, directly to customers, via affiliates and even drop shipping for companies that don't want to deal with order fulfillment! In other words, if you have a website, you can buy stock from Ravi wholesale and resell it. However, if you just want to market the products from the CuffLinks.com site, you can do that and CuffLinks.com will fulfill the sale and send you a commission check for your lead! The bottom line: regardless of whether you want to sell on your own site, a friend's site, through Facebook or you want to work with a third-party wedding-planning, tuxedo-rental or high-end men's clothing site, Ravi has found a way to help sell cuff links through all of these markets.

When I was growing up, there used to be a TV commercial for Shick razors in which billionaire Victor Kiam says, "I liked the company so much, I bought it." Well, I'm no billionaire, but after ordering from CuffLinks.com and being so impressed, and after meeting Ravi and being further impressed, I decided to invest and am now a proud co-owner! The lesson here, of course, is that no matter how small the product, or how narrow the niche, the Internet provides smart entrepreneurs a platform for reaching customers like we've never seen before. Just ask Ravi, who despite his incredible talent and penchant for hard work, always keeps his sleeves down, not rolled up – because you never miss an opportunity to market CuffLinks!

Scan the QR code or go to GetRichClick.com/cufflinks to learn more and save!

Affiliate Models: One time Vs. Lifetime Commissions

There are two popular variations of the basic affiliate model:

- **Two-tier programs**. These programs offer commissions based on sales and sales recruitment; they are similar to the old "Amway" business model – now called Quixtar. Not only can you, as the affiliate, generate income from sales, clicks or leads, you can also get paid for the activity from other affiliate sites you have referred to the merchant.

- **Residual or Lifetime programs**. You may find merchants with a subscription business model offering residual programs. For every visitor you send who becomes a client, you receive a regular commission for as long as that client keeps purchasing the merchant's goods or services.

Businesses can create affiliate programs around actions that are important to them – not all businesses sell products, but they all have sales goals. Perhaps a business wants to encourage newsletter subscriptions or promote registrations for a conference. If you understand how affiliate programs work and the accounting technology behind them to monitor the activity of affiliates, you can help businesses create the affiliate marketing programs that meet their needs.

Affiliate Program Networks

You can do the work of researching merchants that offer affiliate programs, or you can turn to affiliate networks. These are brokers that mediate between you and the merchant with whom you'd like to affiliate. In return for their services, affiliate networks typically get a small override from each of your commissions.

Affiliate networks are attractive because they have access to a wide variety of affiliate programs and can match you with merchants you may not have considered. They also make sense if you are among those who would prefer not to manage the details of your affiliate arrangements.

Creating and managing an affiliate network is a way to apply the *Get Rich Click* mindset: make money by simply connecting two parties that can benefit from each other.

CLICK TIP The concept I'm about to describe can work for any industry, but let's look at wristwatch affiliate programs as an example. Start by creating a website called "My Top Ten Gold Watch Sites" (mytop10goldwatchsites.com).

Next, do your homework: determine what criteria make for a really good online wristwatch site.

Then identify the top-ten wristwatch affiliate programs on the Internet. Enroll in the various watch sites' affiliate programs. Make sure you understand what action a referred visitor must take for you to earn your commission.

Design your site so it looks professional and appealing. Create copy that explains what a particular gold watch site offers and why the site made your top-ten list. Pay careful attention to search optimization strategies that will allow your site to place higher in organic search engine results (see Chapter 5).

Then embed your affiliate links. Visitors to your site click on a link. When they buy any product from ANY of those 10 links, you will receive your commission.

How to Find an Affiliate Program

There are three primary ways to locate affiliate programs for your website:

1. Consult affiliate sites like ClickBank.com or cj.com.

2. Work with a large affiliate network that provides the platform for dozens or even hundreds of advertisers.

3. Research individual merchants to see if they offer an affiliate program.

We have compiled a list of resources to help you connect with suitable affiliate programs at GetRichClick.com/affiliate.

Through these companies, you can market the whole merchant site or a specific product from the central site. The activity you generate is tied to your personal affiliate code, and the respective merchant sends you a commission check.

CASE STUDY:
Creating a Revenue Stream

My friend Adrian Morrison makes a great living in the affiliate marketing world. He has over 70 different campaigns running at the same time, and they're all bringing in revenue.

Here's one example. Adrian was buying traffic from Facebook for $.02 per click and selling those leads to an advertiser who wanted to build an e-mail list. The advertiser was giving away two tickets to the movies – at a wholesale cost of $2.00 – and paid Adrian $1.35 for every lead that signed up. It took about five clicks for every sign-up, which works out to the following:

•**Advertiser pays $2.00 for wholesale movie tickets**
•**Advertiser pays out $1.35 to Adrian**
•**Adrian pays Facebook $.02 per click, or $.10 for every five clicks**
•**Adrian nets $1.25 per e-mail sign up**

This cycle occurs 400 times per day – which means $15,000 per month profit on this single campaign.

There are thousands of ways to make money in the affiliate business. The trick's knowing what traffic is out there to be purchased, at what cost and what type of traffic the affiliates want. Then you put those pieces together – and keep the profit for yourself.

25+ Different Firms That Want to Pay You!

The affliate program market is also referred to as a cost-per-action (CPA) market. Go to GetRichClick.com/affiliate to find a list of websites that pay other site owners for a variety of actions such as buying, clicking, filling out a form or sending them a lead.

Before using any of these firms, you should ask for references so you can talk with other site owners to learn whether they are happy with the services these businesses offer. You might also want to ask your accountant and/or lawyer to review their terms and conditions and explain all the information listed in the "fine print." When you use an affiliate marketing firm to bring revenue to your business, that firm becomes your business partner. You need to know as much as you can about them.

For a great list of affiliate programs, see page 231 later in this book.

CLICK TIP ▷ Many credit card companies and online colleges or universities will pay you an affiliate commission of $5 to $25 for each referral that completes an application. These commissions can possibly double if the company approves the application.

Make Money or Save Money: Both Put You Ahead

Some merchants allow their affiliates to buy products for themselves essentially at wholesale prices. To take advantage of this, create an affiliate link on your website and then use that link to buy products for yourself. That means you are buying from your own affiliate link at the retail price minus the commission you get back.

You might also ask your friends and family to buy from these links. It's a great way to start to profit from the Internet immediately. Be aware, however, that some merchants have restrictions on this type of buying. Make sure you read the fine print on your affiliate agreement.

How to Generate More Income Per Sale

Choose affiliate programs that pay higher commissions. Some of the categories that pay the most include:

- Loans
- Insurance
- Credit card sign-ups
- Digital products
- Surveys
- Casinos
- Financial

Affiliate Programs for Nonprofit Organizations

Affiliate marketing is an excellent way for nonprofits to raise funds.

Imagine, for example, that a fourth-grade class is selling wrapping paper, popcorn or boxes of candy. The class might also consider an affiliate program to offer products that are appealing to a larger audience. The class can do this through a merchant that would become the designated affiliate.

The merchant will require an affiliate coupon code at the time of purchase and would then pay a commission to the affiliate. The fourth-grade class would raise funds for the school without taking possession of the product, having to warehouse the products, having to deal with delivery of the products and not have to deal with any part of the product fulfillment.

The customer would get a product that was probably more useful than wrapping paper, popcorn or candy, and the school might actually make more money over the long run.

An organization could support this fund-raising strategy year-round to receive ongoing commissions. This is simply the difference between realizing profit from a onetime sale versus a sale that creates long-term, recurring revenue. Many schools set up a similar program with the local grocery store so that each time a parent shops at that particular store, a small percentage of the purchase goes to the school or the parent-teacher association.

It would be very easy to set up a website to make money for the school PTA selling school supplies via affiliate links and designate the parent-teacher association as the affiliate. Each purchase through one of the affiliate links then earns the parent-teacher association a commission. You can maintain this fund-raising for as long as your association would like to earn money.

Every affiliate program you promote can be a source of income. If you promote a software application that earns you a $20 commission on each sale, 100 sales could make you $2000. Not bad for selling a product that isn't even yours!

Panning Amazon's River of Gold

When Bill Clinton's highly anticipated memoir, *My Life* (Knopf, 2004), was released, one Amazon Associate made money by taking advantage of the book's media exposure and popularity. What's more, he did it without a website of his own. You can follow this same strategy with any item Amazon sells. It's smart, easy and profitable!

Here are the steps:

- Go to affiliate-program.Amazon.com/gp/associates/join. Then follow Amazon's application instructions to become an affiliate.
- Choose an Amazon product to market (it doesn't need to be a book).
- Obtain the proper affiliate/associate coded link for the Amazon product.

- Purchase a domain name related to the Amazon book from one of the many domain name providers online. (Note: In the *My Life* example, the entrepreneur purchased two available domain names: billclinton-mylife.com and mylife-billclinton.com. I do not recommend this part of his plan. You could easily get sued, have to pay legal fees, lose the names and be forced to give back the money made from the concept plus additional penalties.)
- Create a Google ad like this one:
  - *Bill Clinton – My Life*
  - Preferred Amazon Affiliate
  - billclinton-mylife.com
- In the Google ad, he redirected his web address (billclinton-mylife.com) to the Amazon Associate link for the page Bill Clinton – My Life.
- He sat back and watched his Amazon Associates commissions build. For Bill Clinton's *My Life*, Amazon paid an Associate commission of $1.53 for each sale of the discounted $35 book.

Choose a book you think others will buy. If you like *Get Rich Click*, sign up at Amazon, get your affiliate link and send an e-mail to your friends. Include your affiliate link to this book's product page at Amazon. They buy, you make money and I sell a few books to put my daughters through college!

Get Rich Click Money-Making Summary

Amazon sells a lot more than books. Its Associate program pays commissions on anything you sell, including electronics, clothing and many big-ticket items. Many non-book items actually pay larger commissions.

1. Become an Amazon associate.

2. Find a book title or product to sell.

3. Secure the Amazon Associate coded link for the product.

4. Purchase a related domain name for the product (but not a name that might infringe on trademark or copyright).

5. Run a Google or Facebook ad campaign or market the product to a list or group you believe might want to buy the book.

6. Redirect the URL to the Amazon web page.

7. Receive your commission.

Affiliate Processors and Networks

I've described making money on the Internet as the "gold rush" of the 21st century. Millions of entrepreneurial businesses sell a variety of tangible and intangible products online. Millions of entrepreneurs have quit their day jobs and are now spending less time making significant money operating their own Internet businesses. I'm particularly fond of two companies that help people accomplish these goals.

Too Many Offers? Which One Is Best? Try JOUNCE.com™

Network affiliates have so many product choices and opportunities it's actually a problem choosing which offers are the right ones for you and your business. The truth is, it can be hard to wade through all of the possibilities and determine which networks offer the best deals. That's where jounce.com comes in.

Jounce, founded by former software entrepreneur Tyson Quick, is essentially a search engine of product offers for network affiliates. Users can browse, search by category or enter a very specific product (green iPhone case, for example). They can search by which networks they belong to and how much they're looking to earn. Jounce then spits out a list of from 50 to several thousand matching offers. The goal is to ease the time-consuming process of finding the right product by aggregating offers from hundreds of different networks.

Jounce currently has 60 affiliate networks indexed in its platform, including heavy hitters ClickBank, Commission Junction and Link Share. Quick plans to include more than 400 networks over time.

Networks benefit from investing in Jounce because their products are promoted directly to affiliates instead of to customers – thereby increasing the advertising ROI enormously.

A few network affiliates have been resistant to Jounce's business model, preferring instead to maintain exclusivity for certain affiliates. But according to Quick, most have concluded that it's beneficial to get the word out to as many potential affiliates as possible.

"We'll add statistics tracking what kind of click-throughs you're getting and what kind of conversions you're getting. We'll build a drag-and-drop website that will allow you to do [split testing] on different sales pages," explains Quick. "We'll let the technology automatically adapt to what sells best and start doing that for you. We ultimately want to save affiliate marketers as much time as possible, because that's what generates income."

In the meantime, Quick is becoming a successful Internet entrepreneur in his own right. Jounce currently has eight full-time and two part-time employees, four of whom live outside the United States including a lead program developer in Russia and a search specialist in India. If all goes as planned, international start-up Jounce could forever simplify the way affiliates all over the world do business.

Scan the QR code or go to GetRichClick.com/tyson to watch Tyson's interview.

The Largest 25 Jounce™ Affiliate Networks

1. Commission Junction cj.com

2. Linkshare linkshare.com

3. ClickBank ClickBank.com

4. Share-A-Sale shareasale.com

5. Google Affiliate Network google.com/ads/affiliatenetwork

6. Clickbooth clickbooth.com

7. PepperJam pepperjam.com

8. EpicDirect epicdirectnetwork.com

9. buyat buyat.com

10. Media Trust mediatrust.com

11. Affiliate.com affiliate.com

12. Copeac copeac.com

13. Neverblue neverblue.com

14. Market Leverage marketleverage.com

15. Adknowledge adknowledge.com

16. Monetizeit monetizeit.com

17. QwikMedia qwikmedia.com

18. Tatto Media tattomedia.com

19. Peerfly peerfly.com

20. Convert2Media convert2media.com

21. NDemand ndemandaffiliates.com

22. MaxBounty maxbounty.com

23. Amped Media ampedmedia.com

24. Market Health markethealth.com

25. Adscend Media adscendmedia.com

CASE STUDY:
ClickBank – a Great Way to Make Easy Money

ClickBank is one of my absolute favorite websites. Because all their products are downloadable digital content, the merchants at ClickBank can offer huge commissions for every sale you make – as much as 90 percent in some cases. ClickBank is the largest marketplace of online digital content. They sell over 25,000 eBooks, software programs, videos and hosting programs in over 200 countries every day and have paid over $1.6 billion in commissions to their affiliates! Because the products are all digital, publishers have little or no overhead and no product fulfillment costs. This allows them to offer higher than average commissions to affiliates.

Technically, ClickBank is known as a leading third-party affiliate processor. The company processes payments on behalf of companies and entrepreneurs (vendors) who have products to sell and pays predetermined commissions to affiliates who generate sales on behalf of those vendors. As a ClickBank affiliate you operate as a virtual business, selling products through your own sites, e-mails or other marketing efforts. You don't have to have a website to make money affiliating with ClickBank.

How to Become a ClickBank affiliate partner:

1. Sign up at ClickBank.com.

2. Search the ClickBank marketplace for products to promote.

3. Create your hoplink affiliate code. What is a "hoplink"? For an affiliate to earn credit for a sale, the customer must first follow a ClickBank hoplink. The link takes the customer to the vendor's Hoplink Target web address, and automatically credits the affiliate with that referral. ClickBank provides easy-to-follow instructions.

4. Incorporate the hoplink into your marketing campaign.

5. Promote your link and/or product.

6. Earn a commission on every sale you generate.

When you market as a ClickBank affiliate from a website, choose ClickBank products that are related to your site's content or to the nature of your business.

Uncle Sam's Money

Review: This may be one of the best affiliate programs available. The core product (government grants) is highly desirable. This product and affiliate program has been around for several years – a lifetime by Internet standards! Customers get 13 free bonuses with purchase, and the free bonuses alone are worth significantly more than the base price.

- Very high commission rate: 75 percent commission payout ($27.96 payout).
- Very low return rate: less than 3 percent total returns.
- Highest selling grant program on ClickBank.
Ranked # 1 in ClickBank Finance Category: indicates high sales/click ratio.
- Ranked in top 10 ClickBank programs under Money & Finance category.
- Very high demand product.
- Great free bonus package attracts many purchasers.
- 90-day "no questions asked" guarantee generates higher affiliate sales.

Final Verdict: This affiliate program really has it all – the highest sales volumes, best overall core product, superb bonus package, the best customer service and much more. This winning combination generates high affiliate sales and low return rates, which means the best profit margins for any potential affiliates. This program is simply the best of the best and receives a Top Rating for Affiliate Programs - 9.9/10 and our Top Rating for overall rating — 5 stars.

Product Price: $39.95
Your Commission: $27.96   *Source: ClickBank.com*

CASE STUDY:
Commission Junction

An online affiliate marketing company owned by ValueClick, Inc., Commission Junction is one of the largest affiliate networks in North America.

Commission Junction matches merchants or service providers who sell products or services on the Internet with affiliate partners who would like to promote them. Much like vendors at ClickBank, the merchants are often publishers, and each product link has an assigned fixed or percentage-based commission.

Internet Retailer's Top 500 Guide to Retail Web Sites found that more marketers used Commission Junction than they did the next two affiliate marketing providers combined. The report also said performance marketing continued to be one of the most cost-effective channels for driving online revenues. As a result, top retailers continue to use Commission Junction.

Fifty percent of the top 500 retailers run affiliate programs through Commission Junction. Commission Junction powers more of these affiliate programs than any other single network provider and is the preferred provider in the majority of the marketing categories Internet Retailer tracked, including apparel/accessories, Books/CDs/DVDs, computers/electronics, flowers/gifts, hardware/home improvements, health/beauty, office supplies, specialty/nonapparel, sporting goods and toys/hobbies.

Commission Junction solidified its reputation by building a solid base of advertisers who represent a wide range of large retail markets as well as thousands of niche markets.

This variety of offerings has made the company particularly appealing to affiliates who tend to build small but loyal followings, yet want to make a profit.

Putting Your Ideas into Action

● **Create a website or an e-mail newsletter reviewing books each week or once a month. Include your Amazon Associates affiliate link in each review that points to the book on Amazon. You can do this for virtually any subject. Each time a visitor to your site clicks your link and buys, you make money. This works well for students, entrepreneurs and even members of book clubs.**

● **Create a website dedicated to affiliate programs. Sites like Memolink (memolink.com) and MyPoints (mypoints.com) participate in a wide variety of affiliate programs (usually Pay-Per-Click or pay-per-lead) and then pay their visitors a percentage of the commission on each click or reward them with prizes.**

● **Become a ClickBank Affiliate. It is by far one of the easiest ways to make money online.**

● **Consider creating your own product and listing it on ClickBank so that others can sell it for you.**

● **Realize that making more money or saving more money BOTH add to your bottom line!**

For More Information, go to www.GetRichClick.com.

8

Domain Names

*I created the slogan "Domain Names are Internet Real Estate™" back in 1995. I have amended it to read "**Domain Names and Websites are Internet Real Estate™**." A good domain name creates mindshare™. You can own it, lease it or put up a virtual shopping center.*

1-800-Flowers and the Value of Mindshare

I learned the value of mindshare years ago from reading the story about the toll-free telephone number 1-800-FLOWERS. Jim McCann created that firm out of a phone number! He and I have met on several occasions and discussed his 1-800-Flowers story and my Business.com story. Mindshare is the name of the game when so many transactions take place in the digital economy.

The "1-900" pay-per-call telephone number business took off after local pay-per-call market of "976" numbers were all the rage. I saw that having the right number/name was essential, and I wanted to get a specific one. I got on a plane to New Jersey to ask Bell Communications Research to release 1-900-932-8437, which happened to spell 1-900-Weather. I wanted it to be released to a specific long-distance carrier that I had a deal with.

But when the powers that be realized what I was about to get my hands on, the number magically disappeared from the database of available numbers! I had no legal recourse, but I did learn a valuable lesson about the name game and the value of this type of "mindshare."

Just like those phone numbers, domain names and websites today are truly mindshare or Internet "real estate." The world is just starting to understand demand, supply and value in this market. When I bought "Business.com," I purchased an asset with a value I could build upon. I bought it thinking I'd turn Business.com into a magazine with the domain as its online component. I could also sell it to someone who might want it more than I did.

As it turned out, "Business.com" was well worth its purchase price. I learned from my experience with the 900 numbers. More importantly, instead of thinking at the level of an entrepreneurial transaction, I was thinking of a total business model. This – plus luck, timing and the ultimate "disruptive" technology that allows business to be conducted easily on the Internet – made a huge difference.

Today advertisers are increasingly savvy, demanding better results and more information. Companies are getting smarter and more strategic about maximizing their share of the advertising dollar. New players are always entering the market, bringing new business models and fresh perspectives. And a good domain name is part of the game. Today there are more than 175+ million registered domains around the world, and the secondary market for domain names is robust.

TIMELINE OF BUSINESS.COM
From $0.00 to $345 Million

1992 – Business Systems International, a small British firm selling telephone and computer systems, obtains the Business.com domain name. There is no cost to BSI; domain names were free of charge before September of 1995.

1995 – Marc Ostrofsky buys the name for $150,000 from BSI. A record price at the time. The press wrote many derogatory editorials including the line "a fool and his money were just parted."

1999 – Ostrofsky sells the name to an Internet start-up for $7.5 million; the sale makes the *Guinness Book of World Records*. Ostrofsky demands "put rights," which allows him to buy stock in the firm at a later date or keep the cash, whichever is larger.

2004 – Ostrofsky exercises the "put" rights and gets stock in the new Business.com "business to business" search engine.

2007 – Business.com is sold for $345 million. The additional stock Ostrofsky receives as part of the original sale puts the final value of the original sale at well over $10 million.

The buyer was RH Donnelley, a large firm in the "yellow pages" business. The logic was brilliant. In one simple transaction, this "old world" printed yellow page business supplier added new clients, got $50 million in new revenue to the company, a great online component and the best domain name in the world for any company wanting to do business on the Internet.

The Business.com transaction helped create a market with thousands of active domain name investors who buy, sell and trade domain names on a daily basis.

The Race Is On

It's interesting to sit back and watch firms spend large sums annually on Internet advertising and buy Keywords to match their market needs – yet they fail to realize the business advantages of owning the domain name for the market they are targeting through advertising.

I happen to own a few good domain names such as Photographer.com, Consulting.com, Bachelor.com and MutualFunds.com. To this day, not one major firm has tried to buy MutualFunds.com. It baffles me daily. Hundreds of mutual fund firms market themselves on the Internet, buy "Keywords" from Google and Yahoo! and spend millions of dollars getting potential clients to come to their site. But none has tried to buy "MutualFunds.com" from me – yet. (In Europe, one smart public company did buy the domain FUND.com for $9,999,950.00.)

Many large firms use advertising agencies that, by definition, are not in the business of taking chances. These agencies are charged with being prudent when it comes to a client's marketing and advertising dollars. But the right domain name is an asset on a firm's balance sheet.

Simply capturing those users who type the words "Mutual Funds" into their browser's web address field could increase sales and save money in search engine advertising. Better yet, this direct navigation traffic – when a user bypasses a search engine by navigating directly to the site – is highly targeted. The domain owner captures prequalified leads often meant for competitors! (See Chapter 3 for more on direct navigation and search.)

Corporations and Their $1,000,000+ Domain Names

Below is a list of generic domain names owned by major corporations:

ContactLenses.com (1 800 Contacts)

Contacts.com (1 800 Contacts)

EyeCare.com (1 800 Contacts)

Glasses.com (1 800 Contacts)

Flowers.com (1 800 Flowers)

21st.com (21st Century Insurance)

InfantFormula.com (Abbott Labs)

RA.com (Abbott Labs)

Director.com (Adobe)

Flash.com (Adobe)

Aluminum.com (Alcoa)

Open.com (American Express)

Tires.com (America's Tires)

Checking.com (Amtrust)

HomeEquity.com (Amtrust)

Games.com (AOL)

Love.com (AOL)

AskJeeves.com (Ask.com)

AcidReflux.com (AstraZeneca)

GERD.com (AstraZeneca)

Mobile.com (AT&T)

AutoRental.com (Avis Budget)

RentaCar.com (Avis Budget)

Loans.com (Bank of America)

Book.com (Barnes & Noble)

Books.com (Barnes & Noble)

Archery.com (Bass Pro Shops)

Hunting.com (Bass Pro Shops)

Aspirin.com (Bayer)

Impotence.com (Bayer)

MultipleSclerosis.com (Bayer)

FastAccess.com (BellSouth)

Coat.com (Burlington Coat Factory)

Platinum.com (CA)

Security.com (CA)

Auto.com (Cars.com)

Car.com (Cars.com)

Warehouse.com (CDW)

Finance.com (Citigroup)

Burgers.com (CKE Restaurants)

Bleach.com (Clorox)

Grease.com (Clorox)

Salad.com (Clorox)

Computers.com (CNET)

Download.com (CNET)

Downloads.com (CNET)

Gaming.com (CNET)

Help.com (CNET)

Labs.com (CNET)

MP3.com (CNET)

News.com (CNET)

Radio.com (CNET)

Search.com (CNET)

Store.com (CNET)

TV.com (CNET)

Incontinence.com (ConvaTec)

Buffet.com (Country Buffet)

Checks.com (Deluxe)

Malts.com (Diageo)

Rum.com (Diageo)

Scotch.com (Diageo)

Animal.com (Discovery Comm.)

Dig.com (Disney)

Go.com (Disney)

Video.com (Disney)

Beauty.com (Drugstore.com)

IceCream.com (Dryer's)

Gossip.com (E! Online)

Pipeline.com (EarthLink)

Half.com (eBay)

Rent.com (eBay)

ADHD.com (Eli Lilly)

BipolarDisorder.com (Eli Lilly)

Fleas.com (Eli Lilly)

RentalCar.com (Enterprise Rent-A-Car)

CollegeGameDay.com (ESPN)

Movie.com (Fandango)

Movies.com (Fandango)

401k.com (Fidelity)

Funds.com (Fidelity)

Retire.com (Fidelity)

Snacks.com (Frito-Lay)

VirusProtection.com (F-Secure)

Florist.com (FTD)

AutoLeasing.com (GE)

CarLeasing.com (GE)

Women.com (GE)

ReInsurance.com (General Re)

Asthma.com (GSK)

Bipolar.com (GSK)

Depression.com (GSK)

Diabetes.com (GSK)

Heartburn.com (GSK)

HeartHealth.com (GSK)

Helix.com (GSK)

Osteoporosis.com (GSK)

Reflux.com (GSK)

RestlessLegs.com (GSK)

SkinInfection.com (GSK)

Sleeplessness.com (GSK)

ToothBrush.com (GSK)

WholeLifeInsurance.com (Guardian)

Acne.com (Guthy-Renker)

TaxCut.com (H&R Block)

Easter.com (Hallmark)

Greetings.com (Hallmark)

Stores.com (Hammacher Schlemmer)

PantyHose.com (Hanes)

Casinos.com (Harrah's)

Game.com (Hasbro)

History.com (History Channel)

Motorcycles.com (Honda)

Scooters.com (Honda)

Chips.com (Intel)

Netbook.com (Intel)

PC.com (Intel)

Apps.com (Intuit)

Banking.com (Intuit)

Baby.com (J&J)

Cancer.com (J&J)

Cholesterol.com (J&J)

GetWell.com (J&J)

Hepatitis.com (J&J)

Obesity.com (J&J)

Pregnancy.com (J&J)

ThePill.com (J&J)

WomansHealth.com (J&J)

Gift.com (JC Penny)

DrySkin.com (Kao Brands)

CreamCheese.com (Kraft)

Dessert.com (Kraft)

Mayonnaise.com (Kraft)

Pickles.com (Kraft)

TennisShoes.com (K-Swiss)

DryWall.com (Lafarge)

RE.com (LendingTree.com)

RealEstate.com (LendingTree.com)

Floors.com (Mannington Mills)

PetCare.com (Mars)

Priceless.com (Mastercard)

FirstAid.com (McAfee)

Construction.com (McGraw-Hill)

Sweets.com (McGraw-Hill)

Flu.com (MedImmune)

Back.com (Medtronic)

Pacemakers.com (Medtronic)

Alzheimers.com (Merck Serono)

Fertility.com (Merck Serono)

BoneLoss.com (Merck)

CervicalCancer.com (Merck)

Word.com (Merriam-Webster)

Document.com (Merrillcorp)

GPS.com (Microsoft)

Investor.com (Microsoft)

Juice.com (Microsoft)

ManLaws.com (Miller Beer)

Economy.com (MIS Quality Management)

Do.com (MSN)

Navigation.com (Navteq)

Heat.com (NBA)

Vitamins.com (NBTY)

Meals.com (Nestle)

PurplePill.com (Nexium)

Z.com (Nissan)

LifeInsurance.com (Northwestern Mutual)

AlzheimersDisease.com (Novartis)

GenitalHerpes.com (Novartis)

RespiratoryHealth.com (Novartis)

Shingles.com (Novartis)

Lettuce.com (Nunes Co.)

Salads.com (Nunes Co.)

Vegetables.com (Nunes Co.)

Winery.com (NY Times)

OfficeSupplies.com (Office Depot)

School.com (Office Depot)

Retail.com (Oracle)

Sales.com (Oracle)

Think.com (Oracle)

Lodging.com (Orbitz)

Trip.com (Orbitz)

Cavities.com (P&G)

Clean.com (P&G)

Conditioner.com (P&G)

Dandruff.com (P&G)

DentalCare.com (P&G)

Dentures.com (P&G)

Dish.com (P&G)

Dishes.com (P&G)

Laundry.com (P&G)

Nails.com (P&G)

ShowerGel.com (P&G)

Toothpaste.com (P&G)

Towels.com (P&G)

X.com (Paypal)

Coffee.com (Peet's Coffee)

Circuses.com (PETA)

DogFood.com (PetSmart)

Dogs.com (PetSmart)

Pet.com (PetSmart)

Pets.com (PetSmart)

Arthritis.com (Pfizer)

Vitamin.com (Pharmavite)

SemiConductors.com (Philips)

Speech.com (Philips)

DriveInsurance.com (Progressive Insurance)

Pharma.com (Purdue Pharma)

Q.com (Qwest)

Fund-raising.com (Reader's Digest)

Film.com (Real Networks)

RheumatoidArthritis.com (Roche)

Weightloss.com (Roche)

Dictionary.com (RR Donnelley & Sons)

Reference.com (RR Donnelley & Sons)

Thesaurus.com (RR Donnelley & Sons)

Allergy.com (Sanofi-Aventis)

Hypertension.com (Sanofi-Aventis)

Influenza.com (Sanofi-Aventis)

Parkinsons.com (Sanofi-Aventis)

Stroke.com (Sanofi-Aventis)

IcedCoffee.com (Sara Lee)

Ticks.com (SC Johnson)

AllergyRelief.com (Schering-Plough)

Food.com (Scripps Networks)

Beds.com (Select Comfort)

LNG.com (Sempra Energy)

Benzene.com (Shell)

Ultrasound.com (Siemens)

Gasoline.com (Speedway SuperAmerica)

Network.com (Sun Microsystems)

ServiceProvider.com (Sun Microsystems)

Shades.com (Sunglass Hut)

Educate.com (Sylvan Learning)

Van.com (Symantec)

Tacos.com (Taco Bell)

Gout.com (Takeda)

Trademark.com (Thomson)

Lasik.com (TLC Vision)

Toys.com (Toys R' Us)

Reservations.com (Travelocity)

Vacations.com (Travelocity)

AntiVirus.com (Trend Micro)

Trailer.com (U-Haul)

BakingSoda.com (Unilever)

Eat.com (Unilever)

MouthWash.com (Unilever)

Sauce.com (Unilever)

Softener.com (Unilever)

Soup.com (Unilever)

Data.com (United Business Media)

Plaster.com (USG)

Weather.com (Weather Channel)

Weddings.com (Wedding Channel)

ConsumerFinance.com (Whirlpool)

FoodProcessors.com (Whirlpool)

TrashCompactor.com (Whirlpool)

Ammunition.com (Winchester)

DrugFacts.com (Wolters Kluwer)

ColorPrinters.com (Xerox)

Documents.com (Xerox)

Corporations are not always disclosing the prices they paid for the name of their market. Johnson & Johnson purchased baby.com for an undisclosed amount. Sony purchased the name psp.com for seven digits. Lots of firms are buying names without fanfare or press releases.

I own eTickets.com and offered it years ago to Continental Airlines in exchange for free tickets instead of money. The Vice President of Marketing at the time said to me, "Why would we want that? We already have a domain name." He thought he had a grip on the situation and I clearly didn't. He just didn't understand the value of traffic. Today the name is worth 100 times my offer to Continental.

Today, domain names routinely sell for $1 million or more, and prices are going up daily! Domain name sales are for the name only: that is, the Universal Resource Locator or URL, which is the actual web address. While Sex.com sold for $13 million, Porn.com sold for $9 million and Diamond.com sold for $7.5 million, these firms had established websites, income, clients and advertisers. These were sales of businesses, not just domain names.

LARGEST OF DOMAIN NAME SALES
Domain Name Price (US)

Sex.com $13,000,000	Savings.com $1,900,000
Fund.com $9,999,950	Express.com $1,800,000
Business.com $7,500,000*	Seniors.com $1,800,000
Israel.com $5,880,000	Olimpic-sochi.ru $1,800,000*
Casino.com $5,500,000	Fly.com $1,760,000
Slots.com $5,500,000	Telephone.com $1,750,000
Toys.com $5,500,000	Dating.com $1,750,000
AsSeenOnTV.com $5,100,000	Auction.com $1,700,000
Korea.com $5,000,000	DataRecovery.com $1,659,000
Property.com $5,000,000 ***	Deposit.com $1,500,000
Clothes.com $4,900,000 ****	Tandberg.com $1,500,000
YP.com (a.k.a. Yellow Pages) $3,850,000	MarketingToday.com $1,500,000
WorldWideWeb.com $3,500,000	Cameras.com $1,500,000
Altavista.com $3,300,000	VIP.com $1,400,000
Answers.Travel $3,300,000	Feedback.com $1,225,000
Vodka.com $3,000,000	Vista.com $1,250,000
Loans.com $3,000,000	SS.com $1,250,000
Candy.com $3,000,000	Photo.com $1,250,000
Wine.com $2,750,000	Scores.com $1,180,000
CreditCards.com $2.750,000	Kredit.de $1,169,175
Pizza.com $2,600,000	Chinese.com $1,120,008
Tom.com $2,500,000	Mercury.com $1,100,000
Money.co.uk $2,400,000	Cruises.co.uk $1,100,000.
Coupons.com $2,200,000	Bingo.com $1,100,000
Autos.com $2,200,000	Flying.com $1,100,000
Computer.com $2,100,000	Cruises.co.uk $1,099,798
Britain.com $2,000,000	Zip.com $1,058,830
Celebrities.com $2,000,000	Wallstreet.com $1,030,000

Fish.com $1,020,000

WebCam.com $1,020,000

Invest.com $1,015,000

Beauty.cc $1,000,000

if.com $1,000,000

Rock.com $1,000,000

SportingGoods.com $1,000,000

Websites.com $1,000,000

Topix.com $1,000,000

Success.com $1,000,000

Cyberworks.com (and .net) $1,000,000

Guy.com $1,000,000

Poker.com $1,000,000

Souchi.life $1,000,000**

Poker.org $1,000,000

* The final sale value for Business.com, including cash and stock, totaled over $10 million when the company was sold in 2007 for $345 million.

** Souchi is the capital in Russia and site of the 2014 Winter Olympics.

*** The final sales price for Property.com was not disclosed but we believe it is approximately this amount.

**** Bought by ZAPPOS as per a public filing upon their sale to Amazon.

This list could not have been created without the hard work and support of Ron Jackson at DNJournal.com.

In the Internet real estate business, a domain name is the equivalent of land. It's the location upon which a business is built and where business is conducted.

Real Estate Versus Internet Real Estate: The Power of Leverage

Physical real estate is a long-term, known investment. To purchase $100,000 of land, you might put up $20,000 and borrow the remaining $80,000. If the property doubles in value in a year, then it's worth $200,000. Your $20,000 just made you approximate $100,000 not including the costs you would have had to pay on the interest for the $80,000. Not a bad return.

Internet real estate doesn't work the same way . . . yet. Because this is a new, relatively untested, dynamic market, banks and other financial institutions generally don't loan money against a domain name. Some, however, are starting to do just that – because of the substantial cash flow some Internet real estate properties command.

Andy Bernstein is the undisputed king of finding, owning, financing, managing and operating small, strip-mall shopping centers. His firm, Bernstein Investments (GreatShoppingCenters.com), understands the real estate business extremely well. To Andy, the real challenge isn't finding investors but finding and creating good deals.

Andy and I enjoy a good debate comparing the commercial real estate business with the Internet-based real estate business. Let's look at some of the differences:

Location Versus Mindshare

Andy Bernstein buys great locations he believes can appreciate significantly or generate substantial cash flow. Internet-based real estate offers an additional benefit: mindshare. A great domain name gets more traffic to the site associated with it than a hard-to-remember domain name with no relation to the target market. If you wanted cuff links, chances are you'd go to CuffLinks.com. If you wanted Venetian blinds, you'd go to Blinds.com. If you wanted information on mutual funds, you might start researching at MutualFunds.com. An estimated 12–15 percent of those on the Internet type the term into the address field of their browser, hit return and arrive at the site with this URL. That's called direct navigation, and the mindshare associated with the domain name alone generates customers.

Local Vs. National and International

Andy's real estate serves a local community. But anyone who has an Internet connection anywhere in the world can access a website. If you have a laptop, PDA or cell phone with an Internet connection, you can access Internet real estate on the move.

One Versus Many

Each piece of physical real estate is unique. No two properties share the exact same qualities. But in Internet real estate, you and 500 others can have the same word in the domain name of your websites as long as each of you has a unique modification – for example, JustBlinds.com, UniqueBlinds.com, MiniBlinds.com and 3DayBlinds.com.

> # A website is the virtual equivalent of a brick-and-mortar store. It can be as simple as a one-page site or a complex portal of products, services and affiliate links.

Cost of Entry

It's expensive to build or buy a shopping center. You can buy a domain name for as little as $1.99 these days. With hosting, some programming skills or a "merchant solution," and a way to process payments, your Internet real estate can be up and running, ready for business, in very little time for very little expense.

Internet-based real estate has its equivalents and then some:

Location = Domain name.

Secure transactions and privacy = The customer feels secure supplying The Experience.

Andy notes the 10 things that make for a good experience at one of his shopping centers include: personal and financial information.

Traffic = Site traffic can fluctuate in minutes or days, often by a factor of 1,000 and more. Limitations depend on how effectively the business's computers can handle the traffic volume.

Parking = Unnecessary on the Internet, although I do cover "parking of a domain name" later in this chapter.

Ingress and egress = Did the site download fast enough, or was it so slow that the client left and went to another property? Andy would lose a customer to a neighboring shopping center; you have to compete with every seller in your market who is connected to the Internet.

Lighting and landscaping = The look and feel of a Website is vital to the client's experience.

Music/sounds = Shopping centers and malls often play music or incorporate fountains to create a soothing atmosphere. Websites can incorporate sound and video (though some users find music intrusive and animations distracting).

Signage = While Andy's shopping centers spend money on advertising, promotions and public relations, the majority of the long-term traffic depends on the location and the tenant mix. On the Internet, marketing is king, even over and above a great domain name. Anyone can dramatically change the traffic with good publicity, marketing, Pay-Per-Click advertising, securing new affiliates to sell or resell products and search engine optimization.

- Location
- Parking
- Tenants
- Lighting and landscaping
- Security
- Signage
- Neighborhood
- Traffic
- Music/sounds
- Ingress/Egress

Traffic Is Key

Andy and I can spend money to attract traffic to our sites, but on the Internet small changes lead to dramatic increases in traffic. Andy's physical real estate stays put. He can paint it, change the construction a bit, add or delete parking. He can put in a Home Depot and triple the number of people that come to his shopping center. But there's a limit to how much he can change the shopping center to attract more traffic. A good programmer and a great marketer can change the traffic to this site by a factor of 1,000 in a few days or even minutes.

CORPORATE AMERICA . . . WAKE UP!

Ninety-nine percent of corporations have yet to figure out that they should own the one or two domain names that will give them the most free traffic: the generic name for each of their products or services. The name of their topic, their industry. They spent millions on marketing, advertising and PR but few have yet to realize the value of these assets.

They spend hundreds of thousands of dollars per year on banner ads and Pay-Per-Click campaigns, yet the vast majority do not even consider buying the one asset that will yield the highest quality traffic. Why doesn't:

Palm or **Apple** buy **PDA.com**

Sony or **Panasonic** buy **TV.com**

Dell or **IBM** buy **Computer.com**

Fidelity or **Morningstar** buy **MutualFunds.com**

Kodak or **Fuji** buy **Photographer.com**

Expedia or **United Airlines** buy **eTickets.com**

The American Heart Association buy **HeartDisease.com**

The Amazing World of Buying and Selling Domain Names

Buying and selling used to be the only way to make money with domain names. Before 2003, speculation was the name of the game: people generally bought domain names they thought would be popular and would draw traffic. Then they'd wait until an investor wanted the name so badly he'd ask you to name your price. Today, paid search makes highly trafficked domain names worth the investment in the multibillion-dollar domain name business. This kind of traffic creates an income stream for the lucky domain name owners.

CLICK TIP ▷ To my knowledge, there is no service provider that rents out the e-mail portion of a domain name owned by another company. Why don't YOU create such a service and split the income with the domain name owner? Those who own domains ALL have the same objective as any real estate owner: to find an asset's "highest and best use."

If You Build It, They Will Come . . . and Pay You, Too!

Once you have your Internet real estate, how can you use it to make money?

5 Ways to Profit from a Domain Name

1. Sell it. Sell the name for a profit.

2. Rent it. Rent the name, or just the traffic from the name, to a firm willing to pay for that traffic.

3. Build on it. Put a website on the domain name.

4. Lease it out. Lease the name to a firm that wants the name and the associated traffic. For example, you could lease the name MutualFunds.com to Fidelity for three to five years. They would control what goes on the site.

5. Park it. When you own a domain name but don't want to put up a website until the time is right, you can "park it" with a parking service. A parking service works with Google, Yahoo or one of several other players in the market to sell advertising or "clicks" that take a potential customer from your domain name to an advertiser's website. The parking service puts up a "parking page" on your domain and then pays you every time someone comes to your site and clicks on a link.

This is a good strategy, especially for sites with a lot of direct navigation traffic.

New Revenue from Domain Names:

If you want a simple strategy for making money with a domain name, here is one idea that 99.9 percent of domain name owners overlook.

Some firms rent out the use of their domain name e-mail addresses. A firm called NetIdentity.com created a wonderful business model around this concept. Let's say you own Doctor.com. You could charge a doctor $19.95 a year for "your name@doctor.com." As a domain owner, it costs you nothing to do this and generates a great, long-term, recurring profit stream. Ninety-nine percent of the "domainer" community (firms that own thousands of domain names) do not do this yet. You might discuss this idea with firms that own great names to see if you can set up and manage this profit-making opportunity, splitting the revenue with the owner of the domain.

The Investment:
Short-Term Versus Long-Term Viability

Ten years ago, no one had heard of the term "swine flu." Now, because interest in the topic drives large amounts of traffic to the website, swineflu.com is worth a lot more money simply based on the increased amount of Internet traffic it gets.

If you wanted to purchase swineflu.com from its owner, you would need to consider:

- How much the seller wants versus how much income the site can generate
- Whether the name (or the topic) will be around for the next 2 or 20 years. Is it a passing "fad"?
- The rate of return on the money spent to maintain the site
- Whether the underlying asset (the domain name and/or website) will be worth more or less in 2 years? 5 years? 10 years? 50 years?
- How high will the name rank in search engine listings – first or 20th or 200th?
- Will increasing traffic to this domain name or website be cost effective?
- How much direct navigation traffic does the name get?

DIVERSIFY

Own both kinds of real estate.
But if you don't have the cash or credit
to play in the physical real estate game,
a few choice domain names may provide
a good return on investment.

A piece of physical real estate may change a little, it may have different tenants, cash flow, look, feel and owners, but for the most part, it's here to stay. In contrast, a domain name may be in vogue today and passé in 90 days. However, a more valuable piece of Internet real estate – or a domain name such as bachelor.com, photographer.com, consulting.com or mutualfunds.com, which is based on terms with staying power – is more like physical real estate due to its common use and mindshare, in everyday life.

I'm one of the Top 100 dot-com companies
who are actually making a profit!

The big domain name owners who have hundreds if not thousands of domain names work closely with Yahoo! and Google to set up their "linked" sites. Smaller entrepreneurs can set up their own websites with the appropriate ad links from Yahoo! or Google and reap commissions as well. (See the Google Ad Sense section in Chapter 4.)

9 PARKING SPOTS

The businesses below will park your domain and send you a commission check for the traffic you generate from that domain:

DomainHop	Fabulous	Sedo
DomainSpa	Hitfarm	SmartName
DomainSponsor	ParkingDots	TrafficZ

CLICK TIP ▷ Caution! You're thinking, "I can do this! I have a domain name I want to buy right now that will make me rich." But virtually every single word in the dictionary with good traffic potential is off the market. Some might be available from domain name resellers, but the domain name market is no longer the instant gold rush it was between 1995 and 2000.

For those of you who watch the market, who watch for trends and pay attention to the new words, concepts, ideas and market changes, there is going to be a domain name out there that draws web traffic. And that leads to income.

The Engineering of A Seven-Figure Success

It was a book that jump started Kristof Lindner's seven-figure online success.

An engineer at a plant manufacturing company in Germany, Lindner was inspired by Eben Pagan's book, *Double Your Dating*. "I got that book and I found marketing fascinating, I found the content fascinating… I thought, [Pagan's book] is so good and it's selling well in the US… why don't we have it in Germany too."

With no prior online marketing experience, Lindner did the unthinkable. "I flew to LA. I spoke to Eben Pagan about how we could do a German version of this product, and we figured out a licensing deal." Within weeks Lindner's online business selling Pagan's ebook was up and running.

Two and a half years later, Lindner, age 32, has eight employees, seven active sites that sell a total of thirteen products and ebooks—and 100,000 online visitors to his sites each day.

Lindner's success is no accident. He continuously studies online marketing and his sites' statistics on Google Analytics. He also uses Alexa.com, which provides traffic statistics for a given site. Alexa, he adds, is "very helpful for analyzing what your competitors or what other people in your industry are doing."

Having expanded his business to other self-help topics like fitness, Lindner studies each new opportunity in depth, always learning from his competitors' success. "We find those pages that have really high volumes of traffic… and analyze what they do on their site. Then, he says, "we add those elements, to make [our web pages] better."

While the online opportunities are abundant, he sees a lot of entrepreneurs who don't spend enough energy on marketing. "Instead of taking the time and putting some energy into traffic generation, they start working on other content, for example," he says, explaining why some struggle to achieve his level of success online.

As a ClickBank vendor and affiliate, Lindner has found the community to be his biggest asset. "The people are so open in this market… they don't see each other as competitors. They see, hey if you, start growing your list… I might benefit from it later." In fact, he adds, "If you don't have money and you want to generate some traffic when you're just starting out… find people in your business niche that have a list, that have already customers that might be interested in your product."

It's great advice in the collaborative world of online marketing, where your success can become others' success as well.

Scan the QR code or go to GetRichClick.com/kristof to watch Kristof's interview.

International Domain Names (IDNs): New Kids on the Block

The Internet advertising boom is heating up overseas. There are incredible opportunities in those markets. As Google and Yahoo! bring online advertisements to more countries, overseas domain names have become more valuable.

International Domain Names or IDNs are not Latin Alphabet-based letters and do not use ASCII characters. They are names based on the language of each country that is launching an IDN setup. For example, in Israel, a Hebrew IDN name system uses Hebraic characters; Russia is using domain names with Cyrillic characters. Chinese, Korean and Japanese sites now have kanji-based domain names. No one knows exactly how this will affect the domain name resale market.

From dailydomainer.com: *"Many folks think IDNs (International Domain Names) are the next great domain gold rush. The concept is that not all of the world uses English character (ASCII) keyboards. Lots of the best IDNs are taken already and the waters are still a bit murky in terms of which standards will get adopted, but get out those Cyrillic keyboards and foreign dictionaries if you're interested. And tread carefully."*

Domain Name Extensions

Extensions are categories of Internet domain names. There are several of them to choose from, presented here in order of popularity:

.com stands for commercial and is the most widely used extension in the world. Most businesses prefer a .com domain name because it reflects their business presence on the Internet. However, the .com extension, in the early days, was one of the few available, so many nonbusiness sites have a .com in their url.

.net stands for network. Internet service providers use this extension as do web hosting companies and other businesses directly involved in the Internet. Some businesses choose .net domain names for their intranet websites.

.org stands for organization. This extension is popular with nonprofit groups, schools and trade associations.

.biz—**small business** websites often choose this business extension.

.info signifies a website that offers "information." It's the most popular extension after .com, .net and .org.

.us is for United States websites.

.cc was originally the country code for Coco's Keeling Islands. It is unrestricted, and anyone, from any country, can register a name with this extension.

.tv designates rich content/multimedia websites. Media and entertainment sites commonly use this extension.

.name is the only domain extension specifically designed for personal use. It is suited to people who want easy-to-remember e-mail addresses and personal websites.

.co.uk indicates a commercial domain name (similar to a standard .com extension) in the United Kingdom. It is unrestricted, and anyone, from any country, can register a name with this extension.

For a complete list of domain name extensions, go to GetRichClick.com.

The New Mobile Phone Domain: .mobi

.mobi domain names became available for public registration in 2006. They're dedicated to delivering the Internet to mobile devices via the mobile web.

In its short life, .mobi has already made headlines with several six-figure purchases, including flowers.mobi for $200,000, sportsbook.mobi for $129,800 and fun.mobi for $100,000. It's still a bit early to determine its appeal, but early sales prices indicate an interest.

In the early days of the Internet, I founded a company by the name of idNames.com. My former partner Allen "Pinky" Brand was the President of the firm. idNames.com was a company that helped firms obtain their domain name in countries around the world. He is now the Director of Global Domain Sales for dotMobi. Pinky explains that many large firms have invested in the .mobi initiative because they could benefit if the extension takes root among consumers and businesses. The jury is still out on whether the .mobi domain will really take off or not, but it certainly has its following.

Mobile Advertising

Google and other companies are looking at advertising opportunities on mobile devices. Many believe mobile advertising will be more effective than online advertising, especially for local advertising. Handset maker Nokia hopes the .mobi extension will encourage sales of Internet-friendly cell phones, especially in developing countries where more people have cell phones than personal computers.

Mobile devices still have usage issues with the Internet that are quickly being addressed, and the mobile Internet is becoming a part of popular culture. Some sites, such as Google.com and Weather.com, can detect whether an Internet connection is coming from a mobile device and redirect the connection to a site that is specifically formatted for these devices. In other cases, mobile users can get error messages when trying to access a .com site that has not been formatted for viewing on mobile devices.

Watch the mobile advertising market take off in the coming years. Get to know it, understand it and figure out how you, too, can play in the growth of this market as it takes off. More on this later in the book.

TYPO.com:
Understanding the Misspelled Word Game

I am very much against making money off misspellings, although many play this game. You will recall that domain names get traffic. Some people buy misspellings of popular websites – Starbuckks.com versus Starbucks.com. These names are trademark names and only trademark holders should purchase them. The main search engines are continually improving their algorithms to generate relevant results. Google maintains policies that ensure as rich a search experience as possible and justifies their policies publicly. As long as there are typos and misspelled words, in the age of the Internet where traffic often works off of Keywords, there will always be a few folks that make money from such tactics.

CLICK TIP ⟩ Google analyzed misspellings of the first name of pop singer Britney Spears over a three-month period from information provided by their spelling correction system. There were more than 500 ways to misspell her name. To see the list Google compiled, visit google.com/jobs/britney.html.

When a Company Should Buy a Misspelled Domain Name

Is it JC Penny's, JC Penneys, JC Pennies? Sometimes it makes sense for a business to purchase misspelled variations of its own domain name. Take J.C. Penneys, the department store retailer.

Lots of people don't remember there's a second "e" in the store's name. In this case, the marketing team for this firm should look to purchase:

A. Pennys.com **D.** Jcpenneys.com

B. Penneys.com **E.** Jcpennys.com

C. Pennies.com **F.** Jcpennies.com

While there are hundreds of other ways to misspell this company's name, the six names above are the most popular "other ways" for people to misspell the actual website address.

The corporation could simply redirect the traffic from these sites to the real jcpenneys.com.

The additional traffic and subsequent sales would go a long way toward paying for the purchase price of these new corporate assets.

FYI – The firm uses none of the above as their primary domain. They obtained and use JCP.com as their primary web address.

Some misspelled words have been bought and sold for a lot of money. For example, forclosures.com sold for $150,000 (foreclosures is the correct spelling) and mortage.com sold for $242,400! (mortgage is the correct spelling). Note that these are "generic" names and not private company or "trademarked" names.

Although many search engines often direct users to a search result with a suggested proper spelling, bad spelling can still lead to site traffic. Perhaps you've seen the phrase "Did you mean: *correctly spelled response?*" in your Google or Yahoo! search results. Google does not redirect typos. Google results appear with the spelling of the word as you entered it into the search engine, so it's definitely worth targeting those pages so you show up at the top as a site with the relevant info!

A final thought. I would warn readers not to buy misspelled names of well known people, brand names, slogans, company names, product names, popular websites or other words that are trademarks, copyrights or any form of intellectual property. High-profile businesses with financial backing can take you to court for using these generic domain names if you just own them, even if you are not using them. If you purchase names that violate the law, even the "spirit" of the law, you will most likely be sued at some point in time and could lose a lot of money including, but not limited to, all of the money you made from the name since the first day you owned it.

Putting Your Ideas into Action

- Make a list of at least 50 domain names related to an interesting topic. Don't try to psych out the market by using a variety of Keywords and even putting those Keywords together. Stick to domains you would want to visit if they turned up in a search.
- Visit a site like Network Solutions to see which names on your list are available. For the small price of buying one of those names, could you develop a website that would make the name (and others on the same topic) more valuable? Are you ready and able to do this as a *Get Rich Click* strategy?
- With the possible exception of International Domain Names, a buy and hold domain name strategy will not work today in the majority of cases. It's too late in the game. But there are still huge opportunities in buying developing domain names, just as physical real estate can be bought and developed.
- Visit SEDO.com to see several hundred thousand domain names for sale. Don't buy a name at the asking price. Make an offer and expect to haggle until both parties are happy with the buying price.

For More Information, go to GetRichClick.com.

9

Content Is King!

How can you make money with a simple videotape or a PDF word document?

There are tens of thousands of people who have authored books, articles, speeches and other content that can and should be sold electronically.

Thanks to the Internet, these days you can take a videotape, send it overseas when you go to bed and it will be a transcribed Word document in your "inbox" when you wake up. Imagine, you can now sell that as an eBook less than 24 hours after the video was made! There are so many copyright holders out there with content. They have no clue how to sell it online.

Help them get their content on the market, and both of you will make money in the process.

eBooks: Easy, Fast, Long-Term, Recurring Income

eBooks – electronic books – are becoming increasingly popular, especially with the advent of Amazon's Kindle. The Kindle employs e-ink technology and adds wireless functionality to the device, so Kindle owners can shop for books on Amazon and download them without access to a computer. Amazon has managed to create an impressive library, and it is now evident that the Kindle, the Sony reader, the iPad and other similar devices will transform the entire publishing industry forever.

Knowing this to be a certainty, think what opportunities are being created due to this huge industry shift? There are so many changes that are taking place now – basically anything and everything is about to change in the publishing world. Even the term BOOKS. If in the future, physical books are a rarity and eBooks are the wave of the future, will our children be telling their friends it's a good book or a good read? Figure out that one, buy the domain names and maybe you, too, could hit the intellectual property lottery!

10 Reasons Why eBooks Can Help You Make Money and Save You Money!

1. eBooks are CONSIDERABLY less expensive to publish and distribute than physical books.

2. Many eBooks are available online as free downloads, as samples, marketing hooks or bonuses.

3. eBooks are easier than traditional books to produce. The author or publisher creates the electronic book once and sells the same digital file over and over and over.

4. There are no printing or binding costs.

5. Because the product is delivered electronically online, there are no shipping, distribution or book warehousing costs.

6. Reselling the rights to an eBook can encourage a viral effect.

7. eBooks can be revised easily.

8. Your target market may prefer reading online. eBook customers often prefer convenient desktop viewing.

9. Delivery of an electronically downloaded book on a Kindle is virtually instantaneous, which satisfies those who want their content now.

10. The up-front costs are the same whether you sell the eBook to one

11. person or one million people.

CLICK TIP In the very near future, expect eBooks used as electronic "premiums or incentives." A firm may buy 100 or 1,000 electronic "codes" to download a chapter or an entire book.

A Profitable eBook Strategy

Here's how to to create an eBook or an electronic document that a customer can download for a fee, providing the author with a great stream of income:

- Start with an idea related to your expertise, hobby, passion, business, product or service or some other subject of interest to you and your target market.
- You can create a "niche" book or one with a broad-based appeal. The larger the potential audience, the larger the number of potential clicks you may get.

- Keywords help direct more traffic to your book, creating more sales.
- Research your Keywords using one of the popular online Keyword search tools (see Chapter 4).
- Look up the subject online to evaluate your competition and determine the popularity of your subject.
- Research and brainstorm ideas and information. This is the basis of your writing. Do not plagiarize or copy another's work. In the age of the Internet, it is EASY to find work that has been taken from another!
- Consult other websites, books, periodicals and other resources to help develop your ideas.
- Organize the information in a logical and interesting way.
- Create your document using a simple word processing document.
- Add graphics, charts, appendices, and design a cover.
- Proof, refine and finalize your work.

10 Ways to Market Your eBook

1. Consider selling the book in two different ways. First upload the book for sale to a website like ClickBank.com so they can easily sell it for you – managing all of the back end, credit card processing, etc.

The second option is to create your own website and choose and purchase a domain name related to the topic of the eBook.

2. Consider buying related domain names and Keywords and redirect that traffic to your site.

3. Obtain website hosting for the domain(s) and the content of the book.

4. Create a full-blown website or one as small as a one-page sales letter.

5. Establish a merchant processor account such as Paypal.

6. Decide how you are going to deliver your eBook: by autoresponder, shopping cart or by redirect through a download link on a web page.

7. Market your book by writing articles on blogs or on social media sites like Facebook, Myspace and LinkedIn.com.

8. Consider marketing your book via social media sites such as Facebook, Twitter and LinkedIn to get FREE traffic and then use paid sites such as Google and Yahoo to buy Pay-Per-Click traffic for a few cents per click.

9. Collect payments.

10. Fulfill orders. If physical materials, marketing literature or even a physical version of the book is to be sent out, consider outsourcing these "moving parts" to another firm.

Additional Tips:

Consider offering a very generous commission to individuals who want to sell your eBook. You might have a 40 or 50 percent commission to those who want to resell your book to their audience. Smart entrepreneurs are always looking for more products and services to sell to their audience.

Remember, in the digital world, there is relatively NO COST to sell an additional product that is in digital form. It's better to sell 10 books for a $10 fee ($100) than it is to sell 3 books at a $20 fee ($60). Besides, you will create an instant following for future products and services that you can sell to the reader down the road. If you plan to sell additional products to your buyers, getting more names into your database is the smarter choice.

CLICK TIP ➤ Another way to play in this lucrative eBook market is to find professionals who want to be published but often don't want to deal with the sales and marketing side of the equation. Doctors, lawyers, researchers, business owners and psychologists have written articles, papers or other intellectual property that can be digitized and sold as a digital download. You can help them put their data on a service such as ClickBank.com, manage the process and split the income. It's an easy way to make money over a long period of time.

Here are a few other things you may want to think about when you are ready to market your eBook:

- Consider the extra value of offering reprint rights.
- Offer a printed version of your eBook – or maybe a personalized "signed" copy of the book for an additional fee.
- To generate interest, offer a free sample chapter on Amazon, as a gift or possibly in exchange for giving you their e-mail address.
- Make your eBook a free item with another purchase, or discount it with a purchase, or bundle it with other e-commerce or digital products.
- Consider giving away an eBook that has links to other affiliate products or additional products and services that you are selling.
- Offer monthly updates or annual subscriptions.
- Sell your eBook on eBay, Amazon or other sites.
- Create your own affiliate program to sell your eBook and remember, give them a good reason to market your book vs. another book by offering very generous commissions.

E-mail Marketing in the Digital Age

There are an estimated 1.3 billion people worldwide who use e-mail. But you can also use e-mail to make money. E-mail is essentially the electronic version of writing a letter. So when you think about using e-mail to make money, think how you might make money with a traditional letter. You are still sending a message, albeit through a different delivery system at a lower cost.

The goal of all marketing is to deliver the right message to the right target audience at a frequency that persuades a prospect to take action. E-mail is no different. However, in permission-based e-mail marketing (and you should only solicit people who have given you permission to contact them), relevance is critical. Those who opted-in to your e-mail list for a newsletter or notifications of new products and special offers have expectations you need to fulfill. If they are going to take action on your e-mail, they need to perceive the relevance and value of your offer.

This is often at odds with how you define relevance as a business. After all, your business marketing goals are not your customers' goals. To be successful at e-mail marketing these days, you need to develop all your e-mail communications with your customers' definitions of value in mind.

In *iMedia Connection*, Simms Jenkins, Chief Executive Officer of BrightWave Marketing, provided a list of points that can help you evaluate your e-mail campaigns.

Ask yourself or your client:

- What are the business goals of the campaign?
- What are the other marketing tactics and their approaches?
- Will these new approaches complement an e-mail marketing campaign?
- What is the key message or value proposition to be communicated?
- Is there a "call to action" so you profit from your marketing?

In the permission-based age of e-mail marketing, direct marketing tactics are becoming much less effective. People are drowning in unsolicited e-mails and their spam boxes are stuffed. If you want to be noticed, if you want to build that miniscule conversion rate into something impressive, you have to rethink your e-mail marketing strategies.

Done properly, digital e-mail marketing offers an unprecedented opportunity to deliver the right message to the right prospect at the right time. Every click online is a measurable event. With web analytics software, you have the ability to monitor the effectiveness of the interactions between your prospects and your messages. Testing and gathering data is an essential component of e-mail marketing today.

Simms Jenkins offers these important questions to help you shape and optimize the performance of your e-mails:

What aspects of your campaign do you want to test (subject line, message, creative, offer)?

- How do you want to segment your campaign based on your database (gender, ZIP code, customer versus non-customer)?
- How do you plan to treat your e-mail subscribers based on their "performance" (users who clicked, users who didn't open, users who signed up in the past 30 days, etc.)?
- How will you follow up based on their "performance" (send follow-up message to those who clicked on the call-to-action but didn't convert, users who did not open or click, etc.)?
- How will you measure success?
- What's next after this campaign?

CLICK STAT: The Radicati Group estimates over 183 billion e-mails are sent every day. That works out to more than 2 million e-mails sent every second. Over 70 percent of these are spam and viruses. There are 1.3 billion e-mail users worldwide – in other words, one in six people on earth use e-mail!

7 Easy Ways to Make Money with E-mail

Here are seven ways you can use e-mail to generate income. Remember Attention, Interest, Desire and Action (AIDA) are the four principles marketers use in sales letters and can be used in lucrative e-mail marketing.

1. Subscription newsletter. Prospects and customers often want to hear about someone's news, product, service, ideas and tips. One way to supply this information is via a paid subscription e-mail newsletter.

2. Paid advertisements. Include paid advertisements in your e-mail newsletter (paid subscription or free). Many companies, individuals and entrepreneurs market to the same people you target. Charging these people for advertising space in your newsletter generates income for you.

3. Direct mail. You can use e-mail the same way you would use traditional printed direct mail. Market your products and services to your opt-in list (a list of people who have given you permission to send them e-mail).

4. Software. Using software or a service like "Constant Contact," you can automatically send e-mails to your permission-based list on a regular and predetermined timetable (once a week, once a month or once every two weeks). Programs like this are vital to effectively market online. Such a service will help you market and close sales even while you are sleeping.

5. Online learning. Online learning is becoming increasingly popular. Creating fee-based educational lessons (e-courses) is another way to make money via e-mail. You can even use software, as described above, to automatically deliver the lessons.

6. Create a database. Use the e-mail list to create a great database. Collect as much information as you can about the person. You can sell this information over and over. The more information you obtain about the owner of that e-mail address, the more money you can make from slicing and dicing that list to sell to others.

7. Surveys. Do surveys for others or for yourself, then sell or package the responses into categories that other e-mail marketers will want to buy from you.

The optimal formula for making money with e-mail is to use a combination of these strategies. For example, place ads in a paid e-course or offer a link to a free audio download in your e-mail marketing message.

No spam please! Send e-mail only to those who have expressed interest in you, your company or your products and services.

Make Money Reading E-mails, Playing Games, Searching or Answering a Survey!

You have probably come across websites that promise "big money" for doing very little. The truth is, you will not make "big money," but you can earn money or gift cards for reading e-mails, answering a survey or even playing a game.

I was an initial investor in a firm called MyPoints.com. We sold out to the current owners who have built the business into a major player in this unique marketing space.

At MyPoints, you can earn points for doing what you already do online: shopping, reading e-mails, playing games, searching the web, taking surveys and more! With your points, you can get gift cards for nearly 100 different stores and restaurants, gas cards, airline miles and hotel discounts. You pick the rewards you want and the gift cards are quickly delivered to your door, free of charge.

Another firm you might consider is InboxDollars.com. The firm asks you to provide information about yourself on demographic points such as geography, gender, age, income and education. This information means you will be asked to participate in areas that most interest you. At the same time, the information allows advertisers to reach a relevant audience and pay only for performance that meets or exceeds their expectations.

CLICK TIP ▷ **When you are selling your products and services, sending a free e-course, audio file, some research, a video, a written speech or even a digitized photograph can serve as a bonus or incentive to prospective clients. You can also use these low- or no-cost items as giveaways to entice those prospects to become your customers.**

These are only two of many firms that offer opportunities like this. Here are a few tips for you to consider before you sign up with one of these firms.

1. I *strongly* suggest diligent research on any firm that offers to pay you for reading or participating in their marketing campaigns.

2. Read the "Learn More," or "How It Works" and "FAQ" carefully to fully understand their offers.

3. Be certain you understand how and when you will be paid.

Opt-in Mailing Lists – Campaign and Marketing Strategies

The sad fact is, even the overall effectiveness of opt-in, permission-based e-mail marketing is in decline as the percentage of unsolicited mail increases dramatically. Lee Traupel, CEO of Linked Media Group, suggests counteracting the decline with these strategies while deploying opt-in e-mail campaigns very selectively.

1. Buy opt-in e-mail lists from legitimate top-tier broker/list managers who are well established, are not "oversending" messages to list subscribers and who are constantly refreshing their list quality by adding new subscribers.

2. Ask them how many messages ("frequency" in ad speak) are sent to each list recipient per month.

3. Ask how many new subscribers have been added to their lists.

4. What is the percentage of new members added per month?

5. Are they using "third party" lists to augment their own?

6. Are their lists "double opt-in" – meaning, you sign up and then must reply to a sign-up confirmation to be added to a list?

7. What is their privacy policy and how strictly do they adhere to published industry standards?

8. Utilize plain vanilla text link advertising.

9. Find websites or portals that have traffic that is comprised of customers who are in your market segment.

10. Then, add a text link (banner ad or graphic button if you will) to a page or pages and negotiate a media buy that is based upon a "cost per click" basis; i.e., paying only for traffic that clicks through to your website.

FYI: Nearly every third-party Internet marketing firm DEMANDS "double opt-in" lists to avoid problems with spam. If you don't double opt-in on the names in your database, the big marketing agencies won't use their servers to mail (e-mail) to YOUR lists. The reason? They don't want those servers to be blacklisted for spam. Keep your lists "clean" and be certain to double opt-in.

Traditional and Online Marketing

Search Engine Ranking has come of age in the last 12 to 24 months – you can now easily create and deploy a traditional (title, description, Keywords inserts in content, submissions and optimization) search engine ranking process that is augmented with a Pay-Per-Click ("PPC") process. Deploying both ensures you derive long-term (traditional rankings) and short-term (Pay-Per-Click) results, with the latter being driven by the amount of funds you have in your marketing budget.

Creating Inbound and Outbound Links

Creating and deploying a "link strategy" campaign (i.e., having your site link to another site and / or having that site link to your site) is one of the best self-sustaining interactive marketing processes available. This process is not based upon the more traditional "reciprocal links" procedure. It incorporates some web-based competitive analysis. Start by analyzing the links that are pointing back to your top three to five competitors' websites and then establish relationships with these sites and also submit your site to top- and second-tier directories to augment the number of links.

Podcasting

The editors of the *New Oxford American Dictionary* pronounced "podcast" their word of the year in 2005. The word itself is a merger of "iPod" and "broadcast." Today, the word has entered mainstream usage as a term identifying a series of audio or video files intended for syndicated download.

In the basic podcasting model, a podcaster creates digital audio or video files, uploads them to a host and makes them available through syndicated subscription. Anyone wishing to listen to or view these files simply subscribes to the podcast and downloads installments to an Internet-capable device. Those who subscribe to iTunes podcasts just plug in their iPods, and iTunes automatically downloads the latest podcasts in the series. Other podcast distributors provide notification when the author has made a new installment available.

Early podcasts were audio, presented in a radio-like format. Today, podcasts are also available in video formats, and anyone can use a podcast to communicate information to someone anywhere in the world.

Podcasts and Business

Corporate podcasting is quickly becoming part of the technology landscape of business. Podcasts are easy to create, portable, and users can listen to or view them any time without distraction. Think of all those mobile workforces and businesses where it's almost impossible to gather staff in one place to disseminate the latest training, product update, success story or message from the boss. This is a perfect situation for podcasting.

Podcasts are appropriate for any company involved in educational audio and video. IBM uses podcasts for both internal and external communication (for example, investor relations information). Some firms use iPods to bring learning to employees, while others use audio files to disseminate education and tutorials.

Getting started in podcasting is relatively easy for any individual or business. All you need are a USB microphone, a computer and sound recording software for your computer. You can find free recording software as well as dedicated applications online. EPodcast Producer (industrialaudiosoftware.com) markets itself as a "professional podcast production studio" software. It offers the following features:

- Produce high-quality audio podcasts
- Record, edit & upload from one award-winning program
- Built-in Skype recording, on-screen teleprompter
- Create iTunes tags and RSS feed for iTunes Directory
- Assign up to 36 music and sound effects to on-screen and keyboard function keys
- Full DSP audio editing effects
- Rip music from CD and burn CDs for archiving
- Two FREE sets of non-synthesized, pro sound effects
- Comprehensive online text and video tutorials

Podcasting is here to stay and fits into the *Get Rich Click* approach to getting the word out in as many ways as possible.

Ever have one of those days when you're not sure
whether you're in the zone, out of the box, under the gun,
over the hump or behind the curve?

What's a Wiki?

In 1994, computer scientist Ward Cunningham created a program called WikiWikiWeb, as a way to share programming techniques. He named his creation after the Hawaiian word for fast.

A wiki is a piece of server software that allows Internet users to freely create and edit wiki content using any web browser. Nontechnical users refer to wikis as "open editing" or "group-owned" websites or "the democratic use of the web."

The best known wiki is Wikipedia, now the seventh-biggest website on the Internet. Wikipedia is a collaboratively written encyclopedic reference developed and maintained by its readers. Every day, users are creating, adding to and improving content.

Built in the manner of Wikipedia, Wikihow.com is a how-to guide that was built in a similar "collaborative" method as Wikipedia. With over 50,000 articles covering a wide range of topics, Wikihow had over 15 million unique visitors per month at the close of 2008. Other popular wiki sites include ShopWiki, WikiTravel, Productwiki.com and Wikicompany.org.

At Productwiki.com, consumers share their experiences with products, stores and services.

Making Money with Wikis

Wikis draw their inspiration from the days when early developers of the Internet saw it as a communitarian way for people around the world to share information. But as more people adopt a *Get Rich Click* mindset, wikis are increasingly generating income through advertising. Wikis using the advertising model often work with Google AdSense or offer their own paid advertising space.

Wikipedia primarily supports itself through grants and donations, which is a viable way to generate revenue if you have supporters interested in what you are doing. Wikihow and Productwiki both raise money using Google AdSense.

The advantage of the wiki model is that content is created (for free) by its readers. Because content within a wiki is thoroughly linked with other content, wiki articles receive great rankings and place high in the results in search engines.

CLICK TIP ⟫ **Wikis are a fantastic way to build a community quickly for personal reasons or for business reasons. The content is added in by others for free and you simply add Google's AdSense to make money. Create your own wiki quickly @ Wiki.com.**

Since wikis encourage contribution from anybody interested in the wiki subject area, writing content, grammar and style are sometimes amateurish. Wiki owners outsource editing, moderation and facilitator duties to professionals in many cases.

Businesses are beginning to embrace wikis as corporate tools. Some of the most common uses include:

- Content management
- Project management
- Developer networks
- Managing software development
- Technical documentation
- Knowledge bases

Here's how several companies have incorporated a wiki into their workplaces:
- Google uses a wiki for internal management purposes.
- Pixar uses a wiki to manage their client interface.
- Sun Systems uses their wiki for collaborative documentation creation.
- Sony Ericsson's Developer World Wiki is a place for people developing applications using the Java ME application platform and Symbian/UIQ3 pen-based interface to get information on how these technologies are used in Sony Ericsson phones and share ideas & information.

One strategy for making money with wikis is to learn what wikis are capable of doing for businesses, and how businesses might make use of them. Then offer your services to design, maintain and edit a business's wiki.

Finding the Profit in Personality

Melford and Concetta Bibens' lives look nothing like they did a few years ago. "We've gone from being typical store front business owners to now being almost semi-retired because we're working a lot less hours, and making a lot more money, thanks to the Internet," Melford explains.

Former owners of a retail gym and day spa business, Melford and Concetta saw the writing on the wall at the start of the economic downturn. As their competitors slashed prices, "we had a real hard time keeping a 10,000 square foot building" Melford admits.

The Bibens wasted no time. While struggling to keep their gym afloat, they began creating content to sell online—mostly e-books and other products related to business opportunity, real estate, health supplements, and more. They soon began selling those products on ClickBank, the largest online marketplace of digital products.

Three years later, the Bibens are highly sought after super affiliates, a level of achievement that typically translates into the multi-millions. Some of that success may result from their mindset. "You have to treat [your website] like a business," Melford Bibens says. The alternative is to "treat it like a hobby and make hobby money."

From the start the Bibens zeroed in on one crucial component of effective marketing—building their brand. "Our brand got popular because we are who we are. We are just normal folks who, you know, figured out the right things to do and figured out how to teach other normal folks how to do it," Melford explains.

That ability to connect with their audience is especially powerful in today's affiliate marketing environment. "If you can't put personality behind your product, a saleable personality… don't get into the game." Also, Melfords advises, "if you're not doing video, you're not going to be a top seller on ClickBank or any other merchant account or product base."

The Bibens, whose products have achieved top 20 bestseller status on ClickBank multiple times, should know. After all, getting to that level of success on a network as large as ClickBank quickly converts to big dollar profits.

With their gym now closed, the Bibens have just a few employees running their multi-million dollar online business. It's a life they're thoroughly enjoying. As Melford Bibens says, they're "just normal 40 something year old couple, kids, dogs, you know, living that real American Dream."

Scan the QR code or go to GetRichClick.com/melford to watch Melford's interview.

Contextual Advertising

When you see text on a website or even an e-mail, you may see "hotlinks" or hyperlinked text to a website. Those words are linked by placing static html links on them. These links are in the category of text-based (contextual) advertising.

The Perfect Advertising Medium?

The Perfect Advertising Medium? Users of Google's gmail are familiar with the concept of contextual advertising. Every time a gmail user receives a message, Google scans the content of the e-mail and inserts contextual ads that are related to the context of the e-mail – placing the ads in the column to the right of the e-mail. These links are, in theory, highly relevant to specific words that appear in your e-mails.

Text Link Ads (GetRichClick.com/tla) places text-based ad links on high-quality, high-traffic web properties. The firm says its clients have seen a dramatic increase in targeted traffic, brand exposure and organic search engine rankings with their service.

For example, if I send an e-mail to someone saying I am interested in a trip to Milan, Italy, the words "Milan, Italy" might be hyperlinked to a travel agent's website. It might also be an airline or it might be a hotel. The idea has incredible potential in a world where the Internet is the primary tool for communication.

The blog Making Money (makemoneyonblog.blogspot.com) says:

TextLinkAds is a site that pays publishers on a flat monthly rate per each link sold, which is very different from contextual advertising options such as Google Adsense or Yahoo Publisher network. When you sign up as publisher for TextLinkAds, TextLinkAds will use its own algorithm to determine if you would be qualified. The algorithm is based on your site's page rank, Alexa's ranking, and the number of pages being indexed by the search engines.

Once you are accepted, you can decide on how many link spots you are offering. After that, TextLinkAds will do all the jobs for you. TextLinkAds will even decide how much you charge your advertisers based on its own internal algorithm. When an advertiser decides to buy your link, the ad will automatically show up in your designated spot.

Since TextLinkAds is not contextual advertising, they can be used with Google Adsense without violating Adsense policy.

Text Ad Networks: Profit from Eight Options

A handful of text ad networks are popping up. They are services that work with content websites that want to generate income. These networks find advertisers who want to reach clients by placing ads such as the link on the words "Milan, Italy."

Contextual ad networks sell performance-based marketing on a cost-per-click basis by placing ads on the text within a web page. Ads could also appear on top of or next to a photo of Milan, Italy. The concept is the same: get the client who is interested in a trip to Milan to click on the text (or photo) and take them to an advertiser who wants to reach this audience.

Some contextual ad networks include:

1. Google's AdSense Program
2. Quigo.com
3. ADster.com
4. Text-link-ads.com
5. AdGridwork.com
6. Microsoft's AdCenter
7. ContextWeb.com
8. Miva.com

Most networks offer contextual-based ads that can run in the text portion of their client's web pages. You can place the ad on a run-of-network basis, which means the ads will run on any web page that appears in their network of websites. Alternatively you can purchase text ads on a subject-by-subject basis.

CLICK TIP Because contextual ads are highly targeted and perform as well or better than Pay-Per-Click search engine marketing, you have an opportunity to work for websites that want to implement text-based ads or for text-based ad networks that want to sign up websites. To learn a lot more about this wonderful opportunity, look up Contextual Ads on Wikipedia.org.

What Is a Widget?

The hottest little application to hit the Internet in the last few years is the widget. Once you understand what widgets are and how they operate, you will understand there are so many ways to profit from this growing market that the thoughts alone will keep you up at night.

Think of a widget as an application, a small piece of computer code, that allows the user to customize his or her website, home page, social networking account (such as a Facebook page), your desktop computer or your mobile device. Most of us have used widgets without knowing what they are. They often take the form of on-screen tools such as clocks, event countdowns, auction tickers, stock market tickers or daily weather reports.

You can integrate many applications from a third-party website by incorporating a small snippet of code. The code brings in "live" content – advertisements, links, images – from a third-party site without the website owner having to be involved. These apps often sit on a website like a banner ad, but are interactive in nature and allow the user to engage with the application.

Google, Facebook, Apple, Wordpress, Microsoft, basically any platform website that promotes a more personalized user experience, offers downloadable widgets to their clients. ShareThis.com allows users to share an article, photo, video or other bit of content with their friends and families with just one click.

CLICK TIP ▷ **The Three Magic Words: "Check This Out"**
The homepage for Emerge Digital says: In Social Media, these are the words that matter most: "Check this out." They are right on the money. I just could not have said it better myself!

Those are the words that Internet users age 7–37 (and some of us who are quite a bit older) use to share something they found that is cool, amazing, "hot," shocking – or, most likely, a web application they want their friends to experience. If only I had purchased the domain name CheckThisOut.com. : (

Widgets in Business

As companies begin to use widgets in their marketing efforts, the field is growing fast. The opportunity for anyone who understands this market is enormous!

You do not have to be a technology wizard to make money from this. You do need to understand what buyers want and what sellers have – and how to put the two together.

A company called Emerge Digital helps businesses create these widgets. Emerge Digital's website says, "The viral nature of desktop & web widgets and social media apps will extend your budget farther with unmatched results." To prove it, they show a list of applications they have created for firms such as Burger King, Kraft, Tribune Interactive, Visa and others.

Emerge Digital has three distinct areas of products they create for clients:

1. Desktop and Web Widgets
2. Social Media Applications
3. Branded Games

Here are three simple yet unique web widgets Emerge Digital has created:

1. University of Illinois Athletic Department

PROBLEM: UIC athletics wanted a way to encourage students and alumni to buy into the collegiate experience on a daily basis.

SOLUTION: Emerge Digital developed a downloadable widget for a desktop computer so users can follow university news, get the latest team scores and find out about school functions. Fans can also take advantage of links on the widget to shop for UIC gear and tickets. Best of all, though, sponsored links on the desktop/web widget have turned the campaign into a revenue source.

2. *Chicago Tribune* Interactive

PROBLEM: To create a campaign that nurtures an association between the *Tribune* and the sports fans who have strong feelings for their sports teams.

SOLUTION: Emerge Digital connected the *Tribune* to the vast community of fans in the online social network through a free Facebook application or widget. Facebook users get to root, root, root for the home team by displaying buttons on their profile pages or sending them to friends long after the final out.

3. Burger King and Kraft

PROBLEM: To create a game or downloadable widget to persuade online users to participate in a fun, interactive experience (the game) and share the experience with their friends, all while promoting Burger King shakes and Oreo cookies in a creative way.

SOLUTION: Emerge Digital designed an easy, interactive game that was more fun than a sugar high called "Down the Pipe" for the Burger King/ Kraft "Sundae or Shake?" campaign. The object of the game is to catch the falling Oreos before they smash on the ground and catch as many humongous falling straws as you can. Oh, and you catch all these falling objects in a big Burger King Oreo Shake cup. Consumers are actually playing with the client's products, eager, desperate even, to catch the good things inside it. This gives players positive feelings for the two brands (Burger King and Oreo) and quite an appetite, too.

Make It Once, Sell It 1000 Times: Big Money with Widgets

I believe the market for widgets and iPhone apps is moving so quickly and generating income so fast that these small, often one-man money machines who know how to create the code do not understand how to leverage their position into more and more sales by extending into more and more places. They simply get paid for the first product, take the next order, create the product, take the order, and so it goes.

They are leaving incredible amounts of money on the table by not selling that same application to thousands of other (similar) clients. That is where you come in.

Let's take the application that Emerge Digital created for The University of Illinois.

Do you think every school district knows about this? If so, do you think they know where to get such an application? Do you think having such an application for all of their students would be valuable to them? Do you think you could make money putting a buyer who wants a product together with a seller who already has the product?

Ask yourself, do you think a firm like Emerge Digital would like to sell another 50,000 versions of the very same application to every high school, college, university or trade school in the United States?

There are several ways to do this.

1. Buy the rights to that product and sell it yourself to a few firms at a large price or a lot of firms at a much smaller price.

2. Work with the firm as an outside sales agent to go out and sell to other colleges and universities. Cut a deal to get the rights to the software, and then you can sell at a markup over what they want to be paid for each product sold.

3. No money? Go to the firm, tell them you love their product and see a bright future for it. Tell them you want to go out and find other firms to buy it. Ask whether they will let you work for their firm on a commission-only basis (if not a small salary).

These are only three of the many ways you can find to sell repeat copies of this software application.

In a television interview, the CEO of Emerge Digital said, "It's like we're riding on a train going down the mountain and laying down the tracks as we go." These unique software applications are being created for one firm, but pertain and can be sold to thousands. The technology folks in this world know how to create the product, but often have no idea how to market it over and over, repeating the sales process without having to repeat the creation process.

Putting Your Ideas into Action

Get Rich Click **Money-Making Idea with EBooks**
- Write, market and sell your own eBook.
- Market and sell an affiliate's eBook.
- Write eBooks for others.
- Market eBooks or digital products for others and split the revenue.
- Outsource anything fulfillment of any part of the order.
- Turn to guru.com or elance.com to find people to do any part or all of these issues.

Learn how precise "contextual" advertising can be for getting new clients to your blog or website.

Be *certain* that any and all names that go into your database have gone through a double opt-in process or third-party e-mail marketing agencies won't mail to your lists.

For More Information, go to GetRichClick.com.

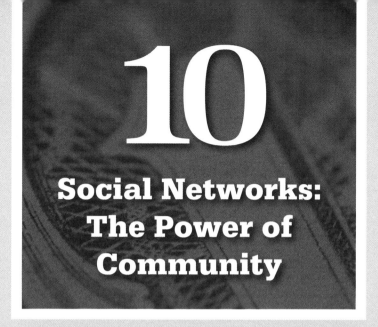

10
Social Networks: The Power of Community

We are social creatures; the experience of community is important to us. What we don't (or won't) do in person, we often choose to do online. This has brought the term "social networking" into being. It also has the power to drive huge profits to those that know how to use it well.

Blogs

Blogs (a contraction of "web log") exist in many forms. Most blogs (which may be public or private) target a specific interest. They're made up of entries posted by the blog owner and other contributors, since blogs generally allow comments by the readership.

Technorati, a blog research firm, provides these statistics:
- There are 175,000 new blogs added to the Internet every day
- United States blogs had 77.7 million unique visitors
- Facebook has 500+ million users
- MySpace blogs had 75.1 million unique visitors
- Worldwide, 184 million Internet users have started a blog
- Worldwide, 346 million Internet users read blogs
- Seventy-seven percent of Internet users read blogs
- Bloggers post information to their blog 1.6 million times per day, which equates to more than 18 updates a second.

Businesses are now embracing blogs to promote their products and services and to generate income from advertisers. A sculptor of fashion dolls, for instance, may create a blog "written" by his latest doll, humanizing her character and her voice, and crafting a personality that is the doll's alone.

A consultant may post articles and observations that reinforce their expertise and help explain their services. In an effort to encourage a one-stop customer experience, some blogs include news aggregators that search for relevant content and offer it to readers.

With overall web advertising expected to grow to $23.6 billion in 2010, more and more ad dollars will move to blogs. For the growing cadre of bloggers, this presents a money-making opportunity. The number of blogs on the Internet has exploded: based on data the blog search engine Technorati.com collects, 175,000 new blogs and 900,000 posts to blogs appear every day. As marketers and advertisers look for new opportunities online, you can bet blog advertising increasingly will become big business.

Entrepreneurs might also consider offering a service that manages blogs for small and large corporations. Fresh content encourages people to return. There are money-making opportunities to write a business's blog, manage the database, help with the advertising and make certain the right companies, people and divisions are given attention.

Getting Started

Businesses such as WordPress (wordpress.com) and Google's Blogger (blogger.com) make it easy for anyone to start publishing the same day, for free. They'll even host your blog, or you can choose to maintain your blog on your own hosting service. The ability to customize your blog may be important to you. WordPress, in particular, makes it possible to create complex blogs that allow you to incorporate features attractive to your readership. In fact, many websites have developer-modified WordPress software as their foundation.

Monetizing a blog can bring in hundreds or even thousands of dollars a day.

Making Money with Blogs

While some blogs publish to disseminate information, others intend to create that loyal following marketers crave. Your blog should provide some type of value to your readers. If you supply value, you ought to make money from the value you supply. Here are some ideas for making that happen:

- **Google AdSense.** Placing relevant ads on your blog through Google AdSense is often the easiest way to generate income. Generally speaking, those interested in your blog content will also be interested in relevant advertisements.

Since Google pays for clicks on these ads, the cost to you is nothing. A well-placed, relevant Google AdSense program on your blog will generate income and profit with very little extra effort on your part as long as you have good traffic to the site. More traffic typically means more income.

- **Donations.** Those who visit your blog regularly probably like what you have to say and value what your blog provides. Many are happy to support your efforts – some through monetary donations. Give visitors a way to express their appreciation through voluntary contributions; this can result in income for your blog.

- **Affiliate programs.** Advertising and promoting other people's products, and earning a commission on the sale of these products, is the basis of the many affiliate programs on the Internet. Chances are, you can find an affiliate (pay-per-purchase) program relevant to your blog's subject or your area of expertise. Placing ads on your blog for affiliate products can earn you significant commissions.

- **Selling your own products and services (including subscription products).** A blog is a great place to market your own products and services. Instead of earning an affiliate's commission, you can earn a full profit margin from the sale of one of your own products. Your products might include books, CDs, eBooks, subscriptions to newsletters or services like consulting, coaching or teleseminars.

- **Selling advertisements to others.** Depending on the number of readers or site visitors, you may have the right target audience for other advertisers. If you avoid conflicts of interest between the products you sell and advertisers, charging others to advertise on your blog site is an excellent source of income. The more traffic you have, the more attractive you are to advertisers, which justifies higher prices for ad placements. Don't overload your blog with advertisements; instead, place them strategically throughout your site.

- **Selling or renting your database of blog followers.** Mailing and e-mail lists have value. Selling or renting your database of readers who follow and contribute to your blog is a source of revenue. Remember, though, that your blog's followers may prefer you keep their names private; disclosing your policy right on your blog page or offering an opt-in option is always good practice.

- **Multiple streams of income.** You can always pursue more than one money-making strategy. Creating multiple streams of income is just smart in any business venture. Broadening your income base also broadens your appeal to your audience and increases your opportunities to generate more income. Diversity on your income stream is also smart so that if one income stream goes away, you will have others to keep the ball rolling.

Daily posting is critical to building a loyal following and a sense of community. Be careful not to post too often. It's usually best to post one strong, focused topic each day. Save your other ideas for a day when you haven't got a topic in mind.

Word Of Mouse™ Marketing

Word Of Mouse™ Marketing (WordOfMouse.com) is defined as taking the benefits of a normal "Word of Mouth" marketing campaign via groups, associations, schools, friends, family and others you typically trust and adding the power of the Internet to get the word out. Add to this audios, videos, photos and graphics and the combination of these various mediums makes for a marketing campaign that is hard to beat.

Below are a handful of ways to use this medium to gain competitive advantage.

● **Word of Mouth.** If you include an easy way for readers to share blog or social media postings with friends, family, colleagues and associates, readers will spread the word for you. "Share This" and "Send to Friend" links are simply ways to let your readers do some marketing on your behalf.

In fact, check out one of my favorite sites called ShareThis (sharethis.com). It's an amazing and easy-to-use "widget" that allows you to share your address book, articles, text, videos, photos, music – even your list of friends – with other friends or other websites. Another way to make money might be to keep up with new ideas like ShareThis and help firms incorporate such good ideas into their own business ventures. You will find a "share this" tab on GetRichClick.com.

● **Social News Sites.** Like share-this links, social news websites allow your readers to discover and share posts on your blog with a larger audience. Readers submit links and stories (and can comment on these) and vote on blog entries. Including a social news link in your blog entries can improve your visibility. Digg and Yahoo! Buzz are two popular sharing sites.

● **RSS.** Real Simple Syndication is a web feed format that allows readers to subscribe to online content like blog posts, news headlines, video and audio. From the blogger's perspective, it is essentially a syndication tool. From the reader's perspective, it is a tool that enables them to stay abreast of content that interests them. Readers can access these feeds from their desktop computers, mobile devices or computerized device that is connected to the Internet.

Twitter Users: "Asleep at the Mouse?"

Micro-blogging lets users create "community" through brief text updates, typically no longer than 140 characters. Twitter (twitter.com) is the most popular of the micro-blogging platforms; Jaiku (recently acquired by Google) and Plurk are also popular.

Twitter describes itself as "a service for friends, family, and co-workers to communicate and stay connected through the exchange of quick, frequent answers to one simple question: What are you doing right now?"

Twitter COO Dick Costolo said Twitter is attracting 190 million visitors per month and generating 65 million tweets a day. Many are "asleep at the mouse" and don't tweet much, if at all. According to Sean Garrett, Vice President of Communications at Twitter, 20 percent of tweets – or roughly 83 messages per second – contain a reference to a product or brand.

Unlike other social media platforms, Twitter users generally don't count on getting replies to their tweets. No one expects to sustain actual conversation. But if you like a particular tweet and wish to share it with your own friends, you can "retweet," or forward, the message. Creating the type of messages that others want to "retweet" to others creates a "viral" effect that has become known as "viral marketing."

Internet Advertising and Marketing BUYS customers.
Blogging and Social Media Marketing EARNS customers.

– Marc Ostrofsky

"How Can I Make Money from Twitter?"

Twitter is basically a "push" medium. A user pushes messages out through Twitter to his network. The catch is that the messages, called TWEETS, can only be 140 characters long. In short, you can use Twitter to capitalize on the relationships and attention you receive from others. This makes Twitter a new and exciting promotion and marketing tool.

Darren Rowse of Problogger (problogger.net) uses Twitter to promote his blog and has more than doubled traffic to his blog since he started "tweeting." He has devised three ways to encourage participation:

- Rather than simply announce a new post by title, he asks a question; instead of saying "Banner Ads Are Dead," he asks, "Do you think banner ads are dead?" Then he provides a link to his blog entry.

- When an entry gets lots of commenting attention, he lets his network know things are getting interesting.

- On slower traffic days, he occasionally asks his network whether an entry is worth a "Stumble" or a recommendation to his network to "discover things you like on the web." You can find him at StumbleUpon.com.

Rowse believes it's important not to overdo the self-promotion, so he makes sure he is always offering more value than he is soliciting. As much as Twitter can help, he believes it is easy to abuse the tool and damage your reputation. That's when "tweeple," or people on Twitter, will just stop paying attention to you.

Many businesses are turning to Twitter to help them connect more intimately with their customer base, develop loyalty, extend innovation processes and promote a word-of-mouth marketing element. Dr. Keri Pearlson (@kpearlson on Twitter), a tech and Internet consultant and the person who got me into the

Internet back in 1994, is always one step ahead of the market. As a major user of Twitter and other social networking sites, she works with major corporations and businesses on how to use social networking and other technologies to gain competitive advantage in their market.

Keri has lots of ideas for using Twitter to gain a competitive advantage in the Internet-driven business environment. These are just a few:

- Solicit feedback on projects
- Offer discounts or coupons to prospective clients
- Ask your audience questions to get back quick answers
- Discuss ideas for jointly written articles
- Announce job offerings
- Ask for hiring recommendations
- Identify specialists
- Build a new database of clients that use Twitter
- Direct traffic to your firm's website or another site
- Share links to articles or videos on topics of interest to your audience
- Announce and update event information
- Encourage testimonials from clients
- Get quick feedback from clients and potential clients
- Chart your time management with continuous updates
- Give "personal commentary" to your clients on a shared concern
- Tell clients and suppliers what you think about a product or service
- Alert customers to new products or services . . . even up to the minute
- Announce, manage and coordinate events

**My name on Twitter is Getrichclick.
Be sure to "follow me" to get the latest
up-to-date and innovative ideas
on great ways to make money and
save money that come across my desk!**

48 Twitter Business Tools to Help Achieve Your Relationship-Centric Goals

David Nour is the author of *Relationship Economics*, *The Entrepreneur's Guide to Raising Capital*, and *The Social Networking Best Practices* series. He is a senior management advisor, and a featured speaker for corporate, association and academic forums, where he shares his knowledge and experience as a leading change agent and visionary for Relationship Economics® – the art and science of relationships. To learn more, please visit: relationshipeconomics.net.

David is one of the best professional speakers in the country on the subject of Twitter and how to use it as a tool to strengthen business relationships. I had the opportunity to meet David, and shortly thereafter he sent this wonderful list of tools to help "achieve your relationship-centric goals."

By way of introduction, David said:

As Twitter continues to become an incredible tool for building and nurturing online relationships, so will the Twitter business model, its security and third-party applications. Millions more will use it to expand their social circle, promote their business, keep their coursework organized and more.

Some of the tools listed below will help you get there; others will simply enhance your Twitter user experience; most will undoubtedly raise the bar on your efficiency and effectiveness in the manner in which you use Twitter – not as a destination, but as a platform:

Personal Branding: Your name is your biggest brand, so what are you doing to package, market and sell "the brand called YOU"? Here are sites that help you achieve that goal:

1. SumtnSumtn: Bring Twitter-conversation directly onto websites – for everyone – on every page. It opens up as a sidebar and people can log in via Twitter and leave messages. You can also see what messages others have left for the page/site.

2. TweetMeUp: A simple way to organize tweetups (Twitter events/ meetings). You can specify the location and mark it on a Google Map.

3. Twinester: Lets you create or join groups and communities for Twitter. These groups are called nests. There are various categories to choose from. The landing page displays the hottest nests.

4. KeymanWeb: Allows you to tweet in over 200 languages! You don't need to download or install anything. Just log in to Twitter and select your preferred language. A virtual keyboard pops up and you can type away in your favorite language. You can tweet in over 15 Indian languages!

5. Twitroduce: Allows you to make an introduction, suggest a user and receive user suggestions based on your unique interests. Think of Twitroduce as a more effective way to do #FollowFriday.

6. Autopilot Tweet: Provides full Twitter automation software for Twitter marketing. This includes a Twitter Friend Adder / Follower Adder, auto follow, follow by Keywords, follow your followers, auto unfollow and schedule tweets. Autopilot Tweet costs $40.

7. TwitterFeed: Announce your blog post on Twitter with a customized message using TwitterFeed.

Information Gathering: Tweeting with Value-Add. Beyond the gimmicky manners in which some will try to build their superfluous list of followers, I'm a strong believer of expert first – speaker, presenter, author, writer or consultant second! With these tools, you can gather information for market research, blog posts and your own simple curiosity.

8. search.tearn.com: Unique social network for viewing photos and videos on any topic and chatting with Twitter users interested in the same subject. Search on any topic.

9. @myflightinfo: Use @myflightinfo to stay updated on your flight's status.

10. Twitscoop: Twitscoop shares what's hot on Twitter at any given moment.

11. Incoming!: A Twitter search client that lets you cut through the noise and find the tweets that matter to you most – so you can follow your favorite topics or keep track of what users are saying about your company's products.

12. TipTop: Semantic analysis of natural language, which looks at data as a source of tips that help people solve problems. A problem that is at the top of someone's mind can often be solved satisfactorily with a good set of tips.

13. TweetMixx: Provides the latest trends across Twitter by showing the hottest content based on the number of times a link is being tweeted.

14. Tweeps.Info: Helps you keep track of interesting stats about Twitter users, including average tweets per day, commonly tweeted Keywords, social participation ratio and more.

15. TwitCam: Enables you to stream live video, which is connected to your Twitter account.

Relationship Building and Management: Follow and Build Followers Intently. Building and nurturing online relationships must start with the central theme of commonality – something that we can utilize to spark a conversation, a dialogue, a sharing opportunity.

16. Twitter Local: Using Twitter's location-based search API, based on the Adobe AIR-based application, you can see tweets from Twitter users in a specific location.

17. Who Should I Follow?: Using this site, you get good recommendations for Tweeps to follow.

18. Twellow: Find Twitter users in a specific industry using this service.

19. Mr. Tweet: Mr. Tweet is a personal networking assistant for Twitter, helping you find relevant followers.

20. twiggit: Use this service to share the articles you digg on Twitter.

21. TweeTube: TweeTube makes it easy to share videos on Twitter.

Getting Productive: Here are some tools to save time and optimize your Twitter list with some efficiency and effectiveness.

22. Ping.fm: Update your status on 40 different social networking sites from one location!

23. Summize: Retrieve information on Twitter quickly to search Twitter in real time.

24. Twalala: Helps you control what you see (and more importantly what you don't see) in your Twitter stream.

25. Just Signal: Set up a filter using Just Signal to get only the tweets that discuss the Keywords you'd like to read about.

26. TweepSearch: Put your Twitter network to good use and search your followers for specific parameters.

Analyze to Improve: You can't improve anything you don't measure – that includes your return on relationships, influence and impact. Here are some analysis tools to explore . . .

27. Twitter Grader: Learn your Twitter grade, your local Twitter Elite and find new people to follow through Twitter Grader.

28. TweetStats: TweetStats offers a graphical analysis of your Twitter stats.

29. Twitter Friends: Carefully measure your Twitter conversations using Twitter Friends.

30. Twinfluence: Twinfluence will measure your Twitter influence based on reach, velocity and social capital.

31. Tweet-Rank: Learn about the quality of your tweets by finding out which ones won or lost followers.

32. Acamin: Makes it easy to share files on Twitter with your followers.

33. Trendrr: Tracks the popularity and awareness of trends across a variety of inputs, ranging from social networks (like Twitter) to blog buzz and video views downloads, all in real time.

Ubiquitous Computing – anywhere, anytime, on any device: Here are some Twitter mobile applications to consider:

34. Twitpic: Twitpic makes it easy to take mobile phone photos and share them using your Twitter account.

35. MyMileMarker: Keep track of your mileage with info sent via Twitter every time you fill up.

36. Jott: Jott makes it easy for you to tweet without ever having to type, transcribing your voice message to Twitter.

37. TwitterBerry: Mobile client for posting updates to Twitter using your BlackBerry device. It works over the data network, so you don't need to use SMS. Besides posting new Tweets, you can view your friend's timeline, or the public timeline.

38. Pocket Tweets: This iPhone-compatible application helps you get the latest tweets from your contacts, update your status remotely or see what is happening around the world by viewing the public timeline.

39. Fring: A mobile Internet service and community that enables users to talk, chat and interact with others and their online communities, from their mobile phones. Fring allows the freedom to communicate with all popular communities' members (Skype, MSN Messenger, Google Talk, ICQ, SIP, Twitter, Yahoo!, AIM) without boundaries, and regardless of device, network operator, platform or the community(ies) to which they belong.

40. FoodFeed: This Twitter-based food log makes it easy for you to track what you're eating.

41. gtFtr: Use the gtFtr tool to record your exercise activity on Twitter.

42. Xpenser: You can Twitter your expenses to Xpenser and they will be recorded for you.

43. Twittertise: Schedule your tweets and track their click-throughs with this app designed for Twitter advertising.

44. TwtQpon: Create simple Twitter coupons for your business with TwtQpon.

45. Tweeteorology: Find tweets about the weather in any location through Tweeteorology.

46. Glue: Post links to books, movies, restaurants and more on Twitter through Glue.

47. TwitterNotes: Organize your notes using Twitter with TwitterNotes.

48. TwitWants: Buy and sell items on Twitter. You need to tag your tweets appropriately for it to show up on TwitWants. To post to TwitWants just tweet about something you want to buy, sell or give away and include #twitwants or @twitwantsdot-com.

The list above is used with permission from David Nour: © 2010 by The Nour Group, Inc. All Right Reserved.

CLICK TIP ➤ More business tips from a Twitter expert: Chris Brogan is president of New Marketing Labs, a marketing agency working with large and midsized companies to improve online business communications through emerging web and mobile technologies. I strongly urge you to sign up for Chris' free newsletter at chrisbrogan.com/newsletters/.

- Tweet about your customers' interests, not just yours.
- Share links to neat things in your community. (@wholefoods does this well.)
- Be wary of always touting your stuff. Your current buyers may love it but others will tune out.
- Twitter is great for getting opinions. When promoting a blog post, ask a question to set up what's coming next instead of just dumping a link.
- Follow interesting people. When you find people who tweet interesting things, see who they follow and do the same.
- Comment on others' tweets and retweet what others have posted. This is a great way to build community.
- Share the human side of your company. If you're bothering to tweet, it means you believe social media has value for human connections. Point us to pictures and other human things.

Social Networks

Social network sites are virtual meeting places where individuals can stay in touch with old friends, meet new friends, share communications (comments, instant messaging, posts, images) and exchange interests.

The form these networks take is varied: modern incarnations of the old bulletin board services (BBS); journaling communities (like LiveJournal); blogs; subject-specific communities (like Flickr); and complex venues that allow for a wide range of social interaction (like MySpace and Facebook).

Three terms to describe
Social Communities:

1. **Social networking** applies to using these websites to link communities.

2. **Social media** refers to the platforms used to get the word out.

3. **Social marketing** leverages these platforms for brand building, lead generation, customer experiences and more.

– Dr. Keri Pearlson is @kpearlson on Twitter

Of course, this form of social networking is Internet-related, so there are many *Get Rich Click* ways to take advantage of the trend and make money.

MySpace, Facebook and LinkedIn.com are currently the most popular social and business networking sites. Their success depends on three primary factors:

1. Stickiness. This is defined as how often a user will come back to a website or how long that user spends on the site once they arrive.

2. Growth. These sites grow rapidly via Word Of Mouse™.

3. User-generated content. Compelling user-generated content attracts more users, which makes it possible for these sites to profit from paid advertising.

The State of the Social Networking Community

Nielsen Online stated that more Internet users are now participating in social networking sites than use e-mail:

- 66.8 percent of Internet users worldwide accessed a social networking community.

- 65.1 percent of the same population used e-mail.

- Search, however, is still a more popular activity than participating in a member community.

- Facebook is the top social networking site in all countries except Germany, Brazil and Japan.

Get Rich Click™
Word Of Mouse™
APPortunity.com™

By now, you can tell I love a play on words . . .

Many of us grew up with the slogan
"Reach out and touch someone™,"
a trademark of AT&T to promote
their telephone service.

In the new digital economy that uses the Internet,
e-mail marketing, iPhones and social networks
to get the word out, I'd like to offer AT&T
a more "up-to-date" slogan I came up with . . .

"Reach Out and Touch Everyone™"
– Marc Ostrofsky

Kids Today Are Growing Up in a Different World

All five of my teenage daughters stay in touch with friends through instant messaging, video chat and Facebook. My identical twins don't even call one another while at college, explaining to me, "Why would we? We e-mail, chat and Facebook one another." OMG! How different is this to the way we grew up?

Facebook and e-mail mean that kids today will never know a life where distance dissolves friendships and contact.

For better or worse, the teenagers of today will never be "out of touch." They will grow up always being in touch with their friends from childhood through college thanks to Internet-based social networking sites like Facebook.

When I graduated from Stratford High School in 1979, I stayed in touch with a handful of friends and later from The University of Texas at Austin and my fraternity, Sigma Alpha Mu. We occasionally would see one another at parties, events and other social occasions. These days, many of us call or e-mail one another.

I had heard of Facebook as an online way for college kids to stay connected, but initially it didn't seem like something I'd get much value from using. When I finally created an account, I was shocked!

Did you know ...
FACEBOOK ACQUIRES UP TO
750,000 NEW MEMBERS A DAY!

If the Internet is the most powerful business tool ever invented, then Facebook is simply the most powerful networking tool on the Internet! It is a remarkable site for people to e-mail, chat, see photos of one another, "tag" a friend on a photo so that the friend is automatically notified they are in the photo you just posted, join groups that have similar interests, hobbies, business issues, political views, pets, tastes, demographics . . . the list goes on and on. And if a group for an interest in a topic doesn't exist, it will shortly, or you can start one in about 60 seconds. (Being the one to start a group has a lot of advantages including the fact that you are the only one who can communicate with everyone in that group at one time.)

I started a Facebook group just for this book: *Get Rich Click*. In this group, you can stay in touch with others who have a similar desire to make money using the Internet as their primary venue for business. The topics in this group cover even more ground than I do in this book: affiliate marketing, new sites to make you money or save you money, new Internet business models, hot ideas, stories about others and more. Adding a Facebook group with the same name as your product, service or website is smart for many reasons.

The *Get Rich Click* mindset understands that any major shift in a specific market influences the development of that and related markets. The sheer magnitude and growth of this one social networking site has the potential to wipe out dozens of smaller, niche sites; those that survive will do so by making significant changes to their business model. Why? Because Facebook is like Wal-mart. They offer much more for much lower prices. They may offer a comparable, if not better, service that is free of charge while many wonderful niche sites such as Classmates.com, Reunion.com and BirthdayAlarm.com may need to restructure the way they operate and bring in income to stay afloat for the long term. As traffic turns away from these sites to Facebook and other similar social networks, the niche sites will be in trouble.

Finally, someone from my high school class created a Facebook group for our graduation class. In only 65 days, the group grew from 30 to over 120 people. That one experience opened my eyes to the power of this medium. If your high school graduating class doesn't have such a page, create one, invite 10 of your closest high school friends and watch it grow. The power of the Facebook experience is amazing, and since it will change the way the world communicates forever, there are amazing opportunities for those that use it and understand it.

CLICK STATS ON FACEBOOK:

Women ages 55 and older are the fastest-growing demographic group on Facebook, with membership numbers up 175.3% since the end of September 2008. The number of males in that age group grew 137.8% in the same period.

More and more every day, the social networking giant Facebook is becoming a large part of the overall Internet experience. There are now more than 500 million users on Facebook, and the users themselves contribute tens of millions of pieces of content daily.

Each day during the month, Facebook users average over 3 billion minutes on the site. They update their status 15 million times and become "fans" of a particular company, brand, product or person 3.5 million times daily.

Statistics courtesy of eMarketer.com

WHERE THERE IS SPENDING POTENTIAL
THERE IS INCOME POTENTIAL

Can Social Networking Sites Generate Income?

Besides creating a given social networking site on your own, the growth, changes and appearance of new sites taking place on any given day create huge opportunities for individuals to profit from helping businesses in their marketing efforts.

Some social networking sites are more niche-oriented than others. In general, as in any other media, those niche-oriented sites have an opportunity to reach a more targeted audience.

Money-making ideas for firms and organizations that are thinking about ways to profit from creating their own social networking site include the following:

- Subscriptions or VIP access to special sections
- Transactions, e-commerce, affiliate sales
- Sponsored search links
- Sponsorship of the site itself
- Income sharing deals with outside vendors
- Access fees to reach a wider audience beyond what users get for free
- Downloadable files (content, photos, videos, music, etc.)
- Paid referrals or links from the site to other sites
- Charge users for additional photo, video, content and other digital storage needs.

The opportunities for association, partnership and targeting needs are many. Here are some examples:

- In its initial marketing plans, Friendster saw the advantages of joining forces with eHarmony.com, a popular dating site. Whenever a Friendster user was referred to eHarmony.com, via the Friendster site, Friendster received a commission from eHarmony.com for the referral.

- Business networking sites have an opportunity to make money from more than just the pure social aspect. Business users frequently are more willing to pay for business services. Many business networking sites are set up to help people find jobs, find business partners, recruit workers, and to refer prospects and customers.

- Job search sites charge employers for job postings; tightly knit social networking sites can narrow this to the point where a job searcher, a member or subscriber pays a finder's fee to the site when a position is filled.

- MySpace, the popular social network for 16- to 34-year-olds, once offered a profile of pop singer Hilary Duff along with a free download of three of her songs. Surrounding the page were ads and pitches for Procter & Gamble's Secret Sparkle deodorant. This product is targeted to the same market that's attracted to Hilary Duff 's music and MySpace.

Much of what is done on the Internet is database driven. With the growth of social networking sites, imagine the opportunity to harvest information from personal profiles. Intelligence of this nature provides the opportunity for very targeted advertising and messaging based on age, gender, interests and location – a true marketer's dream. What was once a concern is now an opportunity.

You can use database information to craft precise, targeted promotional campaigns that are much more effective than standard text and display ads. People reveal a lot about themselves on a social networking site, which is conducive to data collection and target marketing.

Top 4 Reasons You Logged into Facebook Today

Reason #1: **Advertise your business.** While Facebook's advertising platform is still in its infancy, many businesses are taking advantage of the site's ability to efficiently target users based on specific demographic information. Many advertising opportunities are still being explored including "nanotargeting," which is the ability to target a single user via a Facebook advertisement.

Reason #2: **Create an application.** While everybody isn't a developer, Facebook has been extremely effective at attracting new developer talent to build applications on top of the Facebook platform. Facebook initiated the movement toward a more open social web with the launch of their platform two years ago, and they are continuing that movement today. The result has been numerous applications that now are legitimate businesses for hundreds if not thousands of developers.

Many more developers have attempted to build powerful applications on top of the Facebook platform, and despite their failure to attract a mass following, the opportunity provided to developers is frequently too good to pass up.

Reason #3: **Converse with customers.** More important than how you are wasting time is how you are making money and Facebook is a great platform for doing that. Through Facebook Pages, brands have the opportunity to interact directly with their customers, engaging them in a two-way dialogue. Over the next 12 months, we will see a surge in Facebook Pages adoption as new services arrive to make it easier to build a presence. This is just one of the many reasons users log in to Facebook!

Reason #4: **Create buzz.** Guerilla social media marketers (or whatever you want to call them) have a heavy presence on Facebook and other social networking sites and are actively trying to figure out new ways to increase their reach through the site. Whether it's finding more friends, posting more status updates, creating fan pages, purchasing ads, setting up events, tagging users in photos or anything else, many users perform certain activities for the sole purpose of generating buzz.

5 SOCIAL MEDIA SECRETS

The mainstream has fallen in love with Twitter. Facebook grew aggressively and a new wave of companies starting taking social media seriously as a business tool. Below are five secrets to staying on top of it all:

1. Pay attention to the metrics. You can't manage what you can't measure. Chief Marketing Officers are going to pay more attention to metrics and tie in social media more directly to overall business goals, not just web-related goals. When starting up a new project, agree on what the metrics should be and what goals are appropriate.

2. Scale good habits. As you grow, make sure you match your structure, policy and guidelines to your organization size. What works with 2 people won't work with 20 people. All in all your structure should encourage good habits. Your entire team should be motivated to respond quickly, post consistently and talk like a human.

3. Have rules, but trust people. As your social media strategy matures, you'll add in more rules and guidelines. However, you can't have a rule for every situation. You need to trust your team. Lead by example, don't manage with a rulebook.

4. Creativity and personality trump big budget. Social media is definitely one of those areas in life where more money doesn't always win. Two of the most powerful ingredients in social media are creativity and personality. They are the key to having a viral message and to being a trusted resource. They are also essential to discovering useful strategies and tactics. You can't be afraid to try something new or go against the grain.

5. Listen. Listen. Listen. Don't focus so much on you and your message. Put that farther down on your To Do List. Focus first on your customers. Hear what they are saying, see what they're up to. Once you've been able to connect, and figure them out, then see how you can help.

The above five examples are from an e-mail I received from Slideshare.com (Check it out . . . it's a great site.)

Unlimited Ways to Make Money with Facebook, LinkedIn and Other Social Networking Sites

Many social media watchers would tell you Facebook should more correctly be considered a social commerce network. The centerpiece of the Facebook commerce network is the application widget (see Chapter 8 for more on widgets). Enid Burns writes for SearchEngineWatch:

Facebook users establish affiliate programs, then market products in a chatty, friendly way (some people in your network theoretically are real friends) through posts on their walls. Applications (widgets) are the primary money-making vehicle. Businesses develop widgets that users can embed in their profiles. Many of these widgets, while they do provide a social service, have profit as their primary motive. A bookshelf widget can link you to a bookseller if you click on any book a user has added (What are you reading now? What have you recently read? What's your favorite book? What book do you recommend?); you can also provide a review of the book. (SearchEngineWatch, February 2009)

What sorts of widgets might help you earn money on Facebook? Here are eight popular widgets:

- **CafePress.** Sell items with your own imprint through your profile
- **e3buy auctions.** Add your e3buy auctions and store to your profile
- **eBay.** Feature anything you are selling on eBay on your profile
- **FlameTunes.** Profile and sell your own music
- **Garage Sale.** Hold a garage sale on your profile
- **Lemonade Stand.** Pick items from selected sites, feature them on your Facebook profile and earn a commission when someone clicks through and purchases the item
- **MusicBlaster.** Feature BlastMyMusic.com artists on your profile. As you promote a band you like, you're earning 5 percent on every song you sell
- **My Merch Store.** Create products with Zazzle (zazzle.com) and sell them from your profile

Of course, you can always come up with the next exciting Facebook widget application and create a profitable business for yourself that way, too. According to Mashable: The Social Media Guide (mashable.com), developers of Facebook applications can monetize their applications using these strategies:

Sell. Develop applications solely for the purpose of selling them to interested parties. You don't have to know "coding." You have to have determination, creativity and know others who know how to create computer code. Look up "create a widget" on Google to find firms to help you accomplish your goals. Try Guru.com or eLance.com for computer-savvy folks to create your "code."

Develop. An indirect source of funds: develop applications under contract for third parties. A number of companies have been posting contract jobs over at Facebook's developer forums. There exists a large gap in the supply and demand of available Facebook application developers; as a result, finding potential clients to charge reasonable rates should not be a hassle.

Advertising. Use advertisements, cross-promotion schemes and affiliate marketing. It is not feasible to use Google AdSense for this since Facebook does not allow JavaScript embedding. AdSense may be embedded through iFrames, which despite being popular among Facebook developers, is against Google's rules. Affiliate marketing is a great alternative to advertisements.

Micropayments. Sell services within Facebook through micro-payment transactions. PayPal payments made for accessing premium services could potentially yield reasonable income depending on the application's purpose, size and prospective users.

Get investment. If you think you have something big on your hands and lack the funds to scale it, apply for investment through a firm called Bay Partners (BayPartners.com) or other investment firms that have expressed interest in funding Facebook apps. This would be the likely course of action for a start-up with plans to expand globally within and beyond Facebook.

I would add to the Mashable list:

Drive Traffic. Facebook is such a strong tool for getting eyeballs to any site. Why not come up with creative promotions for your website, then use Facebook to tell the world about the promotions and drive traffic to your site? Remember, the more traffic to your site, the more income you will make.

Lower Your Costs. I continue to profess that lowering costs is the same as making more money. So, use Facebook to help you lower your costs by asking others for assistance when buying an expensive item or using Facebook Marketplace to sell unwanted items and buy items others want to sell, ranging from cars to furniture.

CLICK TIP Here's a list of Facebook groups you might want to join:

- Affiliate Marketing Opportunities
- Internet Marketing School
- Internet Marketing University on Facebook
- 6 Figures From Home – Starting a Successful Internet Marketing business
- Facebook Domain Name Network
- Facebook's Ultimate Internet Marketing Mastermind
- Top Secret Internet Marketing Strategies
- The International Internet Marketing Alliance
- AdTech Internet Marketing
- Affiliate Marketing
- The Women Of Internet Marketing

A World of Social Networking Sites

I could write volumes on the social media landscape of the Internet and the many opportunities it offers the entrepreneur. Part of the fun is discovering for yourself everything that is out there; with the *Get Rich Click* mindset, you will begin to piece together all sorts of possibilities. I would, however, like to mention two additional networking communities I believe are worth your attention.

LinkedIn: The Business Social Networking Site

Founded in 2002 and launched in 2003, LinkedIn is an increasingly popular social networking destination for business-oriented people. LinkedIn had over 40 million registered members spanning 170 different industries. LinkedIn's primary goal is to help members maintain contact details for people they know in the business community (these people are known as "Connections"); as the home page proclaims, "Stay informed about your contacts and industry. Find the people & knowledge you need to achieve your goals. Control your professional identity online."

Members can use their Connections several ways, according to Wikipedia:

• A contact network is built up consisting of their direct connections, the connections of each of their connections (termed second-degree connections) and also the connections of second-degree connections (termed third-degree connections). This can be used to gain an introduction to someone you wish to know through a mutual, trusted contact.

• It can then be used to find jobs, people and business opportunities recommended by someone in one's contact network.

• Employers can list jobs and search for potential candidates.

• Job seekers can review the profile of hiring managers and discover which of their existing contacts can introduce them.

Beyond the opportunity to keep in touch with present and former colleagues and classmates, LinkedIn provides a venue for securing new jobs and exploring new business opportunities, as well as giving and getting advice.

LinkedIn Groups You Should Join

• *Get Rich Click*
• Internet Affiliate Marketers Association (IAMA)
• AffiliatePrograms
• Digital Marketing
• eMarketing Association Network
• eTail Careers.com
• Guerrilla Marketing Tips for Small Businesses
• WebAnalysts.Info Internet Marketing, Web Analytics, and E-commerce Group

Doctor's Orders: Dr. Keri Pearlson and How to Build Community and Profit from Twitter

- Provide running commentary and "sound bites" of a meeting or seminar you are attending.
- Keep up with clients who tweet their status and thoughts.
- Participate in the back-channel of a meeting and interact with others on the channel.
- Answer customers' questions.
- Find potential customers (search Twitter users and follow those who look promising).
- Provide live coverage of an event.
- Organize meetings.
- Use Twitter to create or reinforce your brand image (ala Southwest Airlines).
- Promote your position on a topic or newsworthy issue.
- Watch and even learn what competitors are saying and how they are using Twitter.
- Sell your products or services by tweeting about periodic specials (like DellOutlet).
- Using Twitter instead of instant messaging or e-mail to reach out to others in your business (or network).
- Monitoring Twitter for tweets mentioning problems with your company and contact the author directly (like Comcast).
- Do quick polling and surveys with staff, clients, suppliers and others.
- Find other interesting people in your community by observing who others are following.

- Reach out to experts to serve on panels or be speakers in your staff meetings.
- Identify people of influence by analyzing statistics about their Twitter use.
- Learn about local tweet-ups and meet others in your local community.
- Read tips that help you gain skills such as communication tips (search for CommsTweet).
- Do research by asking followers to suggest links or answer questions.
- Find references for new products or services (find people who have used a product or service you are considering).
- Follow celebrities and interact with them to further your reach.
- Gain followers (or become a follower) for a cause or charity.
- Learn about viral videos (such as YouTube posts) that are being talked about in social circles.

(Dr. Keri Pearlson is "@kpearlson" on Twitter)

I'm not disorganized – I know *exactly* where everything is! The newer stuff is on top and the older stuff is on the bottom.

"Twittering While Twaveling"

As I was making the final edits to this book, *New York Times* writer Matt Gross said he had used Twitter while traveling to get instant feedback and ask for suggestions on where to eat while in Minneapolis. Not only did he get a great recommendation, he is now offering similar assistance to others. He went on to say Twitter can be a great resource for travelers. I would say it can be a great resource for any industry, business, entrepreneur or individual. Matt now puts up suggestions, photos, videos and anything he thinks might benefit others.

SUCCESS STORY #10

Helping Others Help Themselves – and Making Millions!

It may sound strange, but Cindy Battye makes money online by helping others make money online!

After receiving a cancer diagnosis at the age of 29, Battye decided to battle the disease by keeping her brain engaged. So she launched TrafficBunnies.com, a website traffic exchange. The idea behind TrafficBunnies was for users to display their websites and earn reward credits for viewing other sites. The more sites viewed, the more credits earned. That guarantees all participating sites receive traffic.

TrafficBunnies.com started out slowly, causing Battye to wonder if she had accidentally launched TrafficTortoise! But then she began adding up-sells to encourage users to become subscribers and receive additional services. Community members soon began to see an increase in viewers and sales. Seeing the potential, Battye then added social networking to the site, letting users chat with each other live to build even more business connections. Within just a few years, TrafficBunnies.com boasted 30,000 paid subscribers and nearly $2 million in annual revenue.

Battye soon realized that she had built a mega marketing list that was worth millions. "Once you start collecting names, you can market to those people over and over," Battye explained. It dawned on her that people doing business online would want to learn how to build their own equally valuable lists.

So Battye and her partner, Soren Jordansen, launched ClickBank Pirate, a turnkey application to help people build lists and make "ClickBank marketing accessible and easy for pretty much anyone."

As the largest marketplace of digital products on the web, ClickBank provides money-making opportunities for anyone doing business online, whether as an affiliate or product vendor. Plus, as Battye adds, "I love ClickBank."

If the strategies behind ClickBank Pirates work as well for users as they did for Battye, ClickBank network affiliates will enjoy sweet success. Nearly five years after her cancer diagnosis, Battye, a native Australian, was living in Cyprus, traveling around the world teaching her Internet marketing techniques. Sometimes, helping others help themselves can be both meaningful and profitable!

Scan the QR code or go to GetRichClick.com/cindy to watch Cindy's interview.

6 Degrees of Separation . . .

You've heard the phrase "six degrees of separation"? Some people also call it the "human web." There is 1 degree of separation between you and every person you know directly. There are 2 degrees of separation between every person they know directly. In theory, there are only 6 degrees of separation between you and everyone on the planet. Social networks work on the theory of degrees of separation, seeking to connect like-minded individuals – those with common interests, values and viewpoints – to each other via some type of online social group. Common interests can range from personal to professional.

YouNoodle.com

Fairly new to the social networking scene is YouNoodle, a San Francisco-based company that provides a platform for those with a focus on start-ups. YouNoodle was founded by Bob Goodson and Kirill Makharinsky, both formerly from the University of Oxford. When the two moved to California, Max Levchin, founder of PayPal, invited them to join a start-up.

YouNoodle's unique contribution to the business community is their "Start-up Predictor," which offers entrepreneurs a way to predict the success of their ventures using information about the start-up's concepts, finances, founders and advisors. YouNoodle has plans to develop more decision-making tools for the start-up community.

YouNoodle writes in its FAQ:

> *YouNoodle is an online platform for start-ups, early-stage ventures and the world's top entrepreneurship clubs and competitions. If you're at a start-up, add it to the network to attract team members, get exposure and build a following. Otherwise, create a profile and browse the site to find start-ups you're interested in.*
>
> *We also offer free, powerful tools such as full business competition, event, newsletter, and membership management for the leading start-up clubs, conferences and start-up competitions worldwide.*
>
> *YouNoodle is for you if you're working on or interested in any way with start-ups and university innovation.*

YouNoodle Lets You:

- Discover the hottest start-ups and trends.

- Use Start-up Predictor to compare your start-up to others, and get connected to relevant others.

- Get exposure and recruit for your own start-up.

- Reconnect with and meet new people in the start-up industry.

- Use our competition, event, mailing list and networking tools if you run an enterprise group or competition.

YouNoodle members create profiles, create and participate in events, create communities, interact with members, create and distribute newsletters, design and run business plan competitions and explore the viability of their ideas.

Putting Your Ideas into Action

- To get a following on Twitter, you must be consistent but not intrusive. Some people post a dozen 140-character messages all at the same time. This is a good way to lose your following.

- IMMEDIATELY, sign up for Facebook, LinkedIn and Twitter. Get both PERSONAL pages and BUSINESS pages. NOTE: I have a Marc Ostrofsky page on Facebook and a *Get Rich Click* fan page.

- As previously discussed, sign up and start offering "digital products" from ClickBank to your friends and following on these social networks.

- The fastest way to build your Facebook following is to follow or "friend" others.   Most of the time, they will follow you back.

- Join and interact with like-minded entrepreneurs on Facebook and LinkedIn by joining a variety of "groups" on subjects that interest you. See page 160.

- Stay up-to-date on Social Network Marketing, follow Dr. Keri Pearlson on Twitter @kpearlson, and Marc Ostrofsky @GetRichClick.

For More Information, go to GetRichClick.com.

11

Collecting Your Payments – Fast and Easy

Finding an easy, quick and safe way for your customers to order and pay online is essential to your success!

How the Money Becomes Yours

For you as a seller, probably the most convenient method of online payment is by credit card. But for a number of years customers were hesitant to disclose card information. While these concerns are still present, the major credit card companies have increased security measures that encourage credit card use in online transactions.

To accept credit cards online, you first need a payment processor. This is an entity in the credit card processing network that handles the posting of transactions for authorization, clearing and settlement to customer credit card accounts. It also handles the settlement of funds to merchant bank accounts. You can either apply to a bank to use this network or use a third party to access it.

Another option for online payment is a third party system such as PayPal, which is by far the most popular. Third-party payment processors provide a way to make payment online so you don't have to manage all the components of your own processing system. However, increased fees are associated with this service.

PayPal operates in 190 markets, and it manages over 184 million accounts, more than 73 million of them active. PayPal allows customers to send, receive and hold funds in 19 different currencies worldwide. They allow consumers and businesses to send money to anyone with an e-mail address. Payment can come from a variety of sources, such as credit cards or bank accounts. The person making payment does not share any financial information with the recipient. PayPal is free for buyers. Sellers, however, typically pay a pro-rated fee for the privilege of receiving money through PayPal.

Shopping Carts

A website's "shopping cart" system stores the items your customers wish to buy, and provides a way to check out. The system calculates shipping costs and applicable taxes, and then displays the total so the customer can proceed to payment.

Here are a few things to consider when choosing an online shopping cart program:

- What is your level of technical and e-commerce experience?
- Do you want to be able to customize your shopping cart?
- What sorts of marketing strategies might you want to incorporate in your shopping cart system (currently or in the future)?
- What are your current clients' requirements?
- What are future clients likely to want?
- What is your budget?
- What does the price include?
- What other functions can the shopping cart do for your business?
- Is the shopping cart easy for customers to use? (Shopping cart abandonment is a serious conversion issue.)
- How many individual items can a customer put in the shopping cart?

CLICK TIP ▷ There are many shopping cart options. Go to GetRichClick.com/carts for some of the best.

Your Own Merchant Account Versus Third-Party Processors

To accept online payments, you will also need to set up a merchant account through a financial institution so you can deposit the money you collect from customer transactions.

Your merchant account is unique to you, your business and your website. It is directly linked to the major credit cards you accept for payment. You are responsible for managing your own merchant account and must provide a payment gateway for your customers.

Maintaining your own merchant account makes sense when:

- You have a large number of transactions (lower fees are associated with higher volume).
- You require direct control of the transaction process.
- You require a more transparent checkout process.
- You need to maintain a more professional image/brand.
- You or your technical staff possess expertise in managing the technical side of your payment processing.

When you use a third-party processor, you accept credit card payments through the third party's merchant account. Using third-party processors make sense when:

- You don't qualify for your own merchant account.
- You do not operate a "registered" business (as one is required to do in various European cities).
- Your business is associated with high-risk conditions, including high-risk merchandise, high-risk sites or high-risk geographical areas.
- You have personal credit issues.
- You have a small number of transactions.
- Your technical expertise is limited.

CLICK TIP ▷ **Caution! Online payments are most secure for North American-based transactions. Some international transactions, especially in countries like China, India, Pakistan and the Middle East still have problems with credit card security online. You should proceed cautiously when you consider security issues for certain international transactions.**

Smart Cards and Debit Cards

Smart cards have been popular in international markets and are becoming more common in the United States. A smart card works much like a credit card but is coded with a finite dollar amount that can be replenished from a bank account. A "smart chip" or a magnetic stripe on the back of the card stores the information and prevents businesses directly accessing a customer's bank or credit card accounts. A Visa Smartcard allows you to transfer "electronic cash" from your bank account to the card. You can then use this card, the equivalent of a bank debit card, at various online retailers and sellers.

Many companies such as Starbucks, Borders and Best Buy offer smart cards or debit cards. Gift cards are still the primary application for these cards in the United States, although businesses are expanding their use into areas like memberships and rewards. These cards can have a fixed limit or can allow the holder to continue adding value.

Through its website, Starbucks makes it easy to use their card. I gave my father one as a gift. I set it up online to automatically replenish the amount monthly so he has enough money to buy coffee ten times a month.

Shipping 1 – 2 – 3

You *must* have reliable logistic systems and shipping procedures in place to handle your orders. When customers receive a product late or when you handle shipping inefficiently, customers often do not return the items and usually spread the word about your inadequate service.

The shipping component of online payment processing is usually the last step in checkout. You need to pay attention to the products you offer, how you design your website and how you process payments, but don't forget to plan for shipping your products to your customers. Unfortunately, shipping is one of the last things many merchants consider when they set up an e-commerce site, but it is a critical piece of your selling process.

CLICK TIP ▷ Caution! Do not treat shipping as a profit center. Customers quickly figure this out and resent it. You will lose business as a result. Keep shipping costs contained to build a strong and loyal customer base.

Consider this:

● Free shipping is a leading incentive for consumers to purchase online. Amazon and the leading electronic retailers (Best Buy, Micro Center, etc.) know this, have proven it and practice it daily.

● Flat-rate shipping can serve as an incentive, especially when the flat rate is attractive.

● Most consumers worry that businesses will charge them unreasonable shipping rates.

● Many consumers will abandon or avoid an online purchase because of shipping charges alone.

When you get a supplier to ship an item directly to the customer, you are drop shipping the item. Drop shipping minimizes your involvement and risk, because you neither have to take physical possession nor do you have to repack and reship. Drop shipping eliminates you from the shipping process. You still own the transaction – you have sold a product to a buyer– and you have received the profits from the markup. Suppliers take care of the inventory, warehousing, packing, distribution and shipping – and you don't.

Running a Business from an iPhone

Internet millionaire Matt Bacak has one simple but powerful piece of advice for up-and-coming entrepreneurs: "There's a direct correlation between the size of your list and the size of your bank account." It's a lesson he learned at the age of 12.

After growing tired of wearing shoes from K-Mart as a child, Bacak, who hails from generations of steel mill workers, decided early that he would be a self-sufficient entrepreneur.

His first foray into business was delivering newspapers. Unlike other boys on bikes, Matt quickly realized that he had created a community of people who liked and trusted him. In essence, he had created his first list! So he swooped in for the up-sell: "Would you like me to cut your grass too?" Every neighbor he asked said yes! He had turned leads into customers; that's when Bacak hired his first employee.

Today, as an Internet super affiliate, Bacak takes the same approach with his e-mail list, treating customers like a community. His company, Bleeding Edge Innovations, hosts events and sells newsletters and eBooks that teach people how to make money online, including "The Secret Money Ring," a program on how to build thousands of leads per month.

Bacak builds his list with opt-in pages, or forms that ask users for their personal information. The trick is to send a free sample portion of a newsletter or website, and then ask readers to sign up to receive the whole enchilada. Once you gain leads that are interested in your product, you can build relationships and sell more products.

"There comes a point where your bank account outgrows your list size. That's the point where relationships and trust are being built," said Bacak. "If you build a list and you cultivate relationships, you're set for life," According to Bacak, it's up to Internet entrepreneurs to avoid "leaving money on the table." Specifically, he warns that affiliates must pay attention to Earnings Per Click (EPC) to see which promotions have been successful and why.

Like most super affiliates at Bacak's level, he is a huge fan of ClickBank, which he says, "is the one place you can be guaranteed payments, where you are going to make money. It's one of the best places for beginning newbie to get started." As the largest online marketplace of digital products, ClickBank has paid out a whopping $1.6 billion its affiliates and vendors.

These days, Bacak runs his businesses from his iPhone, and has plenty of time to play in the waterfalls or hike through one of the eight caves on his large estate. Unlike his father and grandfather, who lost their pensions to bankrupted steel mills, Matt Bacak should be set for life.

Scan the QR code or go to GetRichClick.com/matt to watch Matt's interview.

Drop Shipping: The Golden Goose

Drop shipping is, by far, the easiest way to get into business and make money that you will read about in *Get Rich Click*. Drop shipping has two primary benefits: no up-front inventory to purchase and a positive cash flow cycle (the seller is paid when the purchase is made).

Some drop shipping retailers keep "show" items on display in stores, so customers can inspect a sample that they are purchasing. Other retailers provide only a catalog or website.

Retailers that drop ship merchandise from wholesalers may hide this fact to avoid any stigma or to keep the wholesale source secret. They accomplish this by "blind shipping" (shipping merchandise without a return address) or "private label shipping" (shipping merchandise from the wholesaler with a return address customized to the retailer). The wholesaler may also include a customized packing slip with the retailer's company name, logo and contact information.

Many online auction sellers also drop ship. Often, a seller will list an item as new and ship the item directly from the wholesaler to the highest bidder. The seller profits from the difference between the winning bid and the wholesale price, less the auction site's merchant fees.

The seller usually pays the wholesaler using a credit card or credit terms. Therefore, there is a period of time in which the seller has the customer's money, but has not yet paid the wholesaler.

Find the best drop shipping companies at GetRichClick.com/dropship.

Which Shipping Options Should You Use?

If your business is small and offers few products, it is usually easy to manage your fulfillment quickly. So in-house shipping makes sense. Your strategy might evolve as your sales volume increases or as you start offering more products.

Factors you should consider when deciding your shipping strategy include:
- Your industry
- What your competition offers
- The type of products you sell
- The physical dimensions and weights of the products you sell
- Delivery times
- Specialized customer needs

There are several shipping service options you can consider:
- United Parcel Service (UPS) (ups.com)
- Federal Express (FedEx) (fedex.com)
- Canada Post (canadapost.ca)
- U.S. Postal Service (USPS) (usps.com)
- DHL (dhl.com)
- iShip (iship.com)
- Internet Shipper (Internetshipper.net)

YOUR MOST VALUABLE ASSET ...
YOUR DATABASE

Successful business owners in today's "internet economy," both online and offline, all have one common element that is critical to their success — their DATABASE! Database Marketing is BY FAR the #1 common element to successful selling. Below is how we break up our database so we can qualify these leads accordingly:

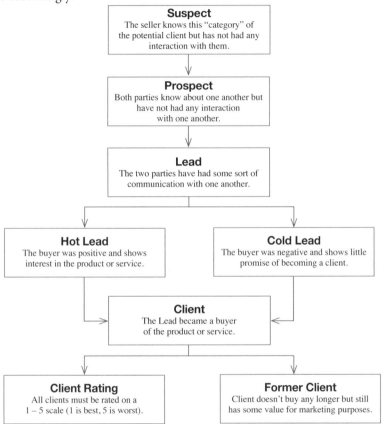

Suspect
The seller knows this "category" of the potential client but has not had any interaction with them.

Prospect
Both parties know about one another but have not had any interaction with one another.

Lead
The two parties have had some sort of communication with one another.

Hot Lead
The buyer was positive and shows interest in the product or service.

Cold Lead
The buyer was negative and shows little promise of becoming a client.

Client
The Lead became a buyer of the product or service.

Client Rating
All clients must be rated on a 1 – 5 scale (1 is best, 5 is worst).

Former Client
Client doesn't buy any longer but still has some value for marketing purposes.

Databases are the most critical part of successful marketing. Sending the right message to the right person at the right time is the ultimate key to successfully turning a potential client into a customer for life.

The second part of the database is "renting" out your names to other firms that don't compete with you. Here is a sample of how you might price renting out names in your database.

Suspect ....$.10
Prospect...$.20
Cold Lead...$.30
Hot Lead ....$.50
* Client..$.75
Former Client...$.60

* Client values may vary based upon your 1–5 rating system.

iShip and Internet Shipper provide e-commerce shipping solutions as well as comparisons between carriers. They itemize size, weight, quantity and location information to calculate the cheapest way to send a package.

Shipping is the last step customers negotiate with you in their transactions, and it can often be a make-or-break step. Providing a good shipping experience is essential to encourage customers to buy again from you, refer you to friends and associates and establish a lasting, loyal relationship.

Your goal should be to develop a loyal customer base; this is your best source for sustaining income.

More Internet Success Stories

Comcate

comcate.com

San Francisco, CA

Founder's age: 18

When Ben Casnocha was 12, he wanted to change the world on his own terms, and Apple Computer's Think Different ad campaign inspired him. In 2001, after a string of ventures, including selling gumballs to his brothers, he started Comcate, a software company that specializes exclusively on improving operations for public agencies.

So far hundreds of small and midsized government agencies around the country have hired the company and installed its web-based software to improve customer service and office efficiency.

Casnocha says Comcate is now focused on one thing: growth. He plans to have Comcate in more than 300 agencies by 2010 and income to exceed $10 million.

There's more to his story. When Casnocha graduated from high school he'd already published a book, *My Start-Up Life: What a (Very) Young CEO Learned on His Journey through Silicon Valley* (John Wiley & Sons).

Comcate's mission statement is compelling:

> *Comcate is the leading provider of web-based software for public agencies. More agencies trust Comcate to help them improve customer service and increase efficiency than any other web-based software provider.*
>
> *Why? Because we deliver MOBILE, AFFORDABLE, EASY-TO-USE AND IMPLEMENT, customizable applications used by agencies serving populations from 2,000 to 3,000,000 people. You can be up and running in days or weeks – not the months required by traditional software systems.*

Polaristar

polaristar.com

New Haven, CT

Founder's age: 21

Brad Galiette is just like any other small business owner, except he founded his $1 million company, Polaristar, in 2003 and ran it from his dorm room at Yale, while he was a junior, double majoring in economics and computer science. Polaristar sells online advertising infrastructure, marketing and hosting services mostly directed at small businesses.

Over time, Galiette has invested a majority of the profits to grow new areas of the business. Polaristar is organized into seven business units. PolariStar LLC has specialized in Internet development and interactive marketing during its history. Through their array of consulting services, marketing products and infrastructure resources, the firm says it is a one-stop-shop for e-commerce needs.

PrepMe

Chicago, IL, and Mountain View, CA

prepme.com

Founders' ages: 24, 23 and 23

Looking to ace the SAT but don't want to hire a coach? Karan Goel, Avichal Garg and Joe Jewell created an online SAT preparation course. Though online tutoring is an optional part of the service, the service starts with a diagnostic test to create a customized lesson plan, then uses artificial intelligence to adapt to each customer's strengths and weaknesses, automatically adjusting the types of questions it asks based on the test-taker's answers. The prep course generally takes three to four months to complete. Its efficiency is the best part of the course, say the founders, because it eliminates needlessly repetitive exercises by constantly updating to focus on areas in which the test-taker really needs improvement.

Their site says:

> Every one of our test prep courses is designed with a rigorous process that starts with recruiting top-scoring students to write course materials. These materials are edited and improved by expert tutors (many of whom have perfect scores themselves) and then revised and tested by our editing team. Next, our technology team builds custom modules to maximize our students' learning experience. Finally, our product management team constantly talks to our students and their parents to enhance their learning experience and make it as enjoyable and stress-free as possible. (About, PrepMe)

The guys are keen to take on heavyweight competitors Princeton Review and Kaplan in an industry worth $730 million. In fact, the tough competition is one of the most exciting parts about building the business for the founders. "That's what makes it fun," says Goel.

Volusion

volusion.com

Simi Valley, CA

Founder's age: 23

Two years before he graduated from high school, Kevin Sproles founded Volusion, a web design firm with three employees, and ran it out of his parents' house. Focusing on installation speed and ease, the company has since evolved into a successful online store builder that sells e-commerce capabilities to businesses. Volusion works to minimize customer frustration and recently created a simplified registration and checkout process. It trademarked the term "Fastest Checkout on the Web."

Their sites says:

> Volusion started out working by request in order to build software to
> fit client's needs and Volusion still builds its software this way. When
> Volusion first started, Kevin often stayed up all night implementing
> a new feature. He notes that his favorite thing to tell clients was,
> "Remember that feature you asked about yesterday? Here you
> go." Volusion developers continually implement new features and
> functionality to benefit those who know it best – their clients.

Volusion continues to grow and to help its clients grow. Realizing the importance of adapting to differing needs, it has designed software that is feature rich and flexible, enabling store owners to meet the requirements of their own unique business model.

Google chose Volusion and other companies to integrate their retailing technology with Google's new checkout system. "We weren't interested [at first], since we were worried they would be competing, but it turned out to be good for both parties," says Sproles.

Putting Your Ideas into Action

● Visit various websites in your industry to get a feel for how they process payments and handle the customer's checkout experience.

● Understand what are some of the factors that make one site easier than another.

● What steps do the sites take to make you feel secure in sharing financial information?

● What can you copy from these sites? What would you change?

● Try to keep shipping costs to a minimum.

● Pass along the savings to your customer.

● Do not treat shipping as a profit center.

● When you have your own success story, please share it with me at GetRichClick.com/shareyourstory!

For More Information, go to GetRichClick.com.

12

The Internet to Go: Mobile Opportunities

You're driving along a busy street and you see a theater. You're in the mood for a movie, but you're not sure what's showing when. You snap a photo of the theater with your cell phone or mobile device and in 10 seconds, you get back information on the movies, show times, admission prices, business hours of operation and amenities. This is already in the works under what is code named "Google Goggles." It is a new VISUAL search capability from a simple photo.

Access to information needn't be limited to a desktop or laptop interface. When 82 percent of Americans and an estimated 4 billion people worldwide are cell phone subscribers, people are turning to the device they take everywhere for instant access to the information they need. Smart businesses know that when, where and how customers want information can make a difference on the bottom line.

The opportunities from these changes are almost limitless.

Back when cameras were first introduced as a cell phone feature, many scoffed. Mobile technology is fascinating, and wide open for those with the Get Rich Click mindset.

Image Recognition

The potential for image recognition technology to merge the real world with the Internet experience is enormous. Basically, all a person needs to do is take a picture using his cell phone, send it as an MMS (a media text message) and retrieve information from the Internet that connects the consumer with the digital media that support the product or the ad, such as micro-sites, audio and/ or video clips, coupons and free samples.

As stated above, "Google Goggles" is about to launch this capability. In the meantime, Mobot (mobot.com) incorporated in 2003 with the goal of creating services for mobile consumer applications, making it possible for people with a cell phone to engage with visual media.

The website says:

We believe that images from camera phones hold a wealth of information – and consumers, when given the capability, will utilize their cameras in new and powerful ways. Some applications of mobile visual search will save consumers time, others will be fun and simply a way for them to interact with the world around them. In all cases Mobot delivers fast, contextual responses so that marketers, game designers, content providers, and retailers can deliver a rich mobile experience to consumers.

Mobot is made up of a team of creative and accomplished people. When we walk down the street, ride in the car, and go about our day-to-day lives, we see a world rich with visual messages . . . a world ready to be **mobotized** (and we're doing it).

We see mobotized cereal boxes, direct mail, headlines, placards, human billboards, brand tattoos, street signs, posters, logos, magazines, coasters, book covers, wild postings, CD jackets, retail signs, and much, much more. We see consumers interacting with brands on their own terms, right at the moment their interest is piqued. And we see a remarkably simple interaction model that enables creative possibilities where previously none existed.

So we've brought together expertise in Internet and mobile content and services, image recognition and marketing to shape a world where mobile pictures are simple and powerful, driving revenue, transactions, impressions, fun, and rewards. (Company, Mobot.com)

Mobot has already worked with applications that allow consumers to purchase ringtones and music simply by taking a picture of a CD cover and to connect to product information simply by taking a picture of an item in a store or from the page of a print advertisement.

Mobile Phones and Personal Digital Assistants have become the Swiss Army Knives of this Generation!

– Marc Ostrofsky

Nokia, the Finnish cell phone manufacturer, calls its image recognition technology "Point & Find":

. . . a unique, game-changing service that enables accessing relevant Internet content simply by pointing a camera phone at a real-world object. It is a quick, easy way to get useful information on-the-go. Using a simple and intuitive interface, it combines the latest in advanced technologies such as image recognition to provide rich content, not just weblinks.

The first beta version of the service focuses on connecting consumers with local movie information. Simply by pointing a camera phone at a poster for a new movie, you can watch the trailer, read reviews, find the closest cinema and even buy tickets.

Consider the *Get Rich Click* possibilities in a world where a simple digital imprint on a mobile device brings instant information. It's real . . . and it's happening now. Simply look at the QR codes being used throughout this book. Download the barcode reader to your mobile phone or PDA and one snapshot of that code takes you to the *Get Rich Click* website!

Music Recognition

The possibilities music recognition technology offered to the mobile world started making popular news in about 2001. For example, London-based Shazam offers a way for cell phone users to identify the music they were listening to in doctor's offices, on their car radios, in elevators, even under noisy background conditions. You just "shazam" the tune (let your cell phone "listen" to the music for about 30 seconds) and the application (resident on your phone) matches the digital imprint to a database of over 100 million tracks worldwide, then returns a text with information about the song and allows you to purchase it. Shazam has been used by more than 50 million people who live in over 150 countries.

The information Shazam provides includes track title, artist name and biography, cover art and reviews. It also offers recommendations based on the song it identifies. You can even send your tagged song information to an "iD" list on your Facebook profile, to share with your friends there. In 2008, Shazam added the iPod Touch (for the second generation iPod Touch) application to round out its offerings to owners of Apple mobile devices – the applications offer a rich customer music interface and connect directly to iTunes for immediate purchase.

Barcode Recognition

The idea that a mobile device could process a barcode and connect you with useful information is a specific application of image recognition in mobile/ Internet technology. Since 2004, Japanese cell phone users have been able to take a picture of a book's barcode, send it to Amazon Japan and receive pricing information. The feature was so popular, Amazon Japan introduced Scan Search in 2006; now Japanese cell phone users can scan book barcodes and connect to the mobile version of Amazon Japan's website, where they can get information and purchase the book on the spot.

Japan is a leader in barcode adoption. Japanese consumers with a camera phone can scan a McDonalds's hamburger wrapper and connect to nutritional information. Instead of using tickets, they can board an airplane using their mobile phones.

There are also applications for scanning billboards or for-sale signs near a house. In Japan, barcodes are becoming ubiquitous; you'll find them incorporated in business cards, magazines, newspapers, flyers, posters, stickers, food products, puzzles and even websites. You just scan your computer screen. The scans can link to a mobile web page, photos, videos and/or a text description of the object.

The barcodes in the news aren't the linear barcodes cashiers scan at checkout. Black and white and square, they can incorporate significantly more information than linear codes. They've been around for several years, though only recently have Americans been able to take advantage of them. Barcodes have the advantage of offering a standardized way to "tag" the real world and connect it to information and consumer activity via the Internet.

In the United States, cell phones have not come equipped with the necessary barcode-reading software; users have had to download the technology themselves. Even in Japan, barcode recognition did not become mainstream until the biggest providers started supporting it by providing a native application. Americans haven't been ignoring this barcode technology, though. Several large technology companies, including Hewlett Packard and Publicis Groupe, are lobbying to move barcodes mainstream. Motorola and Microsoft are researching a wide range of applications for barcodes.

Technology now exists that allows for 2D Barcode software to be easily downloaded to most smartphones. (Similar to the QR Codes you have seen throughout this book.) Nokia now offers a cell phone with a barcode application installed. Homegrown YouTube videos demonstrate how easy it is to take a picture of a 2D barcode, enter it into the application and connect with the associated mobile web content. NeoMedia Technologies (neom.com) is already starting to help businesses take advantage of the new barcode technology. In their words, "It's the future of marketing and advertising and it exists now."

Barcode Reading Applications:

- Kaywa Reader   • QuickMark   • NeoReader
- Zxing Reader   • Upcode   • I-nigma

Unlike the Japanese, Americans don't live in a barcoded world. Yet. But barcodes and cell phones offer another way for us to integrate our real and online worlds in ways few would have imagined 10 years ago.

CLICK TIP ▶ So many websites are not "mobile" ready. There is a **HUGE** opportunity to help companies take their websites and make them easy to access and to navigate from cell phones, smartphones and PDAs.

Sell mobile content such as ring-tones, wallpaper, images, video or music. Offer premium subscriptions and services like a joke of the day, fact of the day, horoscope, news, sports scores or stock quotes and financial information. Other premium subscription items are:
- Sending and receiving e-mail
- Music downloads
- Traditional e-commerce
- Advertising/Mobile AdSense
- Sponsorships of your mobile content
- Teaching others "how to" access, use and benefit from these opportunities

Mobile

Mobile Green with Red Fish Media

Want to try using an amazing new technology – right this moment?

1. Get out your cell phone.
2. Send a TEXT to 23000.
3. Put in the word CLICK into the body of that text.
4. Put a comma (,) next to the word CLICK and enter your
   e-mail address.
5. Click SEND.

Congratulations! You've just used the latest in mobile media marketing called a Five Digit Short Code.

The vendor of this technology, Red Fish Media, helps businesses capture cell phone numbers and e-mail addresses so they can be used for marketing campaigns. And their unique way of doing it really captures the imagination of interested consumers.

Given the proliferation of smartphones with incredible processing speeds and the ability to access unprecedented amounts of bandwidth, anyone doing business online should consider – or should we say, must consider – creating campaigns for these mobile technologies.

Matt McKenna founded Red Fish in 1994 to address the growing demand for SMS and interactive mobile applications. Now the company is a full-service mobile marketing agency that helps clients formulate strategic campaigns to reach potential customers, and develops the technological tools to execute these campaigns, including interactive SMS applications, mobile advertising, text alerts, daily alert subscription campaigns and the BluWater mobile delivery platform, which enables clients to launch and manage their marketing applications through a web interface.

"The advancements in how we communicate and how we conduct ourselves businesswise and socially has been flipped on its head," CEO McKenna says. "Red Fish is part of the communication movement; we empower brands with the element of SMS to improve the way companies engage consumers, ideally increasing response rates, and inevitably their revenues."

Apparently, McKenna is convincing. Red Fish now boasts an impressive client list that includes Starbucks, Google and Nike!

These days, consumers buy when they are literally "on the move." So to avoid being left behind, savvy businesses must move with them. RedFishMedia.com can help you and your business make that happen.

Scan the QR code or go to GetRichClick.com/redfish to learn more about short codes.

Mobile Marketing

Success is always dependent on marketing, and mobile marketing is no different. But mobile marketing has one huge advantage. The mobile channel offers high-speed message delivery, it's interactive, has great customer reach, higher response rates and a focused, targeted market. Since the *Get Rich Click* mindset considers opportunities to save as well as make money, it's important you understand the cost effectiveness related to mobile marketing. Mobile marketing can help you establish brand awareness, generate leads, convert prospects to customers and enhance customer loyalty, making it a powerful new Internet-based medium. This is clearly one of those *Get Rich Click* opportunities you can capitalize on by watching the money flow, the significant players, the competitiveness of the market and the development of complementary picks and shovels that expand the usefulness of this market.

People treat their cell phones like their house keys: they never leave home without them.

Mobile marketing generally has a low cost-per-message. Messages tend to be one-on-one and personal, and response rates are relatively higher. In addition, mobile marketing encourages interactivity and impulse buys. This goes a long way toward developing ongoing, long-lasting customer loyalty that many traditional marketing programs lack or are deficient in.

At this point, real-world-to-Internet applications are still developing; not everyone can access the same features, which are not available for all mobile devices, by manufacturer or even model. WAP, or Wireless Application Protocol, enables a computer or mobile device to access the Internet; it is used for routers as well as in cell phones, smartphones and PDAs.

Mobile Search Opportunities

Mobile consumables currently comprise the bulk of available mobile content, but as mobile search engines improve, access to information is expanding.

Many shopping sites offer mobile versions of their search engines. Think about the demographics: people on the go, all owning one or more handheld devices, are connecting to the Internet anywhere signal strength allows – in cars, on the street, in buses, in trains. That's an ideal target market for mobile search.

Developing Mobile-Ready Websites

Websites for mobile content should be constructed differently for mobile screens than for traditional desktop, laptop and tablet PC monitors. Test the appearance before publishing to the mobile world. There are tools available that show what websites look like on mobile platforms. Use these tools to take your current website and make it available for the mobile world.

One of these firms is volantis.net. Volantis helps organizations solve the complexity of selling and delivering digital content to thousands of unique devices and is one of the leaders in Intelligent Content Delivery solutions. One of their products, Volantis Mobility Server™, is a java-based development and run-time platform that allows web developers to build and run their own mobile Internet applications across over 6,000 devices.

Be aware that mobile Internet access is limited – "small-screen real estate" does not encourage users to type in query strings and typing on a mobile device is an awkward undertaking for many. Over half of mobile searches consist of one word. Another 33 percent consist of two words with three- to four- word searches being 15 percent of the total.

Mobile search engines have experienced a steady growth in unique users, searches per user and average transaction amount. Nielsen Research suggested that mobile search has a ways to go before businesses can consider it a mainstay in general search marketing. This, of course, spells opportunity for those who embrace the *Get Rich Click* mindset and take advantage of it now.

What's Hot in Mobile Searching

Fifty percent of mobile searches represent the following top seven categories:

Categories	Percentage of Mobile Searches
Navigation	16 percent
Music	10 percent
Entertainment	8 percent
Sports	6 percent
Reference	5 percent
Shopping	2 percent

The iPhone and iPad

While mobile search in general may be a slower-growing phenomenon than some expected, the most popular mobile device people used to access mobile search results was Apple's iPhone. The *New York Times* speculated the iPhone could be the device to change the face of mobile search and the mobile Internet in general. I would agree. I use one, and it's a truly amazing product.

Apple got it right. The company knew a wide range of fun, creative applications specific to the iPhone would persuade more people to buy the device. To encourage application development, Apple pays application developers 70 percent of every dollar the company makes selling iPhone applications.

Apple's iPhone and iPad seem to be commanding attention among the application development community. Services like Shazam (see above) have made applications available for the iPhone before they've expanded to other cell phone manufacturers and models. Cleverly, Apple integrated iTunes into the iPhone experience and released the iPhone and iPad Development Kit for enterprising third parties. Within the first 60 days of the iTunes App Store's launch, there were over 100 million music downloads.

There's currently serious money to be made in creating iPhone and iPad applications. Early estimates suggested top applications were making between $5,000 and $10,000 a day. There are too many money-making stories about entrepreneurs to discuss them all here but with the large distribution of these products, good apps that make their founders quite wealthy will continue to be in the press for many years to come.

Rags to Riches iPhone Success Stories

1. Steve Demeter, the developer of the $5 game Trism, spent $5,000 developing the game and in those amazing two months following the launch of the App Store, grossed $250,000. To date the APP has brought in several million dollars. Demeter acknowledges there was some luck involved, but he designed Trism with unique gameplay and high replay value and an online leaderboard for a community dimension. Intelligent marketing, naturally, is a critical component of success.

2. While I was doing the final edits for this very page, The *New York Times* ran a major article about Ethan Nicholas and his wife, Nicole, who were having trouble paying their mortgage and medical bills. Nicholas heard about Steve Demeter and decided to write an iPhone app himself. The 30-year-old had zero experience in iPhone apps but years of java programming experience. After six weeks of working "morning, noon and night," he created an iPhone application called iShoot.

The first day, the $4.99 app made $1,000, and he thought he had won the lottery. The second day, $2,000. The third day, he made $50, and this earning level persisted for several weeks. Then he retooled the app and gave out a "free" version with fewer features but with an upsell to a paid version. So far, he has earned $800,000, called his boss and quit his job. He plans to "milk the gold rush as long as I can."

3. A Greek entrepreneur and two of his friends invested a week of their time and created an iPhone app called iSteam. It makes the face of the iPhone look like a fogged-up bathroom mirror. They made $100,000 in 90 days.

4. Bart Decrem created Tap Tap Revenge, a music rhythm game, and within two weeks of release hit the 1 million download milestone. The game was free to download, and Decrem looked to finance his application through advertising and a premium paid version of the game.

The iPhone and Apple's Development Kit open the market to those who would like to *Get Rich Click*; you don't need substantial capital, simply talent and time. Many liken the iPhone landscape to the early days of the Internet, when excitement was high and the sky seemed the limit.

Remember, if you want to have an iPhone app created, get competitive bids at iPhoneAppQuotes.com.

Keeping an Eye on Mobile Technology

Where can you go to stay abreast of all the developments and communal brainstorming that will allow you to observe the market and gauge your opportunity? Here are two places worth keeping in mind.

Betavine (betavine.net) is an open community for those who would like to make money developing mobile applications. The primary focus is on open-source applications. Betavine's mission: To support the wider development community in imagining, developing, testing and launching great new applications for mobile, wireless and Internet communications. We are platform agnostic and operating system agnostic. (Betavine)

Another resource is MobileFuture (mobilefuture.org). This is a coalition of businesses, nonprofits and individuals who have united to promote and advocate for "an environment in which innovations in wireless technology and services are enabled and encouraged." Their mission is:

To educate the public and key decision makers on innovations in the wireless industry that have transformed the way Americans work and play and to advocate continued investment in wireless technologies. (About Us, MobileFuture)

CLICK TIP ▷ A feature on the MobileFuture website (mobilefuture.org) is MobileU, or Mobile University, which compiles information on the state of wireless applications and mobile services. "We'll teach you to get the most out of your mobile phone and use the newest wireless technologies to make your life more efficient, more productive and more fun." MobileU's categories of material include: staying informed; having fun; blogs; books; and much more.

Putting Your Ideas into Action

Here are a few suggestions to optimize your web content for mobile search engines:

- Keep your titles concise.
- Connect (or link) to legitimate and popular websites.
- Make sure your web design makes it easy for mobile spiders to crawl your site so the mobile search engines can index it properly.
- Submit your mobile site for inclusion to mobile search engines just like you would a traditional website.
- Design sites and content for a wide array of mobile devices starting at the low- rather than the high end.

For More Information, go to GetRichClick.com.

13

Internet Video: Nothing but Growth

Did you know that you drive FREE traffic to your website by Search Engine Optimizing videos you have uploaded on YouTube?

Did you know that the next generation of television sets will be "YouTube Ready" – allowing anyone to view the latest uploads?

Internet video offers some very exciting opportunities for entrepreneurs. Consistent with the Get Rich Click mindset, venturing into Internet video won't make you rich overnight, but it can influence a longer-term, sustainable business model that could eventually generate significant income. This chapter will show you how to take advantage of the growth this market offers.

The Internet Video Business Model

To build real wealth, you need to think beyond onetime transactions and turn them into recurring income streams and ongoing referrals. These create income and build equity. Income is the short-term gain. Equity is the long-term business value that others will want to buy at a later date.

The traditional approach would involve finding someone to shoot the video, edit it and collect a onetime transaction fee. But a *Get Rich Click* business model lets you use the Internet to go beyond a onetime transaction and effectively build a business using free videos posted by others and outsourcing the entire process, from editing to closing the transaction.

MSNBC REPORTS

- Major brands such as Coca-Cola, Smirnoff and Unilever's Dove are creating online video campaigns that rely on word of mouth, often generating millions of views – for far less than it costs to place ads on television.

Income is the short-term gain. Equity is the long-term business value that others will want to buy at a later date.

- Corporations are using web-based video in other ways, too. Tech companies such as IBM and Microsoft use customer testimonial videos in pitches to prospective clients. Firms use video to chat with clients, prospects and suppliers. Kids use video and online "chat" almost daily in their Facebook interactions.

- Enterprise Rent-A-Car, Google and Nordstrom post videos on their websites to help recruit new workers. I saw a watch manufacturer post a video on YouTube.com to help brand the quality of their time pieces and showcase how their watches were made by hand. Viewers got to "watch a watch" being built from start to finish.

YouTube

Google's purchase of YouTube.com did wonders for raising awareness of Internet video. Using simple software application like iMovie and raw iPod video, amateur and casual Internet users from all over the world can post, watch and share original videos online. YouTube now sees more than 20 hours of video uploaded to the site every minute of every day.

How big is the YouTube phenomenon? In March 2008, Digital Ethnography at Kansas State University reported users had uploaded 78.3 million videos over the course of YouTube's existence. Uploads average between 150,000 and 200,000 videos a day. The site has 200 million unique users each month and commands the sixth-largest audience in the Western world on the Internet.

YouTube is not limited to user-generated content:

YouTube has partnership deals with thousands of content providers, including CBS, BBC, Universal Music Group, Sony Music Group, Warner Music Group, NBA, The Sundance Channel and many more. These partnerships and the wide range of content they represent provide appropriate environments for brand marketers and countless opportunities for high-profile placements. (Advertising Opportunities, YouTube)

YouTube promotes the marketing and advertising role it can play for business partners through its "Brand Channel" or "online media kit" (youtube.com/advertise). YouTube encourages companies to understand how to get the most from their video involvement:

• Success depends on participating through your involvement in your message. YouTube is all about people and connections.

• YouTube partnerships make it possible for thousands of content partners, from the world of fashion to the world of television to the world of how-to, to provide premium content to target audiences. YouTube only runs ads on the content or videos from partners with whom they have a direct relationship.

• YouTube's marketing options allow ad buyers to target by age, gender, geography, content category, even the time of day a viewer will see their ad. It's easy to see why this medium is having a major impact on television advertising expenditures.

Pocket Candy from Eye Candy: 10 Ways to Profit with Online Video

Making money using online video content is a strategy that's catching on like wildfire, and it's easier than ever to become an online video producer. Video creates prime opportunities to target audiences and stream online content that will catch eyes and cultivate dollars.

1. Advertising That Runs before the Video. An advertisement that appears before the main content of a video is "pre-roll" advertising. Just as television commercials are a source of income for television stations, these ads are the commercials of Internet video.

Internet users watch video with the same short attention spans they bring to readable online content. Capturing the Internet user's attention and sustaining it is key. Pre-roll advertising should be relevant to video content or at least to the demographics of the viewer. One pick-and-shovel service you might offer is to make advertising relevant and effective for advertisers and purchasers of advertising.

2. Advertising after the Video. Advertising placed after the main content of a video is "post-roll" advertising. Revver.com, for example, offers a post-roll advertising service that produces and provides static image Pay-Per-Click advertising at the end of videos. Revver splits advertising income with the video producer. The business takes its model one step further by combining an affiliate model with its ad-revenue-sharing model. Affiliates can earn money by sharing video, providing a true viral situation to video distribution. Revver says, "We support the free and unlimited sharing of media. Our unique technology pairs videos with targeted ads and tracks them as they spread across the web. So no matter where your video travels, you benefit because we share the advertising revenue with you."

Brightroll.com, an online ad agency helping firms place video content on other websites, uses a contextual advertising model with search engine optimization and Pay-Per-Click advertising. They provide this for both pre- and post-roll ads. Brightroll is considered one of the Internet video industry's largest and most effective performance networks. They work with advertisers to generate traffic, drive online registrations, build an e-mail database and generate leads.

**I created a password and wrote it down like you told me to.
Then I locked it away in a secure folder for safekeeping.
But I need my password to get into the folder!**

3. Advertising Mid-Video. Advertising that appears in the middle of a video is "mid-roll" advertising. Brightcove.com offers this service in addition to pre- and post-roll advertising, and the affiliate sharing model. Brightcove also "offers media management, video publishing tools, online distribution for viral marketing and managed syndication, analytics technology and development tools to help you maximize your online video efforts."

4. Site-Specific Advertising. You can also sell advertising space around the video playback screen in a website. To optimize this scenario, be sure the advertising is relevant to the video.

5. Sponsorships. You can sell sponsorships (logos, ads, public service announcements and links) around the video playback screen. Sponsorships are similar to site-specific advertising but are usually related to nonprofit and public service functions rather than direct advertising.

6. Selling Video Content. Video content can be particularly attractive to training and development companies or to companies interested in staff training.

7. Video Sharing. Video sharing sites pay contributors on a pay-per-view basis. Metacafe.com offers a Video Producer "Rewards Program" that pays $2 for every thousand views a video receives while it runs on their site.

8. Subscription Model. A video content site solicits users to pay a membership fee that is divided among the most successful video content contributors to the site.

9. Video Broadcasting Services. When you create a video and want to get it placed on multiple websites at once, consider using Mike Koenig's TrafficGeyser.com. The site is a one-stop-shopping portal for getting your video on 40+ web distribution sites – all at once.

10. Creating a YouTube Channel. Download speeds are now so fast that video is the final frontier and the true killer app on the Internet. Consider creating a YouTube channel and let me know how you do at GetRichClick.com.

Internet Video and Business

Internet video opens many new options for businesses of all sizes to communicate with prospects and customers. As with all things marketing, high-quality content is essential. Quality is a competitive differentiator that will follow the ad dollars going to a given website.

Anheuser Busch states broadband has given the company an unprecedented direct marketing link to consumers. They've undertaken a project called Bud.tv, an online entertainment network that streams short videos to visitors of the website. The content is free to the user and includes comedy, sports, music and consumer-generated content along with plenty of beer ads.

This was one of the first major online video efforts by a big advertiser, and will undoubtedly influence other big media advertisers to consider video ads and channel more ad dollars to online media. Come up with a fun, interactive game, contest or viral marketing idea for any company that has an advertising and promotion budget, and you can approach its ad agency or solicit the client directly. In these new markets, you never know until you try.

As the quality of video content online improves, viewers will be willing to pay for it. Firms that have "optimized" their video listings for search engines will profit from the increased traffic.

Making Money on YouTube? This Russian Immigrant Nets $15,000+/month

Most people don't even know what the word "etymologist" means, so it's pretty darn impressive that Marina Orlova makes millions being one online!

"Etymologists" study and teach the history of a language. It might sound boring, but it's Orlova's passion so she decided to take her love of words to the masses – and she's done so in the most entertaining of ways.

The 5' 5" buxom blonde Russian immigrant began dressing as a sexy school-teacher and launched videos on YouTube explaining words as simple as "okay" and as complex as "antidisestablishmentarianism." Soon after, she launched a channel and website, both called HotForWords. After only five months, Orlova's YouTube channel gained 300,000 viewers, and since has become a regular guest on Fox News shows like *The O'Reilly Factor*.

But things didn't start out so easily for Orlova. The attractive Russian, who has two degrees in philology (the study of language), began her career teaching English and world literature to high school students in Moscow. Then, hoping to turn her beauty into a modeling career, she moved to the United States, but didn't find much success. Instead she worked for two years as a nanny.

When Orlova finally launched on YouTube, her first few videos attracted almost no hits, and the amount of her YouTube checks added insult to injury: the first was for $20 and the second was for $35. When she called to complain to YouTube about the tiny checks, she was told to "change the category from information to entertainment, that's where all the money is." Orlova heeded the advice and switched. Sure enough, her next check was more than $15,000 for a single month, due to all of the advertising her site attracted.

The increase in income was also due to Orlova's increase in organic popularity. And that was due to her ability to make complex information simple – and engaging. You see, Orlova built a YouTube personality. She starts out every video with her signature "Hello, my dear students," and displays as much cleavage as she possibly can without crossing the line into adult entertainment!

Today, the Internet vocab diva – voted World's #1 Sexiest Geek by both *Wired* and *Maxim* magazines – continues to use her website to teach, as well as to sell-her book *Hot for Words*. Her lesson for today? S.E.X.I. Sells or **S**uccess = **E**ntertainment + **X**itement + **I**nformation.

Scan the QR code or go to GetRichClick.com/marina to watch Marina in action.

Optimizing Video Content for Search Engines

According to Google, more people search for "video" than for "news," "love" or "religion." Videos are also showing up more frequently in regular search results. Google, for example, sets aside a portion of its organic results for video links, offering a few imaged results and providing a link to all video results for that search term.

Optimizing video content for search engines is the next step. The goal of search engine optimization for video content is to make relevant content accessible to those who are searching for it. Basic search engine optimization techniques apply to video as well as static content:

- Use rich file names.
- Optimize the content on the web page that launches the video.
- Submit to search engines like static content optimization.
- Optimize for generic Keywords: (for example, travel Hawaii video, gardening techniques video, smartphone usage video).
- Create a separate video site map.

The bottom line? The growth of broadband has created a huge and burgeoning market for video over the Internet. This market is hot in every sense of the word. There are many opportunities to get in and make a profit if you understand the size of the video market, the coming growth of this market and what advertisers need. It's entirely possible that you can come up with a fun, interactive way to capture the attention of buyers on behalf of those advertisers.

10 Questions to Consider
When Posting Video on Your Website

Should your website . . .
- Post video on your home page?
- Place your video one click away from the home page?
- Place videos deep into your website or more than three clicks or more away from the home page?
- Use online video in an advanced manner: contextual integration of videos, variety of video players, call-to-action tied to the video, etc?
- Offer a "video center" comparable to a corporate TV channel?
- Open a new browser to view the video?
- Display video ads for products in the site?
- Offer a full-screen video option?
- Use a pop-up window to display video?
- Format videos in Flash, Windows Media Player, QuickTime or Real Player?

Putting Your Ideas into Action

- If you've never done so, try shooting and uploading a video to YouTube or Facebook. It's much easier than you might think.
- When you're starting out, don't upload any videos longer than three minutes. Online attention spans are short!
- Be sure to put your website url at the start and finish of all your videos.
- If you are going to post video on your site, consider all of the previous questions so that you maximize download speeds and increase viewership.
- Once you've had some practice in shooting and uploading videos, you can begin sending them to influential blogs in your subject area. This is the best way to get recognition and exposure. Send them also to GetRichClick.com.
- Remember, you can Search Engine Optimize videos on sites like YouTube. Learn the techniques on how to accomplish this. You could then make a living "SEOing" other people's videos for their business needs!

For More Information, go to GetRichClick.com.

"I heard on TV that everyone is getting rich
on the Internet! Is this little slot where
the money comes out?"

14

Get Rich Click for Nonprofit Organizations

In the not-for-profit world, financial resources typically come from donations by individuals, corporations, personal trusts and other organizations. In the vernacular, fund-raising – the income side of a nonprofit business – is an ongoing activity. There are many new and exciting ways for these groups to make money and lower expenses through online versions of their fund-raising activities.

12 + Online Strategies for Making Money with Nonprofits

Online gift-giving is on the rise. On average, through online gifts, charities collect two to three times more than they do through traditional fund-raising efforts. It is estimated online giving in the United States exceeds $3 billion annually. Here are some basic strategies you should implement to take advantage of the surge in online giving:

1. Increased traffic = Increased revenue. Charities and nonprofit groups can make money online in a variety of ways. Send an e-mail encouraging donations to your clients, donors, partner organizations and volunteers. Include a link to your business web address (url). Remember, on the Internet – as in a shopping mall or any other marketing piece – the more traffic you get, the more money your site can take in, provided you know how to convert your traffic into donors. Increasing the number of inbound or outbound "links" on your site will also help increase traffic considerably.

2. List with the search engines. Listing any site with the big search engines like Yahoo, Google and Ask is important. But as a nonprofit, you should also list your organization with the many Internet charity portals or special charity search engines.

Below are a few of the many search engines specializing in finding the right nonprofit organizations to meet a donor's needs:

- Guidestar.org
- NetworkForGood.org
- GreaterGood.com
- Foundations.org
- CharityNavigator.com

CLICK TIP ▶ Just Give (justgive.org) is a site for nonprofit donations. Their goal is to create tools and services that encourage people to make charitable giving part of their lives by connecting people with the charities and causes they care about most. On their site, they offer a "Find a Charity" search engine that combs over one million charities. Donors often review these sites to help them with their research, so it's important to keep your listing up-to-date.

3. Make it easy for people to give. Save the Children (SaveTheChildren. org), a nonprofit organization I happen to like, has a very strong online presence and offers 10 different ways to contribute online. Try to offer your donors as many of these options as possible:

- Gift donation
- Memorial donation
- Monthly giving option
- Sponsorship
- Online auctions
- Emergency support
- A straight financial donation
- Corporate gift donation
- The offer of gifts to be purchased for the benefit of charity
- Sponsorship of a child

4. Set up affiliate programs. You can help not-for-profit companies set up affiliate links for their website. Visitors to the nonprofit site click on affiliate links, and each time a person buys from that affiliate, your organization makes money on the purchase. Think about that. Each time they buy from that affiliate, your organization gets a commission. The possibilities for making money are huge. The income or commission from sales can range from 3 to 5 percent, to 50 percent or more for some digital book affiliate links (see ClickBank.com).

5. Market through e-mail. The most important asset of any nonprofit group is its database – or more specifically, its e-mail list. E-mail marketing to an in-house-generated list of donors is the best way to improve nonprofit earnings. The more names in your database or e-mail list, the more money you will make! Asking supporters to donate directly to the site is the most effective way to make money without incurring excessive fees associated with the fund-raising effort. Almost every charity has implemented such a system. Most alumni organizations at colleges and universities use this tactic and send out e-mails on an ongoing basis asking for money.

6. Sell products. Make it easy for your members and supporters to donate for-sale items to your site or to another site that will sell the items and donate the money to the nonprofit. Your nonprofit can easily set up an eBay Store to sell these items online.

7. Find an unusual hook. Consider having your nonprofit group work with Charity Folks (CharityFolks.com) or Charity Buzz (CharityBuzz.com). These two firms are the leading online marketplace for nonprofit fund-raising, corporate cause-marketing campaigns and celebrity-driven charity initiatives. They offer highly coveted auction lots donated by today's hottest celebrities, musicians, sports stars, high-profile personalities and top-tier brands. Both firms partner with corporations to auction exclusive products and otherwise unavailable items and experiences, enabling them to leverage connectivity to high-profile people and events. All of this is done 100% via the Internet!

8. Auction for charity. eBayGivingWorks (ebaygivingworks.com) is a simple but oh-so-powerful idea: you list an item for auction on eBay (charity auctions are marked with a blue and gold ribbon) and specify what proportion of that item's sale price you want to donate to your favorite nonprofit organization. If you're the buyer, you get a great product and the knowledge your purchase is benefiting a charity. It's a win-win-win.

9. Create a tool for supporters to collect on your behalf. A familiar sight (and sound) during the holidays is the red kettle with its companion dressed like Santa ringing the bell on behalf of the Salvation Army. Just the sound of that bell can act like a magnet and suck all the loose change from your pocket. Depending on where you live, you can incorporate its function in your e-mails. Very cleverly, the Salvation Army has made it possible for you to ring the charitable fund-raising bell for families and friends to donate to online. *USA Today* reported that a U.S. Army sergeant in Baghdad, who had once been an in-person bell-ringer before she deployed, included her virtual kettle in her e-mails to friends.

10. Cross-promote your web address. Whether your organization is printing a business card, letterhead, envelopes, a book, a pamphlet or running a commercial on radio or television, your top priority should be cross-promoting your website. Getting mindshare from clients and potential clients is vital. Promote your web address as often as possible. I've learned the value of doing this myself, with GetRichClick.com.

11. Engage your clients and prospects. Know as much about them as you can, keep them informed, up-to-date and get their opinion on what your group is doing. Do your best to maintain an ongoing interactive dialog – especially with the top 10 percent of your donors.

12. Use the Internet as a strategic marketing tool. It should be the easiest, fastest and most efficient way to make money for many years to come. Develop a systematic approach to relationships. The Internet is not just for accepting online donations. Many people want to help in other ways, too.

Fund-raising in Action:
The Children's Miracle Network

My daughter Shelly entered a "dance marathon" at her university. The goal was to raise money for the Children's Miracle Network of Greater St. Louis. The group donates money to area hospitals to aid children with a variety of issues. The organizers of this event and their website, REALLY, had the fund-raising plans in place – like no other nonprofit I had ever dealt with. Most of the process was so well done, so automated, I was amazed at how well run their site was. In the last two years, they have raised over $250,000 from this dance marathon.

They supplied my daughter with a template e-mail to help her raise money. Their website has informational tabs for everyone involved . . . dancers, alumni, parents, faculty, visitors and businesses. It explains to each category how and why they should be involved in this fund-raiser.

For more information and to see how well a nonprofit website can help your efforts, check out dmstl.org/aboutdm.

Putting Your Ideas into Action

- Just as online merchants must make it easy for site visitors to buy from them, nonprofit sites need to make giving as easy as possible.
- Be sure your online "checkout" process is intuitive, easy to follow, simple to read and that your message gets through loud and clear.
- Make sure you interact with your prospects and clients – clearly and often. The more e-mails you have, the more money you will raise. Remember, it really is a numbers game.
- Most organizations need help with their fund-raising efforts. To the extent your budget allows, consider hiring a professional to help them create and manage the website, e-mail marketing, affiliate programs and test out other unique ways of encouraging donations.
- Ask your supporters to give you inbound links to your website from their websites. Those links are "cash in the bank" and will result in FREE, large-scale, increased traffic.

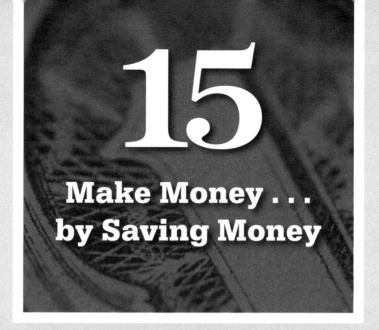

15

Make Money . . .
by Saving Money

There are ONLY two ways to increase your net worth. You can either increase your income OR decrease your costs and expenses. Both options increase your net worth!

Get Rich Click would not be complete without this wonderful chapter on the unique, smart, and fun ways to save money by using what technology offers us!

Whether it's a new iPhone Application that scans a barcode to find the lowest price on an item, a website that compares prices for the latest flat-screen television, or a wonderful site called Groupon.com that sends you a daily coupon to save money for being part of their "collective buying power," this chapter will help you pay for this book 100 times over!

Use the Internet to find thousands of ways to save money on items you buy, places you go, people you hire or things you want. This is the new way to play the personal finance game and win in a very big way.

DOLLARS AND SENSE!

In this chapter we'll look specifically at ways you can use the Internet to reduce expenses, save real dollars, have companies bid for your business and get the best products and services for the money you spend.

Informing you about many unique ways to save time and money is my goal! Please share your own ideas with us at GetRichClick.com/savemoney.

We'll begin with some money-saving websites with a general orientation, and then move onto others that are more specifically focused.

> ## Knowledge is the currency of the information age.
>
> ### – Marc Ostrofsky

LowerMyBills.com

This all-inclusive site provides links to money-saving opportunities of many kinds – everything from lower interest credit cards to mortgage refinancing. As the home page states:

LowerMyBills.com is the one-stop destination that offers savings through relationships with more than 500 service providers across multiple categories, including home loans, credit cards, auto and health insurance, and long-distance and wireless services.

LowerMyBills is really an excellent website! It should be your first stop on the road to making money by saving money. (To be fair, I must state that I was an investor in this firm before it was sold to the current owner. I love this business model because EVERYONE can save money with this site.)

Yelp.com

Yelp has more than 25 million monthly visitors. On the site, you will find reviews and recommendations for all sorts of businesses in hundreds of local areas. As a result, Yelp has been hugely successful with one of the most important strategies of *Get Rich Click*: that is, the users create the content. It has been reported that the owners of Yelp.com were offered half a billion dollars by Google to take over the company – and they turned it down.

Since virtually all the reviews on Yelp include information about the affordability of the products and services discussed, Yelp is an excellent resource for discovering how to save as much money as possible while still getting what you need.

The Yelp business model brings three elements together: users who patronize businesses and write reviews; users who read the reviews and then patronize the business; and the businesses themselves. As you'll see, this is a very powerful triangular arrangement that is being further developed by many other sites.

CLICK TIP ▷ Finding local deals is the consumers' "killer app" for the Internet and the next "big thing" for venture capital investing. Think about creating a LOCAL money-saving website. Start by recruiting friends to help you add content including the daily deals everyone finds on the lowest prices for gas, food, restaurants, electronics, etc. This content can easily be added to your site via a simple text from their cellular phone while they are out and about and find great deals. Sites like FourSquare.com allow their clients to send in text updates via a five-digit shortcode as described in the Mobile section of this book. You can post those deals on your website or automatically send a text to subscribers that sign up to receive instant notifications for the lowest prices on gas or the latest coupon for a half-price offer. You get paid by the business owners via an affiliate link, each time a visitor to your site links to their website or brings in a coupon. Maybe your site (and database of clients) will be the next one that's sold for a fortune!

Shopping Comparison Sites

Many websites compare prices among different vendors selling the same product categories – cameras, clothing, electronics and virtually everything else. Visiting the sites below is a good first step toward making a money-saving purchase:

- PriceGrabber.com
- NexTag.com
- Pronto.com
- Yahoo! Shopping
- BizRate.com
- Google Products
- DealTime.com
- StreetPrices.com
- PriceRunner.com

There are even websites that compare comparison sites like rateitall.com.

WHEN DID I CHANGE THOSE AIR FILTERS?

When was the last time you replaced the air filters in your home? Each time Roy Horlock needs to change the air filters in his home, like the rest of us, he has to go and see what size he needs. Horlock, a serial entrepreneur and friend of mine who has created a host of different business, realized that every home owner needed to change the air filters in their home every eight or twelve weeks. So he created the website called FilterReplace.com to help automate the process. Consumers sign up one time, enter the appropriate number and size of air filters they require, click on how often they wish to receive those filters (every 30, 60, 90, 120, 180 days) and the correct filters show up at their doorstep automatically with a notice that it's time to replace their filters. FREE shipping included, of course! Simple. Easy. Automatic. Long Term Recurring Revenue included!

Groupon.com – the Group Coupon Site

This is a rapidly growing site that "cuts both ways." Groupon brings merchants and vendors increased customer traffic while also bringing discounts to the customers themselves.

Every day the site offers a discounted price on a product or service in cities around the country. Subscribers to the site are notified by e-mail about the "deal of the day" in their hometowns. I personally love this business model. It can be used in almost ANY industry and I expect to see many more sites with this same business plan in various industries.

But here's the twist. The deal only becomes "activated" when a specific number of people participate. As the site's FAQ explains:

What is Groupon? *Each day, Groupon features an unbeatable deal on the best stuff to do, see, eat, and buy in your city. By promising businesses a minimum number of customers, we get discounts you won't find anywhere else. We call it "collective buying power!"*

If I like today's deal – how do I get it? *Click "BUY" before the offer ends at midnight. If the minimum number of people signs up, we'll charge your card and send you a link to print your Groupon. If not enough people join, no one gets it (and you won't be charged), so invite your friends to make sure you get the deal!*

Clearly, the key to success for a site like Groupon is traffic. The more visitors there are, the more benefits the visitors receive.

Alice.com

In the long history of ways to get rich, one of the most potent techniques is to provide a service that most people DO NOT want to do – especially if it's provided quickly and cheaply. That's the rationale behind Alice.com. Most people don't enjoy shopping for laundry detergent or toilet paper, but we do tend to run out of those things. This site is a good way to deal with that problem and save money at the same time:

Scratch Household Shopping Off the To-Do-List

Alice.com provides you a better way to manage all of your household essentials online. You tell Alice what you buy – choosing from great deals on thousands of products – and Alice goes to work. They organize all of your products, find coupons and deals for you, remind you when you might be running low and help you order just the items you need so you can avoid that trip to the corner drugstore or the big-box store. And all this convenience comes direct to your door with free shipping included.

SAVE MONEY ON IPHONE APP DEVELOPMENT

Thinking of a new iPhone app you want to launch? Not sure where to start? Want to get the lowest price for creating that app?

I met entrepreneur Gregg Weiss at the LeadsCon trade show. He told me about his new website that marries two hot new markets – iPhone app development and getting paid for supplying leads to firms willing to pay for potential clients. If someone has an idea for an iPhone application, iPhoneAppQuotes.com makes it easy to go from idea to application. Their developer network lets you take bids from application developers who want your business.

Need a New Mobile Phone App?

1. Go to iPhoneAppQuotes.com.
2. Answer a list of questions about the application you want to create.
3. Put in your budget.
4. Wait for three developers to contact you with their bid.

Each developer pays $25–$39 per lead based on how much the client is willing to spend on the application to be developed. This is a great win/win/win. It's what *Get Rich Click* is all about!

Think about how you, too, can create a similar concept for another market you want to serve. Check out iPhoneAppQuotes.com.

Smartmoney.com

This is a wide-ranging site on financial issues on every scale, from local to national to global. The personal section is hugely informative about money-saving strategies and tactics.

Foursquare.com

Foursquare is geared to mobile users much more than the other sites we've looked at so far. It's similar to Yelp in the sense that users provide commentary on local businesses – but Foursquare presents this commentary in the form of a flowing and dynamic real-time blog roll, like a speeded-up Twitter. People use Foursquare to "check-in," which is a way of telling others of your whereabouts. When you check-in someplace, the site tells your friends where you are and will recommend places to go and things to do nearby. People check-in at all kinds of places – cafes, bars, restaurants, parks, homes and offices.

Through their mobile phones, users can post about their visits to restaurants, stores and other businesses in their neighborhoods via their cellular phone. In return, they earn points in the online game based on the frequency of their activity and their contributions to the site. In this way Foursquare encourages members to visit local business, and the business rewards them with perks – like free drinks and food.

In turn, the businesses publicize Foursquare, build traffic and could possibly buy advertising, too.

As with Groupon, the biggest beneficiaries of Foursquare are the businesses rather than the site's users. But if the site generates sufficient traffic, this is a game that everyone can "win."

Offers.com

This site provides access to coupons and other discounts for online purchases. Founded by Steve Schaffer in Austin, Texas, the site offers are organized by type of offer and category and updated daily. Offers.com operates on an affiliate model, and receives a commission fee from most of the offers. This fee is paid directly to the site from the merchant and does not increase the user's cost.

Here's how Offers.com describes itself:

- *Offers.com helps you save both by sorting through thousands of promos and deals to bring you only the best offers, organized by category and store.*

- *Types of Offers: If you can buy it online, you'll probably find it on Offers.com, your online shopping destination for 7,000+ offers from 1,500+ travel and service companies and retail stores.*

- *Categories: Offers are organized into 150 intuitive categories, from Computers & Networking to Entertainment & Dining Discounts, Clothing, and Tools & Automotive.*

- *Ways to Save: Get the low-down on the best savings opportunities including Online Coupons & Coupon Codes, Free Shipping Offers, Clearance Offers, Free Trial Offers and Free Offers.*

Internet, Cable and Phone Services

If you take the time to closely examine the bills for these services, you will discover that you are probably paying for more services than you use. Stop paying for what you don't use.

High-speed Internet service has become a necessity. It's an essential utility like electricity or gas. But there are significant variations in price from one provider to another – and you may not need all the bells and whistles that some companies try to sell. If you can sign on to the web and access your e-mail, you've probably got everything you need.

If you ever have a problem with your service – and most people do sooner or later – don't hesitate to bring it to the attention of your provider. Very often they will discount your bill, especially if they think you're angry enough to discontinue the service.

If you use your cell phone a great deal, it might makes sense to cancel your landline account as so many young people seem to do these days. Keep in mind, too, that Skype and other Internet phone services are free for domestic calls, and only about 10 dollars a month for worldwide service. To save money on business phone issues, try visiting this site: comparebusinessphones.com.

CrowdSourcing ... CrowdShopping ... CrowdFunding!

The long reach of the Internet is creating an entire new way to use "groups" to interact, communicate, buy, sell, vote, promote and even fund new business ideas. Add to this the amazing power and reach of the mobile phone and Personal Digital Assistant (PDA) markets and the opportunities for new profit-making ideas are endless. What's your million-dollar idea?

There are outsourcing sites for virtually every occupation, as well as for general business needs. Three of the best websites I can recommend are Guru.com, eLance.com and rentacoder.com. Just as eBay is a "broker" or "listing service" for products, these sites play the same role for "services." Whether it is accounting work, an artist, a logo, creating a website – pretty much ANY service you need has folks on these three sites offering to sell their "time" to you for a very competitive price. Often, these suppliers are not in the United States and their rates are as much as 90 percent below the cost of domestic suppliers for similar services.

Reduce Debt

John Cummuta is the author of a very successful multimedia program called "Transforming Debt Into Wealth." His website (Johnmcummuta.com) not only covers the major issues of debt reduction, but also takes a proactive approach toward turning financial liabilities into positive opportunities. This is especially important with regard to credit card debt, which for millions of people is an ongoing concern.

People in debt are faced with increasing costs such as high credit balances and unfair interest rates. It's hard to save money under those conditions. In addition, debt can take an emotional and even a physical toll. It's just a huge energy drain.

On the positive side, debt reduction can be one of the most positive, rewarding, life-changing moves you'll ever make. Reduced debt can improve your health, leading to less stress, lowered blood pressure and fewer headaches. A lower debt burden also can also help maintain or rebuild your credit score, in case there is ever a situation in which a loan is absolutely necessary. Fewer debts can also provide you with more freedom, which you could use to take time off work, pursue an education or even to change careers.

Like hundreds of thousands of people in this country, you may feel you're hopelessly buried under a mountain of debt. But reducing is very doable when it's approached in a systematic way. Follow the guidelines below to get started.

First, face the facts. It's not unusual for people in debt to be totally unaware of the reality of their financial situation. They live in a kind of denial that can make their lives very complicated unless they do something about it. The first step is awareness of the problem. One must face it head-on.

10 Steps to Reduce Your Debt

1. Make a list of all of the companies you owe money to (credit cards, car loans, store credit cards, student loans, etc.).

2. Add up your credit debt and the cost of monthly payments.

3. Now look at the total figure. You may be surprised at the amount. You may even be horrified. But at least you are aware, and that's the first step toward financial freedom and peace of mind.

4. Get rid of your nonessential credit cards. The fewer cards you have, the less temptation you have to spend.

5. Cut the cards into pieces, then phone the card companies and inform them so that there is no chance of credit card fraud.

6. Do not acquire new cards.

7. Keep one card. This card is for emergency situations or travel, and it should be the card with the best rate and lowest annual fee.

8. When choosing which card to keep, pay no attention to the introductory offer, as that does not last long enough to matter. Read the fine print on the monthly bill to determine which card is really the least expensive.

9. Prioritize your payments. High interest and secured debts should be paid first. These include mortgage and car payments. With all debts, exceed the minimum monthly payment whenever possible. By doing so, you can reduce the debt faster and save money by avoiding the accrued interest.

10. Consolidate your debts to the greatest possible extent. Transfer all of your credit card balances to the card with the lowest interest rate. Doing this may seem like a hassle, but reducing interest rates by even a fraction can save you a surprisingly large amount of money.

As your debt reduction program starts to work, use the money you've saved to further pay down your obligations. Being totally debt free is the ultimate goal. It's a high priority mission with you as both the cause and the beneficiary. You have to be willing to go to any lengths to raise enough money to be free of debt as quickly as possible.

TIME = MONEY
Time is valuable as long as work is being accomplished in a given time frame. When workers are idle, money cannot be made, and a business cannot grow.
Time IS Money!

eBook On "Jumping" Lands Young Author Millions

Jacob Hiller turned his interest in jumping into huge Internet sales and millions of dollars.

Hiller was in college- not doing great academically- when he decided to post a YouTube video teaching people how to do what he loved best…jump high.

"I was the young kid who wanted to dunk just like most young boys and I never really grew out of it," said Hiller. "I went from one [system] to another that worked or didn't work, so I developed my own theories on how to get high in the air, then started training other people to do it."

In his first video, he gave some very basic advice about how to jump higher. "I turned on the webcam and said, 'Here's what I did. Here's one tip for you.' I didn't have a master plan. I had one tip to give and then the next week I gave another one," Hiller explained.

The video was so popular Hiller decided to remove his YouTube videos, create a website and sell an eBook. He made what he describes as a "very ugly" website and wrote *The Jump Manual*, a 10-chapter, 80-page book of tips and information on jumping, including instructional video.

Initially Hiller gave *The Jump Manual* away for free until the testimonials began rolling in. Then he sold the eBook for $15 through PayPal on his own site.

The turning point, and large monthly checks, started when he joined ClickBank, a huge online affiliate network. "When we put it on ClickBank, the affiliates were going crazy with it. A few months later we were making a few thousand dollars a month from the e-book," he said. "ESPN had picked us up and *Sports Illustrated* contacted us and *Men's Health* and it just kind of blew up from there."

"By 2010, *The Jump Manual* was selling for $67 with the option of adding monthly coaching services. Hiller estimates that in 2010, he sold up to 1,000 books per month, earning up to $75,000 monthly.

In fact, if the *The Jump Manual* had been published traditionally, his sales would have earned it *New York Times* bestseller status, a feat many hope for, but very few accomplish.

For those interested in selling books online, Hiller advises: "Don't come across like you're trying to sell something." And just as importantly: "Find something you are really passionate about, and that you know can help somebody."

Scan the QR code or go to GetRichClick.com/jacob to watch Jacob's interview.

In *Get Rich Click* fashion, allow me to suggest that you visit eHow.com, a wonderful time-saving website.

Paying for School

The cost of higher education can saddle students – and their parents – with significant debt for many years after graduation. Much of this is avoidable with the right information. Collegemadesimple.com is an excellent resource for all aspects of this issue: Collegemadesimple.com says it can:

- *Help parents of college-bound students navigate through the extremely complex and time-consuming college admissions and financial-aid processes.*

- *Help design plans that allows parents to more easily afford to pay for their children's education and guide them step-by-step from the cradle to college graduation and beyond.*

- *Help students pick the school that's the right "fit" for them (and their parents' pocket books!), which guides them to discover their true strengths and talents. This, in turn, leads students to making sound college selection choices and puts them on a clear path toward prosperous and rewarding careers and lives post-college.*

"HIRE YOUR WEAKNESS"
– Marc Ostrofsky

"Do what *you* do best. Outsource the rest." This has always been one of my key principles, and it's definitely an important aspect of saving money to make money. If you were a professional photographer, you'd certainly need to take a lot of photos in order to make money. You'd also need a "back-end system" online to handle your website, sales process, payments and much more. But maybe that's not really what you're good at. You're just good at taking photographs. Fortunately, sites like ifp3.com can handle everything for a photographer except taking the photos. All the photographer needs to do is sign up, do a free trial, list the photos for sale and wait for the orders to come in. Marketing and getting listed on the search engines is very important to increase sales of your work.

Air Travel

Sites like Travelocity.com and Expedia.com were pioneers in providing access to discounted airfares. Now that those sites are well established, other sites like Kayak.com have sprung up that can sometimes beat the mainstream prices by offering a consolidated, one-stop-shopping option made up of several other websites.

If you have some flexibility in your travel dates, some of the major flight booking sites offer a feature that can save you money. You can enter the price you're willing to pay for a specific trip, and the site will send an electronic "alert" to your computer when that price becomes available. Here's how this feature is described on expedia.com:

Expedia Fare Alert

- *Get bargain fares for your flights delivered right to your computer desktop.*
- *Simply download the latest Fare Alert and a small icon is installed onto your desktop. Set your flight and fare. When Expedia finds a fare that meets or beats your price selection, a small window pops up briefly to alert you.*
- *Fare Alert supports most domestic airports. Look to see if the departure airport nearest your home is supported.*

Bookingwiz.com is a useful linking site to all the various ticketing agencies, both new and old. The site is easy to use and very complete. This can save you money!

eTickets.com

Ticket scalping is a very old enterprise, and it's alive and well online. There are lots of ticket sites, but most of them are controlled by one of two players that consolidate tickets. So if you look closely, you will find THE EXACT SAME TICKETS on most of the sites. In any market, where there are numerous players competing for the same buyer, prices can be all over the board and you can make money or save money by understanding this and buying or selling accordingly. Next time you need event tickets in a hurry, remember to use eTickets.com.

Seeing New Ideas . . . "Clearly!"

As I waited in the doctor's office for my Lasik surgery, I thought of creating an iPhone app that offers an "eye test" and then connects to a local doctor to get your eyes checked. You would get paid EACH TIME anyone signed up to go and see one of the doctors working with your "site." See the chapter on making money with LEAD GENERATION. Wouldn't you know it, the application already exists via a cool app called eyeXam.

From that same playbook, why not create a free iPhone app that helps inform the consumer about a product or service – then offers to connect them to a supplier who pays you for each new client or lead. Think about all the possible connections between the mobile phones and computer databases. You'll be overwhelmed by the possibilities!

MORE WAYS TO SAVE MONEY ONLINE . . .

Real Estate Costs

Yahoo offers a tool that lets you calculate the cost differential between owning a home or renting, depending on what interest rate you get. If you can do this in your head, you're a mathematical genius. Otherwise go to: realestate.yahoo.com/calculators/rent_vs_own.html.

Automobile Prices

This site provides a huge amount of information about prices for hundreds of makes and models: pricequotes.com.

Computers

Just as with cars, there is a major cost differential between a new computer and a used one. Here's an excellent site for exploring the details online: usedlaptops.com.

Personal Financial Planning

Even with all the information that's available on the web, there may be areas of your financial life that you're just not sure about. In fact, there may be a lot of them. Some sessions with a personal financial planner can be of great help, and despite an up-front cost, the ultimate result can save you money. A good place to start looking for a financial planner in your area is the homepage of the national association: napfa.org.

Online Coupons

Do NOT buy anything online without looking for a coupon first. You can also turn this around: go to couponcabin.com and see which stores are offering discount coupons. All the major chains are linked on that site. Then, if you need or will need anything from those vendors, you can make your purchase at a discount. Other coupon sites include: couponmom.com., smartsource.com. and valpak.com/coupons/home.

Putting Your Ideas into Action

Research shows that 60 percent of all Americans are worried about running out of money. Instead of worrying, do something about it. Here are some steps you can take right away to help you Get Rich Click! by saving money: Sites that offer similar "low fare alerts" like the expedia alert range from alerts on domain name availability, real estate prices and mortgage interest rates. A little bit of research can save you a lot of money!

- Saving money is as smart as making money . . . both add to your bottom line!
- Always look for coupons when shopping online.
- Realize there are huge opportunities to create new websites with the convergence of computers, telecommunications, database marketing, Internet and mobile phones. Think of a new iPhone app that connects buyers and sellers.
- Look for "low fare alerts" on websites you visit. Sign up for these alerts and you will be notified when the lower prices become available.

16

The Future

The *Get Rich Click* mindset considers the past, present and future as it can influence current and upcoming trends in the marketplace. Trends are the next indication of hot opportunities, but that doesn't mean you need to discover the next Amazon, Facebook or Google.

Most of those who have profited from the Internet simply built a "better mousetrap." They took a hot market and jumped in at the right time with a competitive or complementary product, service or offering. Many individuals have made their fortunes auctioning on eBay, buying and selling domain names, arbitraging Internet traffic, selling leads or selling other products and services via the Internet. Others are making excellent incomes offering new tools – digital-based "picks and shovels" – to the growing number of companies and individuals who are building websites that attract eyeballs.

When assessing your future opportunities, don't think you have to be first in a growing market. It's never too late to jump into your own business with one or several of the many models discussed in *Get Rich Click*. If, in addition to stellar customer service, you have an offering that is complementary or competitive, it can translate into a loyal following and future success for you. Remember, it's all in the numbers. Get a higher quality and quantity of traffic than your competitors and you should be successful in whatever you do online.

Pay Attention to Trends

Watch the market dynamics. Keep an eye on buying patterns. Learn everything you can, not only from the success stories, but also from the failures. Very often, failures and mistakes reveal valuable knowledge that will increase your chances of future success.

Routinely investigate different trade shows you might attend, and read the trade magazines that appeal to you. Listen to industry experts and relevant speeches any chance you get. These all represent great places to discover trends and learn about the latest and greatest developments in the market as well as the latest and greatest customer needs.

When thinking about future trends, you only have to look at past trends. Remember using the phrase "space age"? We don't hear that phrase much anymore because it has become commonplace. The same thing will happen with "the Internet," or "going online." In ten years, will our "green" movement away from paper-based products have us saying it's a great book or a great "read" because physical books will be few and far between?

Increasingly, people don't think of going online as setting out for a destination in a geographical sense. Instead, they're entering a state of being continuously connected. As more devices are integrated with the Internet, being online becomes necessary to work and play. Just look at people who own an Internet-connected mobile device like a Blackberry, iPhone or Android. Their lives are very different; they are constantly connected to their world and can act sooner, faster and more efficiently. Companies are adapting to such changes but at a much slower pace.

Look overseas for successful websites, trends and other Internet applications. This is such a simple idea, especially for those who are from another country or have friends and family overseas. You can bet that the hottest Internet trends and applications will be coming to a website near you very shortly. Think about creating a similar product, service or venture and have it ready for a larger firm to acquire. Many larger companies prefer to purchase an existing, proven model rather than risk building a competing product or service that may not take root.

Consider some of these current trends:

- Cellular phones that interact with the Internet can help you purchase a soft drink from a vending machine.
- Getting instant directions from the intersection you are sitting at.
- Read your text messages to you as "voice" mail.
- Read the latest magazine you subscribe to (and send the one section you really like to read to your e-mail inbox).
- Send a "text" message to someone in your own "voice."

In the future, the Internet will hold our world together even more . . . and the opportunities are already vast right now! We're only *just* beginning. Think about what applications are coming down the pipe from the merger of telecommunications, computers, consumer electronics, mobile phones, PDAs and the Internet. It's nothing short of a shocking number of new, cool, innovative ways to profit from these mergers!

Already, few people remember a world without personal computers. The younger generation won't remember a world without cell phones or the Internet. My own five teenage daughters have no idea what life was like before people could text each other on a moment-by-moment basis. What has happened, what will happen, is normal, organic change in action. Some might see this as a generational shift, but the changes going on right now represent a complete paradigm shift – physically and intellectually – in how the world works, plays, interacts and communicates.

Telecom + Computers + Internet + Consumer Electronics = Unlimited Opportunity

The reason so many of the new "mega-millionaires" are so young is not just that they get it and have grown up with it, but that they are not afraid of trying it. Using it. Testing it. And pushing it to the limits. In most cases, "it" means the Internet, the iPhone, the iPad and the many applications and new websites and mobile phone apps that make their lives easier to manage and money easier to make. Older Americans can't imagine a home without a phone connected to the wall yet the younger generation can't understand why their parents and grandparents keep paying for a wall phone when the same phone calls can be made on their mobile devices.

Alas, the truth is, they also know if they fail, they don't have far to fall compared to a 45-year-old man with a house, credit card bills, a mortgage, a few cars, two children, two college tuition bills and a full-time job to manage.

Silicon Crispies, a cereal for the New Millennium.

Consider the whole area of digital photography. I recall asking why anyone would choose a digital format over film. Now I am a professional photographer in my spare time (photos at MarcOstrofsky.com) and have not used film in many years. Digital cameras have redefined the photography industry. Sites like ImageKind.com and blurb.com allow even the most amateur artist to buy, sell and create art pieces and professional photo books directly from a digital download. Technology makes it possible to capture any image from a video and present it with the same quality as a digital camera.

Your entrepreneurial spirit, believing possibilities like these can and will happen, helps you understand how to plan a business around them – and the possibilities are endless.

I forecast that in a very short time frame, videographers will "film" a wedding, pull the very best digital "photos" from their digital videos and create photographic quality prints that are just as good as the photographer's shots. That means *NEVER* missing "the shot" and every photo album will be "perfect." Such developments profoundly affect traditional methods for photographing an event and necessitate a dramatic shift in how we think about various artistic media and industries like photography.

As the Internet matures, it will become more of an art form rather than an overt homage to technology. Design, layout and ease of use are becoming more vital to your success on the small screens of computers, mobile devices and PDAs.

Just as silent movies defined a nascent cinematic industry and black-and-white television pioneered its industry, the Internet will mature beyond YouTube, Facebook and Google in a relatively short time.

There will also be challenges. Security will always be a challenge. Bill Gates stated online security was the biggest issue Microsoft and the industry as a whole faces. By now, you know, in the spirit of *Get Rich Click*, challenges turn into opportunities. Where do you want to make money in this high-growth market of doing business on the Internet?

Some countries may not be as accepting of all of this connectivity. Those that don't embrace the vital position the Internet has in a global economy will fall further behind the digital divide I discussed in Chapter 1. Innovation will continue to reward those who pursue it. Innovation is most successful when innovators communicate easily with anyone, anywhere, at any time on a global scale. The Internet lets this happen now, and it will become more widely accepted as a meeting place for brainstorming. This bodes well for innovation.

CLICK TIP ▷ As security methods improve, opportunities will proliferate for anyone who can help firms become more secure by teaching and implementing security methods.

As we've seen throughout this book, we're living in a time of revolutionary change in the way information is shared. And it's getting even more revolutionary by the minute. Desktop and laptop computers have been at the forefront of the revolution for the past twenty years, but they're no longer the cutting edge. Smartphones like the Android, the Blackberry and – especially – the Apple iPhone and iPad offer possibilities that no one even imagined just a few years ago. It's like being able to shoot your own film and show it to your friends (and customers) in your own movie theater. And the theater can be carried around in your pocket!

The Apple iPhone was introduced to the public in January 2007. Now it's the iPad and Droid that are "Hot." Right from the start there was tremendous excitement about the iPhone, and long lines formed at Apple stores where it was available. The iPhone was a cultural event as well as a communication instrument. They were purchased by collectors, eBay resellers, and even a few people who just wanted to talk on their cell phones.

"APPortunity of a Lifetime™"

For savvy web entrepreneurs, creating smartphone
apps are an incredible chance to Get Rich Click.
Your website can be accessible to
anyone, anywhere, at any time.
No computer necessary!

For our purposes, the definition of an app will be functional rather than technical. We won't delve into the process of writing code or any of the other operations that are required for software creation. As far as we're concerned, an app is a piece of software that allows you to reach web users 24/7, provided only that they are connected to the Internet through a computer, tablet PC or a cell phone.

Some of the most popular and profitable early apps were games, and games are still hugely sought after. The game called Farmville, for example, has been played by 50 million people! Farmville is owned by Zynga, a company that didn't even exist a few years ago. Zynga has also created Mafia Wars and Pathwords. Some of these games are free, and some of them (like Farmville) call upon players to make small investments of real cash. For Zynga, the main crop of Farmville is cash!

Do It Yourself

As happened when Apple introduced the Macintosh desktop in the early 1980s, the iPhone offered a vision of unlimited possibilities. A huge step toward actualizing that vision took place when Apple began offering a software development kit (SDK). This made it possible for anyone to independently create apps that could be downloaded onto iPhones.

Now the universe of potential apps has been exponentially expanded. It isn't just games anymore. Business owners and entrepreneurs of all kinds can make their products and services available to the world through smartphones. Best of all, no special technical knowledge is required. There are user-friendly companies ready to configure apps according to your needs.

Here are a few more "million dollar apps" of the kind that have prospered since the iPhone's introduction:

ENIGMO
Sales: $2.5 million
Company: Pangea
Navigate water mazes by pinching, dragging and dropping

ROLLER-COASTER RUSH
Sales: $1.1 million
Company: Digital Chocolate
Tilt a cart through loop-the-loops and steep drops

F.A.S.T.
Sales: $1.8 million
Company: SGN
Engage in aerial combat on your phone

FLICK FISHING
Sales: $1 million
Company: Freeverse
Cast a line by waving your phone in the air, then reel 'em in

OCARINA
Sales: $1.3 million
Company: Smule
Turn any iPhone into a woodwind instrument

iFART
Sales: $750,000
Company: InfoMedia, Inc.
One of the world's most famous iPhone novelty applications

(Source, *BusinessWeek* Oct 22, 2009; Data: Company reports)

Change Is the Only Constant

The landscape of apps is changing faster than any other area of the information economy. There is a constant shifting mix of technical capabilities, rules, regulations and new innovations. The market pioneered by the Apple iPhone is being invaded by new phones from Google and other companies. To be perfectly frank, anything you read here maybe out of date by the time this book is published. So you'll need to do some of your own research online. But that research is absolutely worth doing.

Almost certainly, the real future of *Get Rich Click* is in smartphone technology. If you doubt that, just count the number of people you see staring at their phones as you walk down the street. All of those people are your potential customers. Because when it comes to cell phones, there are so many useful apps, they just can't help themselves!

CLICK TIP ▷ One area I am watching very closely is the HUGE growth in YouTube and other video-based sites that is about to hit. With the growth of broadband worldwide and the next generation of television sets coming out "YouTube Ready," you will see massive amounts of video hitting the Internet allowing anyone to be their own TV Reality Star!

Now and Then: What's Next?

A host of young start-ups have created tools and services for the web-literate. Here's only a fraction of what you can now do online:

- Organize your life with tools Technology Review has created.
- Keep your social calendar at Eventful.
- Organize your to-do items at Goodtodo.
- Read the news (or write your own) at Newsvine.
- Find hours of video entertainment and business information at sites like YouTube and Jumpcut.
- Create and share web bookmarks at Diigo.
- Create podcasts and audio memos at Odeo.
- Publish your own blog or read someone else's at Wordpress, LiveJournal, Xanga, even through search engines like Google (Blogger).
- Manage your company's projects at BaseCamp.
- Conduct online meetings with anyone anywhere in the world, letting participants view the organizer's actual computer screen and sustain ongoing private chats with other participants, with GoToMeeting.
- Share photographs (and get prints) at businesses like Flickr, Buzznet, Photobucket, Bubbleshare and Zoomr. Some of these sites even allow you to share music and videos. All for free. With a *Get Rich Click* mindset, you can put yourself in business, doing any of the hundreds of ideas in this book for other people or companies for a fee.

When we look back, the opportunities seem obvious. What obvious opportunities can you find looking forward? Many opportunities are simple in nature, but it's ultimately out-of-the-box thinking that's at work here – imagining a business, following a deliberate path, adding an Internet component and coming up with a new product or service. It's happening more and more every day.

Think what would happen if an online networking site hooked up with an online video site. You could create introductions instead of the basic written 30-second commercials for your business. Look at what's happening with audiovisual search engines. These are examples of combined business models and ways to *Get Rich Click*.

The Internet is everywhere; it's not only the present, it's the future and you can learn a lot just by looking around. Absorb as much information as you can. Learn from others. The costly mistakes you will make have most likely been made by others. Understand why some models work and others don't. Getting rich won't happen over the course of a weekend, but if you pay attention to the principles in this book, you, too, can be on your way to finding new ways to *Get Rich Click*!

If you can imagine it, you can do it on the Internet. Once you get an idea, plan it, develop it, scale it and get it in front of customers. Taking any of the ideas in *Get Rich Click* and combining them with others may create new products or services the world is looking for.

Now Get Going!

Making money on the Internet is a dynamic undertaking; the playing field is ever changing. There are those who embrace the cutting edge. As soon as you read about something today, someone is probably applying it, refining it, making it better and more versatile. Think twitter.com. Someone is devising a whole new way to accomplish it. Start implementing your business ideas and pursuing areas for which you have a passion. It can be fun and it can make you money.

You have come to the end of this book and the beginning of your new mind-set! You are now equipped with a host of ways for you or your company to make and save money via the Internet. You are limited only by your imagination; and there is no end to what humans can imagine. There is no end to the ways to make money in a world where the Internet is the central way we interact, communicate and entertain ourselves.

Good luck. I sincerely hope you *Get Rich Click*!

My Secrets to Your Success . . .

I've been involved in marketing most of my life, and along the way I've learned some important "secrets." These perspectives are real. They are on target. They make all the difference.

1. **Know what you don't know.** So many people really can't tell you what they don't know – they don't have a clue. Find out what you don't know and bring in the best people who have the knowledge you lack.

2. **Learn from the best (and never stop learning).** Learn from people who are smarter than you. Learn from people who have been there, who have made the mistakes and know the tips, tricks and secrets! Never stop learning. Just remember, it's smarter (and cheaper) to learn on their nickel!

3. **KISS.** Keep it simple, silly (Okay . . . stupid). Don't get caught up trying to become the next Google, Facebook, PayPal or eBay. These success stories receive all the publicity and notoriety but are the one in a million exceptions. More often than not, the other 999,996 situations out there offer great *Get Rich Click* opportunities, too. Think smaller ventures that do make money, require little to no investment and can be done over and over. The best ideas are often simple ones that are easy to clone or adapt to your situation.

4. **Don't get caught up in "it's already been done" thinking.** I hear this all the time: "If it's already out there, why should I do it?" or, "If someone else is selling it, why should I?" With this sort of thinking, there would be only one make of car on the market, one brand of computer and one type of shoe. Very often, creating something new, whether it's a product, a service or even a new business model, comes from recombining pieces that already exist. Add in an element of thinking outside the box, and you might find yourself coming up with the next site that makes money from day one and gets sold for $10 million!

5. **Pay for the best person you can afford.** Make that person part of your support network, whether in a business or as part of your entrepreneurial ventures. One $40,000 employee is often worth much more than two $20,000 people.

6. **Hire the right attitude.** When you come across those rare people who have a great personality, who are energetic and enthusiastic about life, whom you immediately like and want to be around, hire them.

7. **Hire your weakness.** You can probably add and subtract, but a good certified public accountant (CPA) can often pay for himself many times over with efficiencies and strengths. Hire others that have the skills you may not have.

8. **Do what you enjoy and stick to what you do best.** When you pursue things that interest you, things in which you are accomplished, not only is life a lot more interesting and fun, but your riches will come in more ways than one!

9. Ask questions, cultivate contacts. I was the kid in class who always had a question. I've also developed incredible contacts from so many sources – seminars, conventions, conferences, and reading constantly. To be successful in business and stay one step ahead of the competition, you must never stop asking questions, researching your subject and knowing all the players in the game.

10. If at first you don't succeed . . . The last principle comes from Albert Einstein, who said, "Insanity: doing the same thing over and over again and expecting different results." If one approach doesn't produce the outcome you'd hoped for, come at the situation from a different angle. As the nature of the Internet is constantly changing, creative flexibility is a huge asset.

"Its an Internet-ready, tri-mode, LCD color, MP3 compatible, digital wireless communicator. We make them extra big so people will notice how cool you are."

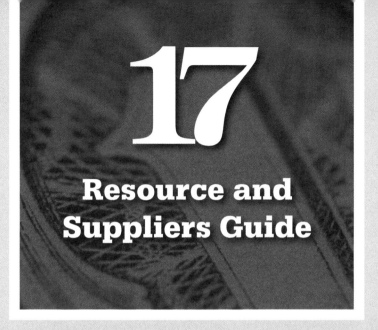

17
Resource and Suppliers Guide

On the following pages are resources to get you started on your road to *Get Rich Click*. It's by no means a complete listing, but it includes a number of the major players.

The *Get Rich Click*
Top 25 Internet Conferences

1. **Affiliate Summit** affiliatesummit.com

2. **Blog World** blogworld.com

3. **AdTech** ad-tech.com

4. **Click Z Events** events.clickz.com

5. **Direct Marketing Days** the-dma.org/conferences/dmdays10

6. **Domain Round Table** domainroundtable.com

7. **EcomXpo** wbresearch.comecomxpo

8. **eTail** wbresearch.com/etailusawest

9. **Internet Retailer** irce.internetretailer.com/2011

10. **Online Marketing Summit** onlinemarketingsummit.com

11. **PPC Summit** ppcsummit.com

12. **Search Engine Strategies** searchenginestrategies.com

13. **T.R.A.F.F.I.C** targetedtraffic.com

14. **PubCon** pubcon.com

15. **Online Retailer** onlineretailer.net

16. **Search Marketing Expo** searchmarketingexpo.com

17. **Streaming Media** streamingmedia.com

18. **Direct Marketing Conference and Exhibition** dma.org

19. **Internet World** internetworld.co.uk

20. **LeadsCon** leadscon.com

21. **The Power of eMarketing Conference** emarketingassociation.com

22. **OMMA – Expo** omma-expo.com

23. **Domain Fest** domainfest.com

24. **Link Share** linkshare.com

25. **Affiliate Marketing Conference and Exposition** a4uexpo.com

The *Get Rich Click*
Top 25 Public Motivational Business Speakers

1. **Jeffrey Gitomer** gitomer.com
2. **Les Brown** lesbrown.com
3. **Jack Canfield** jackcanfield.com
4. **Stephen Covey** stephencovey.com
5. **David Bach** finishrich.com
6. **John Assaraf** johnassaraf.com
7. **Brian Tracy** briantracy.com
8. **Sharon Lechter** slechter.com
9. **Steve Harrison** reporterconnection.com
10. **Marshal Sylver** sylver.com
11. **Marci Shimoff** happyfornoreason.com
12. **Jay Conrad Levinson** gmarketing.com
13. **Tony Robbins** tonyrobbins.com
14. **Mark Victor Hansen** markvictorhansen.com
15. **Mike Koenigs** mikekoenigs.com
16. **Susan Sweeney** susansweeney.com
17. **Joel Comm** joelcomm.com
18. **Robert Kiyosaki** richdad.com
19. **Jim Kwik** jimkwik.com
20. **Yanik Silver** Yaniksilver.com
21. **Stephen Pierce** dtalpha.com
22. **Jay Abrams** abraham.com
23. **Keith Ferrazzi** keithferrazzi.com
24. **Anthony Morrison** anthonymorrison.com
25. **Bill Walsh** billwalsh360.com

The *Get Rich Click*
Top 25 SEO Firms

1. SEO.com

2. iProspect iprospect.com

3. Outrider outrider.com

4. White Hat Media whitehatmedia.com

5. Edit Optimisation editoptimisation.co.uk

6. Leap Frog Interactive leapfroginteractive.com

7. Spark Inbound Marketing sparkinboundmarketing.com

8. Seer Interactive seerinteractive.com

9. Exclusive Concepts exclusiveconcepts.com

10. yMarketing ymarketing.com

11. Seologist seologist.com

12. Qualified Impressions qualifiedimpressions.com

13. First in Search firstinsearch.com

14. DDS Agency ddsagency.com

15. Found Search Marketing foundsm.com

16. Sticky Eyes stickyeyes.com

17. Position Research positionresearch.com

18. Red Spot Design dallasseocompany.com

19. Leverage Marketing, LLC leveragemarketing.net

20. E-Storm International e-storm.com

21. 97th Floor 97thfloor.com

22. Steak Limited steakdigital.co.uk

23. Eye Flow eyeflow.com

24. Yellow SEO yellowseo.com

25. Crexendo crexendo.com

The *Get Rich Click*
Top 25 Websites That Can Make You Money
Right Away (Put You in Business)

1. **Ecrater.com:** ecrater.com

2. **Zazzle.com** zazzle.com

3. **Oodle.com** oodle.com

4. **CafePress.com** cafepress.com

5. **RedBubble.com** redbubble.com

6. **ImageKind.com** imagekind.com

7. **PrintFection.com** printfection.com

8. **RocketLife.com** rocketlife.com

9. **Mercantec.com** mercantec.com

10. **Shopster.com** shopster.com

11. **Blurb.com** blurb.com

12. **Qoop.com** qoop.com

13. **BlastOff.com** blastoff.com

14. **CityMax.com** citymax.com

15. **HomeStead.com** homestead.com

16. **Volusion.com** volusion.com

17. **Customink.com** customink.com

18. **Dawanda** en.dawanda.com

19. **Chacha.com** chacha.com

20. **Etsy.com** etsy.com

21. **Just Answer** justanswer.com

22. **Bitwine** bitwine.com

23. **ClickNWork** clicknwork.com

24. **About.com** about.com

25. **Ether** ether.com

The *Get Rich Click*
Top 25 Facebook Groups

1. Social Income Group
2. Crowd Conversion Social Media Marketing
3. Business Café
4. Web 2.0
5. Affiliate Marketing
6. Make Money Online
7. Facebook Addicted
8. Internet Marketing School
9. 5,000 Friends in 40 Days
10. Twitter
11. Network Marketing Revolution
12. Ultimate Exposure
13. The Women's Prosperity Network
14. Facebook + Twitter + Successful Thinkers
15. Affiliate Marketing Opportunities
16. Internet Marketing University On Facebook
17. 6 Figures From Home
18. Facebook Domain Name Network
19. The Ultimate Internet Marketing Mastermind
20. Top Secret Internet Marketing Strategies
21. AdTech Internet Marketing
22. The Women of Internet Marketing
23. Network Marketing – How to Build Online
24. Advertise Your Business Here and Twitter For Free
25. Ultimate Exposure! ~ Grow Your Contacts List Insanely FAST!

The *Get Rich Click*
Top 25 Internet Marketing Firms

1. **Increase Visibility, Inc** increasevisibility.com

2. **WebiMax** webimax.com

3. **SEOP** seop.com

4. **Intrapromote.LLC** intrapromote.com

5. **ArteWorks SEO** arteworks.biz

6. **OneUpWeb** oneupweb.com

7. **SEO Image Inc** seoimage.com

8. **Customer Magnetism** customermagnatism.com

9. **ThinkBIGsites** thinkbigsites.com

10. **WebMetro** webmetro.com

11. **Weblinx Limited** weblinx.co.uk

12. **Web.com Search Agency** submitawebsite.com

13. **Submit Express** submitexpress.com

14. **WebpageFX** webpagefx.com

15. **Bruce Clay, Inc.** bruceclay.com

16. **1st on the List Promotion, Inc.** 1stonthelist.ca

17. **SEO.com** seo.com

18. **High Position Limited** highposition.net

19. **Direct Hit Solutions, Inc.** directhitsolutions.com

20. **SEO Inc.** seoinc.com

21. **Peak Positions, LLC** peakpositions.com

22. **Elephant Traffic** elephant-traffic.com

23. **First Page SEO** first-page-seo.com

24. **HighPoint Search marketing** highpointseo.com

25. **Elite SEO Marketing** eliteseomarketing.com

The *Get Rich Click*
Top 25 SEO Blogs

1. **Search Engine Land** searchengineland.com

2. **SEO Book** seobook.com

3. **SEOmoz.org** seomoz.org

4. **Matt Cutts** mattcutts.com/blog

5. **Search Engine Watch** blog.searchenginewatch.com

6. **SE Round Table** seroundtable.com

7. **Search Engine Journal** searchenginejournal.com

8. **Top Rank Blogging** toprankblog.com

9. **Pronet Advertising** pronetadvertising.com

10. **Marketing Pilgrim** marketingpilgrim.com

11. **SEO Chat** seochat.com

12. **Search Engine Guide** searchengineguide.com

13. **SEO Black Hat** seoblackhat.com

14. **StuntDubl.com** stuntdubl.com

15. **Graywolf's SEO Blog** wolf-howl.com

16. **SEO by the Sea** seobythesea.com

17. **Link Building Blog** linkbuildingblog.com

18. **Jim Boykin's Blog** webuildpages.comjim

19. **SEO Pedia** seopedia.org

20. **David Naylor** davidnaylor.co.uk

21. **Bruce Clay** bruceclay.com

22. **Blue Hat SEO** bluehatseo.com

23. **SubmitExpress** submitexpress.com

24. **SEO Refugee** seorefugee.com

25. **Small Business Search Marketing** smallbusinesssem.com

The *Get Rich Click*
Top 25 Making the Most of Twitter

1. Tony Robbins tonyrobbins.com

2. Zappos.com, Inc. zappos.com

3. Icanhas Cheez Burger cheezburger.com

4. Woot! woot.com

5. MSNBC msnbc.msn.com

6. SomeCards somecards.com

7. Jet Blue jetblue.com

8. Jack Dorsey twitter.com/jack

9. Threadless threadless.com

10. Jimmy Eat World jimmyeatworld.com

11. Whole Foods Market wholefoodsmarket.comtwitter

12. Stockington stockington.com

13. Etsy etsy.com

14. Cake Wrecks cakewrecks.com

15. Twitt Cause experienceproject.comtwitcause

16. TheNextWeb.com thenextweb.com

17. Daily Candy dailycandy.com

18. Good goodinc.com

19. Twitter Moms twittermoms.com

20. Non Profit Wordpress.com nonprofitorgs.wordpress.com

21. OMG Facts omg-facts.com

22. Mr. Tweet mr.tweet.com

23. Gary Vay Ner Chuk garyvaynerchuk.com

24. The Digital Royalty thedigitalroyalty.com

25. Streamy Awards streamys.org

The *Get Rich Click* Top 25 Blogs
That Will Help You Make Money Blogging

1. **Shoe Money** shoemoney.com

2. **John Chow** johnchow.com

3. **ProBlogger.com** problogger.com

4. **Incomediary.com** incomediary.com

5. **Performancing** performancing.com

6. **Copy Blogger** blogcatalog.com

7. **Make Money Online** makemoneyonlinewithejcooksey.com

8. **Greens Real World Blogspot** greensrealworld.blogspot.com

9. **Entrepreneurs-Journey** entrepreneurs-journey.com

10. **Internet Marketing for Mommies** internetmarketingformommies.com

11. **Lip-Sticking** lipsticking.com

12. **Social Hallucinations** socialhallucinations.com

13. **Bash Bosh** bashbosh.com

14. **Carl Ocab** carlocab.com

15. **Cafe Blogger** cafeblogger.net

16. **Chris Brogan** chrisbrogan.com

17. **Quick Online Tips** quickonlinetips.com

18. **Successful Blog** successful-blog.com

19. **Blog About Your Blog** blogaboutyourblog.com

20. **Blogtrepreneur** blog.entrepreneur.com

21. **Build a Better Blog** buildabetterblog.com

22. **JohnTP** johntp.com

23. **Lorelle on Wordpress** lorelle.wordpress.com

24. **Daily Blog Tips** dailyblogtips.com

25. **I Help You Blog** ihelpyoublog.com

Affiliate Network and Cost-Per-Action Networks

AdBrite adBrite.com

Ad Drive addrive.com

Affiliate.com affiliate.com

AffiliateGuide affiliateguide.com

AffiliateScout Affiliatescout.com

Azoogle Ads azoogleads.com

ClickBank ClickBank.com

Commission Junction cj.com

Commission Soup commissionsoup.com

Ethos Interactive ethosinteractive.com

Flux Ads fluxads.com

HydraNetwork hydranetwork.com

IncentaClick incentaclick.com

KeyNetLinks Keynetlinks.com

Leadger Marketing leadgenmarketing.net

LinkShare linkshare.com

LinkValu LinkValu.com

Market Levarage marketleverage.com

Net Margin netmargin.com

Never Blue Ads neverblueads.com

Offer Web offerweb.com

Partners Edge partnersedge.com

Partner Weekly partnerweekly.com

Performics performics.com

Primary Ads primaryads.com

Python Media pythonmedia.com

Revenue Gateway revenuegateway.com

Revenue Loop revenueloop.com

Rextopia rextopia.com

The Biz Opp Network thebizoppnetwork.com

Traffic Needs trafficneeds.com

ValueClick valueclick.com

Web Jam Ads webjamads.com

XY7 xy7.com

Associations

American Association of Webmasters aawebmasters.com

CTIA – The Wireless Association ctia.org

eMarketingAssociation eMarketingAssociation.com

Direct Marketing Association the-dma.org

Internet Commerce Association internetcommerce.org

Search Engine Marketing Professional Organization sempo.org

Web Analytics Association webanalyticsassociation.org

World of Mouth Marketing Association Womma.org

Contextual Marketing Networks

AOL advertising.aol.comtechnologysponsored-listings

adSter adster.com

ContextWeb contextWeb.com

Miva Miva.com

TextLinkAds Text-Link-Ads.com

Domain Name Registrars and Resellers

Afternic Afternic.com

BuyDomains buydomains.com

Great Domains greatdomains.com

Network Solutions networksolutions.com

Pool pool.com

Register.com register.com

Snapnames snapnames.com

TuCows tucows.com

1&1 1and1.com

Domain Name Parking Firms

DomainSpa domainspa.com

DomainSponsor Domainsponsor.com

Fabulous Fabulous.com

Hit Farm hitfarm.com

Parking Dots parkingdots.com

Register.com register.com

Sedo sedo.com

TrafficValet TrafficValet.com

TrafficZ TrafficZ.com

Drop Shipping and Wholesale Product Suppliers

Cafe Press CafePress.com

DOBA Doba.com

DH Gate dhgate.com

Drop Ship Design Dropshipdesign.com

Drop Ship Review Dropship-Review.com

Drop Ship Sites dropshipsites.com

MegaGoods megagoods.com

Shopster shopster.com

Simplx simplx.com

Worldwide Brands worldwidebrands.com

E-mail Marketing Software and Services

AWeber Aweber.com

Constant Contact Constantcontact.com

iContact iContact.com

Benchmark Benchmarkemail.com

InfusionSoft infusionsoft.com

IntelliContact IntelliContact.com

Lyris Lyris.com

LyriseMail Labs eMaillabs.com

My Newsletter Builder mynewsletterbuilder.com

Streamsend Streamsend.com

StrongMail Strongmail.com

SubscriberMail Subscribermail.com

Freelance Employee Sites

Note: Type "outsourcing" into your search engine for more options in this category.

eLance eLance.com

Bid Job Bid-job.com

GoFreelance GoFreelance.com

Guru Guru.com

Rent-a-Coder RentACoder.com

Internet Advertising Networks
(see also Search Engines Listing on page 236)

Avantlink Avantlink.com

AZoogle azoogle.com

ClickBank ClickBank.com

Modern Click Network modernclick.com

Share a Sale Shareasale.com

Trade Doubler Tradedoubler.com

Internet Dictionary Sites

Note: I've not included a terms or glossary in *Get Rich Click*. So many new words pertaining to the Internet, its related technologies and applications are appearing regularly; a dynamic resource will serve you much better. Two sites do a good job of staying on top of Internet and web-related terminology and jargon.

Search Engine Dictionary searchenginedictionary.com

Wikipedia.com Wikipedia.com

Internet Research Firms

eMarketer emarketer.com

Forrester Research Forrester.com

Hitwise Hitwise.com

InfoSurv InfoSurv.com

Omniture omniture.com

Optimost optimost.com

Keyword Help Sites

Click Path ClickPath.com

Good Keywords GoodKeywords.com

Google adwords.google.com/select/KeywordToolExternal

Keyword Keyword.com

Trellian Keyworddiscovery.com

Omniture Omniture.com

WordTracker WordTracker.com

Magazines and Related Websites

BrandWeek Brandweek.com

BtoB Magazine btobonline.com

Direct Magazine DirectMag.com

DMnews dmnews.com

CNN Business2.0 business20.com

DNForum.com dnforum.com

DNJournal.com dnjournal.com

Entrepreneur Magazine entrepreneur.com

FastCompany fastcompany.com

Internet Retailer internetretailer.com

Revenue Magazine RevenueToday.com

Search Marketing Standard searchmarketingstandard.com

Webmaster Radio WebmasterRadio.fm

Wired wired.com

Outsourcing Sites

Bid-Job bid-job.com

Elance elance.com

Guru guru.com

oDesk odesk.com

Rentacoder rentacoder.com

Payment and Transaction Software and Services

Authorize.net authorize.net

Chase Paymentech Paymentech.com

CyberSource CyberSource.com

iTransact iTransact.com

Moneris Moneris.com

PayPal PayPal.com

Verisign Verisign.com

2Checkout 2Checkout.com

VerePay VerePay.com

Payment Processing Firms

CC NOW ccnow.com

Moneybookers moneybookers.com

Paypal Paypal.com

2Checkout 2Checkout.com

Wirecard Wirecard.com

Pay-Per-Call Service for Websites

Ingenio ingenio.com

PayPerCall.com PayPerCall.com

uPaypercall upaypercall.com

Ziff Leads Ziffleads.com

Search Engines

AltaVista AltaVista.com

America OnLine aol.com

Ask ask.com

Business.com Business.com

CompuServe CompuServe.com

Google google.com

MSN msn.com

Yahoo! search.yahoo.com

Search Engine Optimization (SEO) Firms

AtrinsicInteractive atrinsic.cominteractive

BusinessOnline BusinessOL.com

Bruce Clay bruceclay.com

FutureNow futurenowinc.com

iCrossing iCrossing.com

iProspect iprospect.com

Morevisibility morevisibility.com

SEO.com seo.com

SEOinc seoinc.com

SmartSearchMarketing smartsearchmarketing.com

Submit Express submitexpress.com

Shipping Firms

Canada Post canadapost.com

DHL dhl.com

Federal Express Fedex.com

iShip iship.com

United States Postal Service USPS.com

UPS ups.com

uShip uship.com

Trade Shows

AdTech ad-tech.com

Affiliate Summit affiliatesummit.com

Click Z Events events.clickz.com

Commission Junction University
cju.cj.comeventsevent_overview.html

Direct Marketing Days.com dmdays.com

DomainFest domainfest.com

Domain Roundtable domainroundtable.com

eComXpo wbresearch.comecomxpo

eTail wbresearch.cometailusawest

GnoMedex gnomedex.com

Internet Marketing Conference internetmarketingconference.com

Internet Retailer Internetretailer.com

IzeaFest Ideafest.com

Linkshare Symposiums linkshare.comeventssymposium

MediaPost Events mediapost.com

OnlineMarketingSummit onlinemarketingsummit.com

PubCon Pubcon.com

PPC Summit ppcsummit.com

Search Engine Strategies searchenginestrategies.com

Search Marketing Expo searchmarketingexpo.com

SEO Roadshow SeoRoadshow.com

South By Southwest sxsw.com

T.R.A.F.F.I.C. Targetedtraffic.com

Additional Resources

AllWhois allwhois.com

ALEXA Alexa.com

BetterWHOIS Betterwhois.com

Doubleclick.com DoubleClick.com

DMOZ dmoz.org

DomainTools domaintools.com

eMetrics.org emetrics.org

Get Rich Click GetRichClick.com

Internet Advertising Bureau iab.net

Internet.com Internet.com

Marketing Sherpa marketingsherpa.comindex.html

PR Web prweb.com

HighRankings HighRankings.com

Wayback Machine Archive.org

Wikipeida wikipedia.com

Webmaster World Webmasterworld.com

Webmaster Radio WebmasterRadio.com

Yahoo! Merchant Solutions smallbusiness.yahoo.come-commerce

LinkedIn.com Groups You May Want to Join

Get Rich Click

Internet Affiliate Marketers Association (IAMA)

AffiliatePrograms

Digital Marketing

eMarketing Association Network

eTail Careers.com

Guerrilla Marketing Tips for Small Businesses

Innovative Marketing, PR, Word-of-Mouth & Buzz Innovators

Online Lead Generation

Online Marketing Media

WebAnalysts.Info Internet Marketing, Web Analytics, and E-commerce Group

Facebook Groups You May Want to Join

Affiliate Marketing Opportunities

Internet Marketing School

Internet Marketing University on Facebook

6 Figures From Home –
Starting a Successful Internet Marketing business

Facebook Domain Name Network

Facebook's Ultimate Internet Marketing Mastermind

Top Secret Internet Marketing Strategies

The International Internet Marketing Alliance

AdTech Internet Marketing

Affiliate Marketing

The Women of Internet Marketing

Marc Ostrofsky's Websites

Owned in whole or in part

Blinds.com

CuffLinks.com

eTickets.com

SummerCamps.com

GetRichClick.com

WordOfMouse.com

MarcOstrofsky.com

Marc Ostrofsky's Websites Coming Soon

DesignDogs.com

MutualFunds.com

Bachelor.com

BeautyProducts.com

MortgageCompanies.com

InsuranceCompanies.com

Psychologists.com

HeartDisease.com

Photographer.com

Consulting.com

Expertz.com

APPortunity.com

TWO FINAL THOUGHTS:

1. Be sure to add your own stories
   and ideas at GetRichClick.com!
2. Watch for future *Get Rich Click* editions at
   GetRichClick.com!

- *Get Rich Click for College Students™*
- *Get Rich Click for Seniors™*
- *Get Rich Click for Part-Time Income™*
- And other *Get Rich Click* books

****

Watch for the next book written by Marc Ostrofsky:

Word Of Mouse™

301+ Ways to Gain Competitive Advantage Using the Internet for Marketing, Advertising, Sales, Customer Service and Public Relations

****

Be sure to visit:

- GetRichClick.com
- WordOfMouse.com
- MarcOstrofsky.com

Start to Finish
by Marc Ostrofsky

We all start with Questions . . .

From questions come research

From research come answers

From answers come knowledge

From knowledge comes understanding

From understanding comes
competitive advantage

From competitive advantage comes
winning "the game"

Learn, understand, compete and win

Acknowledgements

It's so much fun – and so rare – to have the opportunity to work on something that's a genuine labor of love. For a creative person like me, the Internet is an incredible tool that has (to the chagrin of my lovely wife, Beverle) kept me up very late many nights. I have met, worked with and been mentored by so many wonderful people. I have learned from many of the greatest business and creative minds on the planet. Each has helped me achieve the success I've attained. Each has helped me create this book.

The most obvious mentors in my life are my parents. My dad, **Dr. Benjamin Ostrofsky**, spent 45 years teaching me about business, planning and the value of caution at every turn. He has been a professor for more than 30 years, first at UCLA, then at the University of Houston, teaching business and industrial engineering. Then there was my mother. She was the creative one in the family – smart, outgoing and always thinking outside of the box. She pushed the limits thinking about the future and prompting me to do so. Sadly, she passed away while I was doing the final edits on this book. May her memory always be a blessing.

Thank you to my loving wife, **Beverle Gardner Ostrofsky**. Bev is *brilliant*, talented, creative, fun and loving in so many ways. Her never-ending support and encouragement helped make this book a reality. She truly is the best part of me! I love her dearly.

Thanks to my sister, **Dr. Keri Ostrofsky Pearlson**, an expert on social media and a consultant on the subject. Keri is the author of the book *Zerotime*, and while she was a professor at the University of Texas at Austin, she showed me a wonderful new "thing" called the Internet back in 1994. Thanks as well to her husband, **Dr. Yale Pearlson**, and my niece, **Hana Pearlson** in Austin.

Outside of my family, a special thank-you to **Al Lautenslager** for his help and guidance early on in this long process. You may know Al as one of the authors of "Guerrilla Marketing In 30 Days."

A *very* special thank-you to my three business partners, **Stuart Dow**, **Drake Harvey**, and **David Gardner**. These guys worked days on end finalizing this book so it was as good as we could make it! Thank you, guys! To my Internet company partners: **Jackie Maestas** and her husband, **Moses Maestas**, who run SummerCamps.com; **Jay Steinfeld** and **Daniel Coltar**, the brilliant minds behind Blinds.com; and **Ravi Ratan**, the super-smart entrepreneur who built and operates CuffLinks.com: you are all great business operators and I applaud you. Thank you to **Albert "Albe" Angel** for being a great friend and business associate. I have traveled the world and encountered some of the greatest business minds of our time . . . all of whom influenced me in different ways: **Bill Gates** who shares the same birthdate as I do, **Steve Jobs** and **Steve Wozniak** of Apple, **Nicholas Negroponte** at the MIT Media Lab. I cannot forget the brief meeting I had in New York with the late **Sam Walton** who built Walmart into the powerhouse that it is today. I love to learn from the "big boys" and these are but a few I have met along the way. Then there was the call I received from my former investment advisor, **Loraine Dell**, asking if I would like to help her son with a new computer company he was starting at the University of Texas. Luckily for Michael, I didn't work for him; my guess is that if I had, he would be broke and homeless! :)

I was also lucky enough to become coinvestors and friends with several founders of "Internet incubators." One is a really smart guy named **Bill Gross** who founded Idealab! I can honestly (and respectfully) say that Bill is even crazier and more creative than I am. He really sees the forest for the trees. Thanks to my partners at Business.com, **Jake Winebaum** (Disney) and **Sky Dayton** (Founder of Earthlink!), for creating and then turning Business.com into one of the strongest forces in the "business-to-business" search engine market. They bought my domain for $7.5 million; I reinvested in their concept and we later sold it for $345 million! Thank you to these guys is an understatement!

To my friend **Tony Hsieh**, founder of Zappos, thanks for the meetings and the great info about Zappos that I included in the book. Thank you to the folks in the publishing industry who helped me such as **Steve** and **Bill Harrison**, and the many folks who offered wonderful testimonials including **Steven Covey**, **Jack Canfield**, **Mark Victor Hansen**, **David Bach**, **Steve Wozniak**, **John Assaraf**, **Liz Kalodner**, **Jan Smith**, **Yanik Silver**, artist **Peter Max** and the rest of the wonderful friends I have made along the way.

Trying hard to keep me out of trouble are my lawyers and trusted advisors: **Jim Spring**, **Josh Bowlin**, **Patsy Wicoff**, **David Harris**, **Dr. Clive Fields**, **Karen Bernstein** and **Gil Melman**. A special thank-you to my good friend and closest advisor, **Michael Rubinstein**.

A special thanks to comedian **Robin Williams** with whom I dined the very night I began writing these acknowledgments. The creative juices were certainly flowing at dinner that night! We discussed our first encounter when I introduced Robin to Bill Gates when the three of us were at the Mirage Hotel in Las Vegas for the CES show some years ago. They were like two little kids meeting one another for the first time. It was *so* funny to be watching it unfold. Other friends who helped along the way include **Brian Becker**, **Bruce Eskowitz**, **Mohommid Fathalbob**, **Marc Nathan**, **Dr. Ed Reitman**, **John Eric Thompson**, **Ray Tirado** and the founder of the Houston Technology Center, **Mr. Paul Frison**, **Mr. Dan Levitan** and **Howard Schultz**, CEO of Starbucks. We were partners on my last firm, Internet Reit, along with Texas oil man **Ross Perot**. A special thank-you to all the deadlines met by our friend **Nasir Dadaboy.**

Thank you from everyone at Razor Media Group to our great friends at Clickbank including **Dr. Tim Barber**, **Brad Wiskerchin**, **Dush Ramachandran** and **Neil Hartley**. Thank you to artist **George Foster** for his assistance on the cover of the book. To **Wyndham Wood** for all of her help in the ongoing edits for our newsletters. Thank you to **Pauline Neuwirth** and **Beth Metrick** of Neuwirth Associates for all of their help in making this book a reality. To our friends at Bookmasters especially **Tony Proe** and **Randy McKenzie**. A better late than never thank you to **Chelsea Mollere** and **Rachel Taylor** for their help in getting day to day "stuff" out the door. Thank you **Joseph Fulvio** for your friendship and support. A special thank you to my good friend, **Andy Bernstein**. Andy took the photo for the book jacket and was the basis behind the chapter on Real Estate vs. Internet Real Estate.

To the staff at Affiliate Summit especially founders **Shawn Collins** and **Missy Ward** for their ongoing help in coordinating. Thank you to **Professor Keith Cox** at the University of Houston and a special class of 12 folks that helped us create and manage our "Get a Job or Create a job" viral video into a reality. Thank you to **Allie Herzog** for her day to day management of that project and her help with the entire *Get Rich Click* marketing project. To our friends **David Gonzales** and **Michael Lovitch** of the Austin Internet Marketing Party for their help. A special thank you to **Peter Hoppenfeld** for helping us grow this firm faster than we had expected.

To the folks who helped make this physical book a reality. **Mitch Sisskind** for his wonderful edits. **Connie Senter** and her team for assistance on a variety of design options. They are terrific! **Greg Russell**, my favorite graphic artist – who had the time, energy and most of all, the patience to work with me over eight months to lay out this book so each and every page was the best it could be. To our cartoonist, **Mr. Randy Glasbergen**, for creating such delightful, well-targeted cartoons. I put these in the book because I enjoy a mental break as I read. Randy and I hope you, too, will enjoy these rest stops along the journey. On the promotion side of this book and our new brand called *Get Rich Click*, a big thank-you to **Kevin Small** and the folks from Goldberg McDufie Communications, **Lynn Goldberg**, **Megan Beatie** and **Angela Hayes**.

Last, but certainly not least, I thank my five teenage daughters: **Tracy Ostrofsky**, **Shelly Ostrofsky**, **Kelly Ostrofsky**, **Maddy Grieco**, **Mary Grace Grieco**. A special note of interest . . . my identical twins, Kelly and Shelly, were one of the first sets of identical twins in the world to ever graduate as "co-valedictorians" at a high school. One of those proud moments that will never be forgotten and a truly amazing feat that is hard to imagine.

Nothing makes me happier than to see smiles on the faces of these five young ladies! I love you all so very much! Remember that you are amazing women and you can do anything you put your mind to. Set your goals, make a written plan, keep your head down, never let anyone talk you out of what you love to do and always shoot for the moon – even if you miss, you'll land among the stars!

To all of my friends, personally and professionally, who helped me market and promote this book to their own list of friends, contacts and professional organizations. Thank you for believing in me.

As I was doing final edits on the book, I got an e-mail from my friend **Warren Struhl**, founder of Dale and Thomas Popcorn. He told me to check out a new group he is part of called "YoCEO" that helps entrepreneurs better understand the "game" we all play. I found the following statement on the information page, which I couldn't have said any better:

"In the world of business, the ultimate currency is experience. There are many paths to obtaining that experience, some of them conventional, and some of them not so much. But the conventional paths to experience will only get you so far, and then you have to have the brains, instinct, or pure dumb luck to succeed beyond that."

Well, I don't know about brains or instinct, but I sure am thankful for the "pure dumb luck"! So, dear friends, family, business associates, thanks again for your friendship and your patience; I know I'm a handful – and then some!
– Marc

Index